Missing the Mark

SIN AND ITS CONSEQUENCES IN BIBLICAL THEOLOGY

MARK E. BIDDLE

Abingdon Press
Nashville

MISSING THE MARK
SIN AND ITS CONSEQUENCES IN BIBLICAL THEOLOGY

Copyright © 2005 by Abingdon Press

All rights reserved.
No part of this work may be reproduced or transmitted in any form or by any means, electronic or mechanical, including photocopying and recording, or by any information storage or retrieval system, except as may be expressly permitted by the 1976 Copyright Act or in writing from the publisher. Requests for permission can be addressed to Abingdon Press, P.O. Box 801, 201 Eighth Avenue South, Nashville, TN 37202-0801, or e-mailed to permissions@abingdonpress.com.

This book is printed on acid-free paper.

Library of Congress Cataloging-in-Publication Data

Biddle, Mark E.
 Missing the mark : sin and its consequences in biblical theology / Mark E. Biddle.
  p. cm.
 Includes bibliographical references and index.
 ISBN 0-687-49462-1 (alk. paper)
 1. Sin—Biblical teaching. 2. Bible—Theology. I. Title.

BS680.S57.B53 2005
241'.3—dc22

2005016004

All scripture translations, unless noted otherwise, are those of the author.

Scripture quotations marked RSV are from the *Revised Standard Version of the Bible*, copyright 1946, 1952, 1971 by the Division of Christian Education of the National Council of the Churches of Christ in the United States of America. Used by permission. All rights reserved.

Scripture quotations marked NRSV are from the *New Revised Standard Version of the Bible*, copyright 1989, Division of Christian Education of the National Council of the Churches of Christ in the United States of America. Used by permission. All rights reserved.

Excerpts from Alistair McFadyen, *Bound to Sin: Abuse, Holocaust, and the Christian Doctrine of Sin*, are © 2000 by Cambridge University Press. Reprinted with the permission of Cambridge University Press.

Excerpt from "The Rock" from COLLECTED POEMS 1909-1962 by T. S. Eliot, copyright 1936 by Harcourt, Inc., copyright © 1964, 1963 by T. S. Eliot, reprinted by permission of the publisher.

05 06 07 08 09 10 11 12 13 14—10 9 8 7 6 5 4 3 2 1
MANUFACTURED IN THE UNITED STATES OF AMERICA

Contents

Foreword v

Introduction vii

1. Clearing the Deck 1

2. Sin: To Be More Than Human 16

3. Sin: Failure to Embrace Authentic Freedom 49

4. Sin as Basic Mistrust 75

5. The Objective Nature of Sin:
   Intention Is (Relatively) Insignificant 95

6. Guilt as a Condition and a Consequence: Sin and Systems 115

Notes 140

Subject Index 169

Scripture Index 173

To My Grandparents

Leo (in memoriam) and Ettie Jones Biddle

Foreword

I am grateful to many people for the parts they played in my life while I was researching and writing this book and before. My paternal grandparents, to whom I dedicate the book, taught me a great deal by example and exhortation about the joys and whims of being human. Granddaddy's contagious sense of humor, especially about his own foibles, taught me that human imperfections are perfectly human. In my youth, Granny B, a truly wise woman in the ways of life, helped me to gain some degree of insight into the world's delicate balance as we picked blackberries together down by the spring and dug potatoes in the garden—both always on summer's hottest days it seemed to me. Good things, she taught me, often exact a price in briar sticks and brow sweat. I still learn from her when I visit and we sit drinking coffee. I hope to have the privilege for years to come.

I thank, too, my students at the Baptist Theological Seminary at Richmond, especially my Spring 2003 "Sin" class—who collaborated in an early exploration of the topic—and my teaching assistants, Vanessa Ellison and Richard Vinson—whose extreme competence freed me to devote more of each day to this project than I could have hoped otherwise. My editors at Abingdon, John Kutsko, Robert Ratcliff, and Tim West, have given invaluable encouragement and suggestions.

A number of my family and friends have graciously allowed me to importune them to respond to drafts of sections of the book. In particular and foremost, I thank my wife, Priscilla, who read every word of every draft. My son, Colin, and my stepson, Alec Broen, my mother- and father-in-law, Linda and Bill Lindsey, and my thoughtful friend Carrie Henly read various chapters for clarity and as safeguards against excessive theological jargon. Any error in the book is probably the result of my failure to heed good advice.

I wrote the preponderance of the book during a sabbatical leave from teaching. I thank the trustees and administration of BTSR for their generosity.

My most profound prayer that God may amplify the image of Christ in his children accompanies this book. If it can be an instrument to that end, my boldest hopes will have been surpassed.

Richmond, July 2005

Introduction

> *Every high priest chosen from among men is appointed to act on behalf of men in relation to God, to offer gifts and sacrifices for sins. He can deal gently with the ignorant and wayward, since he himself is beset with weakness.*
>
> Heb 5:1-2

As a rule, religions, philosophies, and the social sciences agree that the world is not as it should be, that there is a problem with human existence individually and corporately. Further, each of these worldviews offers a solution for the human condition suited to its definition of the problem. Buddhism holds that individual existence is an illusion and that, therefore, striving for the satisfaction of needs and appetites is meaningless and is the root of all human pain and suffering. Marxism identifies the problem as the alienation of the worker from the fruits of his or her labor. The solution, then, would be communal ownership of the means of production. Freudian psychoanalysis locates a bifurcation in the human psyche rooted in the conflict between the unruly id and the overbearing superego, a conflict to be resolved by the integration of a balanced ego.

Christianity identifies the human problem as "sin" and proclaims the Good News that God saves and heals. The Christian gospel can be summarized in the deceptively simple statement that *God sent God's Son to save human beings from their sin*. As is often true of such straightforward statements, however, its apparent simplicity masks the complexity and subtlety of the key terms. What is the nature of human sin? Is it a disease afflicting individuals from birth? What are its origins? Of course, whatever "sin" is, salvation must be its remedy. Did Jesus' life, death, and resurrection *correct* what is wrong with human beings? Does it have the potential to *remove* the problem? Does it *mask* sin? How? Just as a physician's diagnosis of an ailment matters with regard to the course of treatment he or she chooses, it matters how the church and its theologians define sin—what is wrong—and salvation—how God through Christ makes it right again.

The Need for a New Sin-thesis

For most people, the very term "sin" evokes images of the moralist listing and decrying specific actions—drinking, smoking, fornicating, etc.—or of the evangelist urging members of an audience to acknowledge themselves to be sinners and to submit to the cleansing blood of Christ. Both the moralist and the evangelist assume a specific, limited concept of sin quite firmly entrenched in Christian tradition. In the West, the dominant model of sin and salvation—developed especially in the thought of Tertullian, Augustine, Anselm, and Abelard—has long relied on a courtroom analogy. Human beings in willful rebellion against God's authority violate God's law. Their crime incurs the penalty of death. God's perfect and absolute sense of justice requires the execution of the penalty. The only means whereby both the pure justice of God can be satisfied and the mercy of God can be made manifest involves God's willingness to assume the guilt and pay the penalty. In order to do so, God becomes incarnate and dies in humanity's stead.

This "sin as crime" metaphor, with its emphases on the juridical, the individual, and willful rebellion, and its interests in assignment of guilt and exaction of punishment, addresses certain aspects of the problem of human existence. Yet, although dominant in the Western popular mind, it does not fully reflect the biblical witness,[1] nor provide a sufficient basis for the church's ministry in addressing human wrongdoing and its consequences,[2] nor take account of the insights of contemporary theological movements,[3] philosophies, and social sciences that do not confirm its validity as a thorough description of the problem of being human. In fact, although the sin as crime metaphor dominates the Western popular mind, academic theologians, especially since the middle decades of the twentieth century, have increasingly recognized its shortcomings and offered a wide variety of critiques and alternative models. Despite decades of this academic reevaluation, however, owing probably to the inertial force of centuries of tradition, the preacher in the pulpit and the parishioner in the pew seem still to be unaware of the inadequacies of the traditional view and of the advent of useful alternative descriptions of the problem of being human. In addition to inertia, the continued dominance of a model increasingly seen as insufficient may also reflect the fact that the various voices of theological critique and revision have as yet to enter into constructive dialogue with one another in any meaningful way. This book hopes to bring to the church's attention the point that a more comprehensive view of sin offers the church enhanced tools for ministry. It will do so, in part, by bringing contemporary voices into dialogue with one another and with the Bible.

The Bible on Sin: A Complex Picture

The dominant Western model of sin does not equate fully with the biblical description of sin, the problem with being human. One well-known biblical example illustrates this point very clearly. King David committed adultery with Bathsheba, the wife of Uriah the Hittite, and commissioned the murder of Uriah to conceal his crime (2 Sam 11). He must have been fully aware in both cases that his actions were wrong, contrary to the express will of Israel's God. He "willfully rebelled." The juridical understanding well describes the nature of his sin. Nathan's message to David was on point: "You are the sinner, you deserve the penalty" (2 Sam 12:7). Likewise, David's admission of guilt and successful plea for forgiveness were entirely appropriate (2 Sam 12:13). So far, as a biblical example of the dynamics of sin, the interaction between the king and the prophet corresponds to the church's conventional treatment of sin: it is a willful crime deserving of punishment, but a merciful God will commute the sentence for one who is truly repentant. The church's only role is to call the sinner to account and to offer the promise of forgiveness to the penitent.

The biblical account goes on, however, to relate Nathan's triple prediction of disaster for David and his household (2 Sam 12:10-14). Although forgiven, David's sin has its own vitality and will replicate in the lives of his children. David, as father and king, has created a system of interactions that will ultimately bring one of his daughters and three of his sons to ruin at the hands of other members of the king's family. The nation will experience civil war and long-term political unrest. The royal court will be torn by intrigue (2 Sam 13–1 Kgs 2).

Legal Models Insufficient for the Task of Ministry

Just as the legal model for sin fails adequately to describe the full scope of a situation such as that created by David's sin with Bathsheba, it also cannot provide a full range of tools for ministering to the full range of human pain and sorrow. The dynamics of sin in everyday life often more closely resemble the complexity of the aftermath of David's sin with Bathsheba than the simplicity of the "sin as crime" model. The church and its ministers regularly confront complex human crises in which something is clearly wrong, sin's effects are clearly evident, but no clear guilt for an act of willful rebellion can be identified. Consider three situations from pastoral experience:

Case 1. A teenager from a troubled home—her mother had been in a series of unstable, abusive relationships—had been attending youth activities at a rural southern church with a friend for a year or so. She professed faith and joined the church in early summer. Everyone was delighted that she had found some direction for her life and hopeful that she would be able to escape the pattern established in her mother's life. The youth minister had heard, although he had no firsthand knowledge, that she was seeing an unemployed high-school dropout notorious in the community as a troublemaker. It did not seem appropriate to intrude. Then, as the holidays approached, she came to the minister's office after a youth function and tearfully announced that she was pregnant. She was distraught. She said that she loved the boy and that she had thought he loved her. Now, he had no interest in establishing a family. Her mother's response to the news had been: "You made your bed, now lie in it." Although she was at least an

Introduction

average student, she could envision no alternative to quitting school. The minister feared the daughter reliving the mother's life: generation following generation.

Case 2. A parishioner came to the pastor in a state of extreme anxiety, seeking counsel. In her teens and twenties, she had rebelled against a strict, fundamentalist upbringing and, among other things, habitually abused alcohol and drugs. Shortly before the birth of her son, she kicked the habit with her new husband's support, and she had since become an active member of the church. A few months earlier, doctors had diagnosed her son, now in elementary school, with a congenital disorder related to her history of substance abuse. It would affect his ability to learn, his attention span, and his ability to process emotions for the duration of his life. Since the diagnosis she had been fervently praying that God would forgive her for damaging her son and that God would heal him. Now she had become convinced that her son's condition was God's punishment and that, since God had not answered her prayers, she and perhaps even her son may never be truly "saved."

Case 3. Over coffee at a Wednesday night fellowship dinner, the pastor offhandedly commented that the church really should consider doing something to help with the basic needs (food, clothing, health care) and, especially, education of the children of migrant workers employed seasonally in the packing plant located in the community. A deacon sitting at an adjacent table, who was coincidentally part owner and operations manager of the plant, overheard the remark. A few days later, he called on the pastor in her office. He had been in a long struggle against efforts to organize a labor union among his employees. A union would put pressure on him to raise wages and offer new benefits. He feared that the business could become unprofitable and wanted the pastor and everyone else to leave well enough alone. Her talk about doing "social work" among the workers' children sounded to him like more labor-organizing liberalism that could upset the apple cart. "Why don't you just preach the gospel?" he challenged her. "This is a church, not the welfare department. Stick to the Bible!"

The conventional understanding of sin offers the ministers in these situations meager tools for ministry. Surely the young girl in the first case was aware of the requirements of conventional morality with respect to premarital sex. Her youth minister could rightly conclude that she had "willfully rebelled," call her to repentance, and promise forgiveness. In truth, however, the situation was much more complicated. The girl had known no constant, reliable, loving relationship with her father or any of her mother's companions. No doubt there was a gaping hole in her psyche. For her, theological metaphors likening God's love to that of a father or a mother were not very communicative of the gospel. Her mother's example taught her not to expect mutuality in relationships, not to pursue long-term goals or to aspire to achievement. Who is to blame? More importantly, what can the church do for the real "victim" in this case, the unborn child, the potential next generation in this cycle? What does the girl need most now, to be forgiven her rash and unwise act or to be healed from the scars left by her upbringing? Is she primarily a rebel or a victim? Has she rebelled against God or succumbed to her insecurities and neediness?

The Bible speaks to a number of aspects of sin as evidenced in these sample cases, aspects often largely ignored in Christian theology and ministerial praxis. The Bible can provide an enriched understanding of the human condition and therefore a vocabulary and theological framework in which to address a wider range of human suffering. Furthermore, many of the insights of contemporary theological movements can be productively linked to biblical foundations. So equipped, the church and its ministers need no longer be reduced to assigning guilt—"who sinned, this man or his parents?" (John 9:2)—but may be about the task of healing and restoration.

The Complexity of the Human Condition Confirmed by Other Approaches

More than any other aspect of Christian thought, theological consideration of the human condition involves an empirical dimension. It is theology done "from below," asking descriptive questions about human nature. Ideally, it should take into account the insights of non-theological examinations of human nature, as well. As mentioned at the outset, psychology (especially its developmental subdiscipline), sociology, anthropology, and the various philosophies and economic theories all make observations concerning the human condition. To be sure, their observations are subject to review and revision—theological approaches that seek to restate Christianity in the terms of some empirical science risk denaturing Christianity altogether—but, if reality is one, the insights of Christian theology into human nature can be expected to correspond to some degree with the reliable insights of the social sciences and philosophy.

Some theologians will likely object that human powers of observation and, especially, of reason are themselves marred by human sin, so that the results of empirical science will be inevitably and irremediably marred and unreliable, as well. Theology, they will argue, must rely exclusively on revealed truth as its source. Such a position classifies sources of truth into absolute categories: true without mixture of error; if false, then absolutely so. The approach taken here will seek instead to acknowledge that the world is the one God's creation, that human beings are capable of recognizing truth, that the quest for truth is a movement toward absolute truth, and, especially, that when revealed truth, which is itself a "treasure in earthen vessels" (2 Cor 4:7), and empirical observation confirm one another, those interested in truth must pay particular attention. In essence, when revealed truth and observed truth coincide, one can have a great deal of confidence that one is on the right track.

In fact, the popular understanding of the Christian doctrine of sin corresponds only in part either to revealed truth as found in the Scriptures or to observed truth as interpreted by the sciences. To mention only a few points manifesting this lack of correspondence, matters that will be treated in greater detail in subsequent chapters, developmental psychology points out that human beings are not born with the cognitive and moral capabilities to be "sinners." As humans become cognitive moral agents, they become sinners. Sociology and systems psychologists call attention to the environments that predispose individuals to attitudes, behaviors, and modes of being that Christianity classifies as sin. Existential philosophy grapples with the givenness of the human dilemma—free but finite—that sets absolute parameters for being human. Any Christian understanding of human nature that fails to explain sin in relation to these and other insights will be parochial and insufficient by definition.

The Procedure for This Inquiry

The approach to be taken in these pages is inherent in these comments concerning the need for an understanding of sin that recognizes the complexity of the human condition and that will equip the church with more adequate tools for ministry to sinners. Three tasks lie ahead: recovery of biblical insights often overlooked in the dominant theological tradition; tests of these insights against those of contemporary theology, philosophy, and the social sciences to confirm their accuracy and currency as descriptions of significant aspects of the human condition; and explication of the value of these insights into sin for ministry to the wide range of human pain and sorrow.

Recovery of Biblical Insights into the Nature of Sin

The Bible, in both Testaments, views sin as a much more complex phenomenon than does the juridical model. If the crime metaphor utilizes a binary logic of individual guilt or innocence, the biblical model operates on the complex logic of organic systems. In analogy to an ecological system, the biblical model sees sin as the disequilibrium pervasive in a system in disarray. On an individual level, this disequilibrium—sin—manifests itself in the person's failure to attain and maintain the balance definitive of authentic human being. God *created* humanity *in God's likeness*. By definition, therefore, authentic human existence involves a polarity. True humanity reflects God's nobility, God's personhood, God's creativity, God's autonomy, God's concern for God's creation, God's interest in relationship. Human godlikeness, however, is a reflection: it is second order; it is derived nobility, imitative personhood, limited creativity, autonomy within limits. Human beings can never be more than creatures, closely akin to the earth from which they were fashioned and to their other creature cousins. Human beings properly inhabit the realm between the dirt and the divine. Authentic human existence—human life as God intended it—aspires to realize its full potential of godlikeness while consistently acknowledging its creatureliness and limitations. Sin is disequilibrium in this aspiration: humanity failing to reflect its divine calling, humanity forgetting its limitations.

The whole problem of sin—of the individual's failure to attain or maintain equilibrium—is compounded in the biblical view by the fact that "system" consists not of discrete individuals but of multitudes of individuals across generations whose actions and choices interact with the efforts of multitudes of other individuals seeking balance. The actions of one reverberate throughout the system, upsetting the precarious balance of all those shaken by the wave of sin. The multitude of choices and actions made by members of the system impinge upon all the individuals in the system, even across time, limiting the freedom of all to make fully free choices and, therefore, to act authentically.

Aware that metaphors, especially as they grow more complex, serve their purposes only to a point, it may be helpful to compare the ecological system of human existence with a modern transportation system. One is not free to take whatever specific route one chooses between two points. Private property cannot be crossed without permission. Rivers and streams must be forded or bridged, swamps bypassed, mountains crossed. Generations of decision-making and habit have already chosen the routes open to a contemporary traveler such that he or she simply follows without deliberation or real alternatives the paths established by previous generations. An animal path became a hunting path became a roadway. Highway builders locate exits at key points that may or may not coincide with the traveler's simplest route to a destination. The traveler is not free to exit the highway across a farmer's field even though it may be the shortest way home. On the roadway, drivers must contend with the decisions and actions not only of previous generations, but also of those traveling the same route at the same time. These other individuals also make free choices within the parameters established by the system. They block one's path, cut into one's lane, drive too slow/fast, have accidents that cause traffic jams and road closures.

Similarly, individuals seeking authentic human existence find themselves born into systems in which their predecessors have created family, cultural, and societal pathways that predispose them toward certain behaviors and attitudes. Typically, a child knows no other model for family life and marriage than that into which he or she was born. Some are born into substantially healthy family systems; others are not. Those who are not encounter, from the very outset of their lives, an imbalanced system, disequilibrium, sin. With no real resources for imagining other patterns, they will likely simply replicate the fundamental patterns they learned as children. The imbalanced system will reproduce imbalance in its individual members. The same or a very similar ecological mechanism operates in cultures that value people according to their social status, the accidents of genetics, gender, and color. From within the system, already in place when individuals encounter it, a given of reality, it is difficult to imagine alternatives, to evaluate the claims inherent in the system. Not surprisingly, cultures reproduce themselves across generations. In the biblical view, this disequilibrium inherent in systems is sin, indeed, "the sin of the world" (John 1:29), the "sin that waits at the door" (Gen 4:7). Obviously, then, the juridical model, which sees sin solely as an individual's intentional act in violation of divine law, cannot account for the complexity of interactions between individuals seeking equilibrium and the turbulent environment, which is the world of family, community, and society.

The complexity of the biblical view is evident at first glance in the richness of biblical terminology. Whereas English and other Western languages have a single term, the Bible employs tens of terms for a variety of sin's aspects. In common English usage, "sin" refers to "transgression of divine law" or to "the human propensity for such transgression," definitions that emphasize the act apart from its consequences or the tendency as a trait of human nature, definitions that imply willful violation of a known standard. Biblical terms and usage involve a much broader spectrum of ideas: the act as a wrong regardless of intention, the real effects of the act loosed on the world as an abiding condition unless and until remedied, shortcomings resulting from ignorance or incapacity, a communal phenomenon with communal consequences, etc. In addition to the etymological variety of biblical sin-language in comparison to Western discourse, the biblical worldview embraces non-Western notions of the inherent value of an act regardless of the actor's intention, of the continued efficacy of an act, either for good or for evil, of the "corporate" dimensions of an act, and so forth.

The complexity and foreignness of the biblical view is compounded by the problem posed by the phenomenon of two Testaments written in two languages. In other words, in order to examine the biblical concept of sin, one must grapple with a three-layered matrix of translational and cross-cultural relationships. How do Hebrew/ancient Israelite and English/modern Western terms and concepts correspond to one another? How do Hebrew/ancient Israelite and Greek/Hellenistic Christian terms and concepts relate to one another? How do Greek/Hellenistic Christian terms and English/modern Western terms and concepts compare? Issues arising from a comparison of the linguistic domains and worldviews of the two Testaments are at least as daunting as the cultural differences between antiquity and current Western culture. A long strand of Christian interpretation, in fact, treats the transition in thought and culture represented by the shift from Hebrew to Greek as a major line of demarcation. The authors of the New Testament, informed by their encounter with the risen Lord, so the argument goes, have come to see the problem of sin in an entirely new light. The corporate dimensions of sin familiar from the Hebrew Bible's discussion of the life of the people Israel disappear in favor of a depiction of sin as the failure to respond to the call of Christ, that is, as an individual, spiritual matter. The ancient Israelite priest's concerns for remedying unintended tragedy in this world give way to a focus on salvation from personal sins as the avenue into the world to come.

Can it be that the authors of the New Testament, including the rabbinically trained Paul, abandoned their Hebrew heritage? This question has a long and troubled history in modern biblical scholarship. Suffice it here to offer a working hypothesis—to be tested below by exegesis of specific New Testament texts—with respect at least to the New Testament authors' understanding of sin: since the authors of the New Testament knew and revered the Hebrew Bible as canonical scripture, they did not feel compelled to restate every aspect of its thought with which they agreed, but, instead, they concentrated on formulating the significance of Jesus in the context of their canonical traditions. As will be demonstrated, New Testament authors did not, in fact, reject Hebrew concepts of sin so much as they argued that all of sin's complexity finds a solution in the life, ministry, death, and resurrection of Jesus of Nazareth.

From the standpoint of theological method, the question arises, of course, as to whether Christian doctrine should and can be equated with wholesale adoption of ancient Israelite and early Christian lexica and worldviews. No one seriously argues that modern Christians must adopt a three-storied model of the universe as a tenet of Christian orthodoxy. Indeed, the semantic difficulty inherent in translating biblical worldviews into modern concepts already confronts the task of doing biblical theology that takes seriously the Hebrew Old Testament and the Greek New Testament. Yet, the common practice among theologians of outlining the biblical position on an issue before dismissing it as antiquated and irrelevant [4] must be avoided for at least two significant reasons. First, Christian theology claims special revelatory status for Scripture; Protestant theology typically extends this claim in the form of its *sola scriptura* mandate. Yet, as James Barr laments in the context of discussions of so-called "natural theology":

> On the whole, people are far more heavily influenced by the strong dogmatic convictions which they have inherited or to which they adhere, and only with the greatest difficulty can they find it in themselves to admit that the Bible actually points in a direction different from these convictions.[5]

Are there biblical perspectives that can be profitably recovered for the church—even if they run counter to Western, post-Enlightenment sensibilities?

Second, fidelity to the church's claim regarding the inspiration and authority of Scripture mandates that Christian theology maintain contact with its source and first expression. It is certainly true that the history of the faith community (Israel and later the church) has been a process of encounter with new situations and new revelations of God's character. The Bible is not an exhaustive statement of God's character, nor does it explicitly anticipate specific challenges that may confront the community as history unfolds. It has been and will be necessary for the church and its theologians to say something new concerning sin—to account for the results of social-scientific research, for example. In order honestly to speak with a distinctively Christian voice, however, the church must speak from its tradition. The church's statements regarding sin may go beyond the explicit perspectives expressed in Scripture, but if they contradict Scripture outright, or omit major scriptural emphases, or speculate entirely without reference to scriptural foundation they are, as Paul put it, expressions of "another gospel" (Gal 1:6-9).[6] While situations change, the gospel contends that God remains fundamentally true to God's character. Evidence does not support the conclusion that cultural and technological progress has been accompanied by moral progress. Human beings still commit murder as they did in the days of King David and St. Paul. Now, however, they use automatic weapons. The notion that modern ideas have progressed beyond the primitive thought of ancient Israel and the early church cannot be sustained. As Barr puts it: "The discovery of the mentality of ancient people might uncover a mode of thinking that, while different from modern modes, [is] valuable and constructive when taken in its own right."[7] Is the dominant model of sin true to the wealth of scriptural insight into the human condition?

The church's preaching, teaching, and pastoral practice typically fail fully to appropriate biblical tradition, relying too heavily on the "sin as crime" model. There is evidence of a growing recognition of the inadequacy of the traditional understanding. In a number of provinces of theological thought, questions have recently been raised as to the adequacy of the conventional understanding of the human condition. Liberation theologians have critiqued the hyper-individualism of the conventional approach, pointing to its pie-in-the-sky promises that tend to aid and abet the continuation of an unjust status quo. Consequently, they emphasize the social and political components of sin as manifest in social injustice and political oppression. Especially since Vatican II, Catholic moral theologians have struggled with shortcomings perceived to undermine Augustine's version of the doctrine of original sin. Several have suggested revisions of the doctrine in terms of the notion that humanity was not created as fully formed, perfect, moral creatures. These suggestions, ironically, in some ways represent a return to a position laid out by Irenaeus and the Greek fathers and largely followed in the Orthodox Church. Feminist and liberation theologians have reminded the church that the definition of basic sin usually offered in classical theologies—namely "arrogance," the will-to-power, or *hubris*—does not account for all manifestations of human inauthenticity.[8] Among the oppressed and powerless, such as the girl in the first case study or the children in the third, the temptation often is not to overreach but to settle for less than full humanity. In fact, in the biblical view and according to liberation theologies, sin manifests itself in its aftereffects that become the perverted system antecedent to individual choice. The result is that the perception and judgment of all involved in the existing, twisted system are themselves so perverted and distorted that one cannot even envision an alternative to the status quo—one cannot choose freedom because the system predisposes one to perpetuate the system.[9] Clinicians have pointed to parallels between the inevitability of sin and the bondage of addiction.[10] Psychiatrists, depth psychologists, and existentialist philosophers and theologians have focused on the ramifications of the conflict between transcendent freedom and fundamental finitude at the core of human existence. At their center, human beings know themselves to be free to grow, to realize ambitions, to imagine new realities. Simultaneously, however, they also know that no one is truly and wholly free, that human beings are limited by their creaturely existence, by the conditions of their birth, by the accidents of genetics, by the values of the dominant culture, by the state of the economy, and so forth.[11] Systems theorists have analyzed the complexity of human interactions, exposing complicity as a powerful force in wrongdoing. Often, even victims, although not guilty of wrongdoing, share to some degree in responsibility for their suffering. Post-Holocaust theology has been forced to acknowledge the reality that the juridical model—individualist and reductionist—cannot account for the sin of the world, which is, in some sense, corporate and cumulative, nor for the tragic component of sin evident in the way in which the acquiescence and complicity of quiet, "law-abiding" citizens contributed quite materially to the horrible murders of millions of innocent people.[12]

For a biblically oriented theology of sin, the need is to test these various insights for consonance with scriptural tradition. Are there, in fact, points of contact between these new perspectives and biblical reflections on the human condition that can serve to ground them in the Christian tradition? Can these points of contact provide a corrective to the frequently one-dimensional preaching, teaching, and pastoral ministry of the church? Do they supplement some usually neglected aspect of the biblical tradition so as to point in some productive new direction?

The Plan of the Book

The crime model alone cannot supply the church and its ministers with sufficient tools to minister the gospel to a world in which sin takes on every possible form, inflicts all manner of guilt on people taught to ignore its significance, and perpetuates itself in ever-widening echoes. The three central tasks of this book (recovery of overlooked biblical insights into sin, tests of these insights against contemporary thought, and explication of the value of these insights on human sin for the practice of ministry in the contemporary world) will involve two phases. The first addresses the essential nature of sin. Since the dominant Christian understanding of sin depends heavily on a certain privileged tradition of reading Gen 3 and Paul, the first chapter calls attention to difficulties inherent in this accepted reading and points out other possibilities inherent in the texts. Three successive chapters address the fundamental question: What is the *essence* of "sin"? Genesis 3 and its later expositions in Ecclesiastes, Romans, and the Johannine literature and certain other isolated texts explore the human propensity for *inauthentic existence*. These biblical texts view authentic humanity as a precarious balance between freedom and finitude. As traditional exegesis of Scripture has argued, one expression of inauthenticity can be overreaching, the attempt to usurp divine status. This dominant view, which defines "sin" as *pride*, as willful rebellion against God and God's will, portrays aspects of the human condition, but does not represent an exhaustive depiction of the essence of human sin. Human beings not only seek arrogantly to transgress the boundaries between authentic humanity and the realm reserved for divinity, they also fail to fulfill the potential of genuine humanity: the human condition manifests *sloth* alongside *pride*. The Bible agrees with contemporary critics of the traditional approach (feminist and liberation theologians, especially) that inauthenticity can also be manifest in the failure to live up to the full stature of human godlikeness. Are these two forms of inhuman existence rooted in some underlying cause or phenomenon? Underlying this dual manifestation of the human condition is the essential human flaw: *mistrust*. Indeed, a range of texts—from Gen 3, through the Deuteronomistic History and the prophetic corpus, culminating in the New Testament, especially the Johannine literature and Hebrews—exposes the basic lack of trust in God, the lack of fundamental faith in God's goodness toward humanity, as the root cause of both humanity's tendency to overextend and humanity's failure to fully realize its godlikeness. Human beings find it difficult to trust that authentic humanity under God is sufficient for them and that, under God, they are sufficient for authentic humanity.

The second phase explores sin's dynamic character, tracing the life cycle of sin as understood in Scripture from the act as an objective reality, through the state of guilt resulting from the action, to the perversion the act introduces into the world. The dominant Christian understanding of sin sees it primarily as a soteriological problem—that is, it pertains chiefly to the conditions that make salvation necessary. Sin disrupts relationship with God in such a way that only God can reestablish relationship and restore well-being; this is salvation. God graciously restores the sinner to relationship in response to repentance and faith, removing or covering the blot of sin. The Bible and common experience suggest, however, that sin is more than a blot on one's record—that it impacts the world, including and surrounding the sinner in real and lasting ways. The Bible views sin and its aftermath as an organic continuum. Common experience, economics, and depth psychology confirm the Bible's wisdom. Contemporary discussions of Western hyper-individualism, of intention as a defining characteristic of sin, and of the complex nexus of social interactions, shared guilt, and complicity will enlarge the exposition of the biblical perspective.

The final two chapters, then, explore the dynamics of sin as act, condition, and cause. In contrast to the dominant view, a balanced view of sin notes that it involves more than a mark against the sinner; sin has real impact on the world. Its effects cannot be remedied merely by a transaction analogous to forgiving a debt. Sin does damage that must, as far as possible, be repaired. Finally, a balanced view of sin notes that sin's impact on the world reverberates throughout the sinner's environment, across space and time. In this sense, sin becomes a cause. It creates a distorted environment that is the precondition for the sins of others.

CHAPTER ONE

Clearing the Deck

> *"To want to give a logical explanation of the coming of sin into the world is a stupidity that can occur only to people who are comically worried about finding an explanation."*[1]

The crime model of sin, dominant in Western Christianity, is insufficient, but it is not useless or wrong. It addresses one aspect of reality from a single biblical perspective, but it requires supplementation and revision. In order to reflect the broader biblical tradition and to speak to a wider range of human experience, it must be supplemented with other perspectives. Sin, the umbrella term for the flaws in the human condition, cannot be exhaustively described by one viewpoint. Since fundamental realities such as the human condition are aspective, subsequent chapters will examine other facets of the problem inherent in human existence. Now the task is to examine the conventional model with an eye to revision in order both to reclaim its valuable insights and to address flaws in the traditional formulation. The ongoing theological enterprise must ever reexamine cherished ideas, testing them against their own central assertions, against the scriptural source of Christian tradition, and against the church's new experiences and changing situations.

The conventional definition of sin in the Western church equates sin with the prideful human attempt to usurp divine prerogatives. In essence, it argues, human beings become so obsessed with their own status and security that they refuse to acknowledge their proper subordination to the deity, and they regard everyone and everything else in creation as having lesser value than themselves. Sin is arrogance, egotism, the natural will-to-live perverted into the will-to-power.[2]

The conventional version of this doctrine relies heavily on a particular reading of Gen 3 and certain passages in Paul. Both this understanding of sin and the related interpretation of Scripture are closely associated with the doctrine of original sin, especially in Augustine's classical formulation. For many Western Christians, "sin," "original sin," and the conventional interpretation of Gen 3, in particular, will seem indistinguishable and self-evident. A number of issues, ranging from advances in scientific anthropology to improved linguistic information regarding Paul's Greek, however, necessitate a reexamination of the doctrine and its basis in the biblical text.

Sin as "Crime" and "Original Sin"

The Augustinian version of the doctrine of original sin links Gen 3 and Rom 5:21 to explain the universality of human sin and the relationship between sin and death. As codified at the Council of Carthage (411–418 CE), the doctrine distinguishes between original sin in the sense of the first, historical action taken by Adam and Eve (*peccatum originale originans*, "original sin as originating"), the flawed nature inherited from the first parents by all human beings, except for one (*peccatum originale originatum*, "original sin as originated"), and *concupiscence*, the disordered will that remains even after baptism.[3] The traditional doctrine makes five central assertions: (1) Human beings were created in a state of innocent perfection. As perfect creatures, they were originally immortal. Death, the essence of human finitude, was not in God's original plan for humanity. (2) Adam's sin brought guilt upon all his descendants. The traditional version of the doctrine understands this guilt to be transmitted biologically through the paternal lineage. Jesus escaped this inherited guilt by virtue of his virginal conception. (3) The penalty for Adam's sin is death. Just as the heritage of sin is universal, so is the penalty. (4) All human beings, except Jesus, are born under the burden of this sin and its penalty. Infants are not innocent. (5) Because of the common heritage, human beings are unable to live in accordance with the will of God. The Mosaic law fails as a means to salvation because human beings are sinners from the outset, even before they actually sin. As sinners, all inevitably sin.[4]

Contemporary Questions for the Traditional Doctrine

Contemporary Western culture perceives a number of difficulties with the traditional formulation of the doctrine. Theologically, in fact, disputes concerning ramifications of the doctrine have accompanied it since its inception. Pelagius, a contemporary of Augustine, was uncomfortable with the determinism inherent in the notion that descendants of Adam are sinners even prior to any exercise of their own free will. During the Reformation, the degree to which the "fall" marred the image of God in which humankind was created became a point of contention. Catholics argued that, while distorted, it was not eradicated; baptism removes the mark of original sin, original guilt, restoring in human beings a measure of the originally intended freedom *not* to sin. Luther and many Protestants, holding that the "fall" produced the total corruption of human nature, that is, the loss of free will, argued that baptism removes neither guilt nor the compunction to sin but is a sign of imputed righteousness.[5]

Contemporary theologians also often find the hierarchical and legal/juridical components of the traditional doctrine of original sin problematic. The metaphor underlying the traditional doctrine places God in the primary role of moral lawgiver and judge, and too easily can have the effect of justifying social and political hierarchies. It offers no theological paradigm to account for the suffering of victims and those oppressed by hierarchical structures; in fact, it implies that suffering is deserved. To describe horrendous crimes such as the Holocaust, ethnic cleansing, serial killings, and pedophilia in terms of rebellion against God while using the same description for relatively innocuous personal behaviors discounts the reality of sin's impact on its victims. The traditional concept focuses on the individual's disobedience to a known will of God, elevating the status of the individual to tragic heights, nurturing the overvaluation of individual free will (precisely the problem it seeks to redress), despite the fact that such Promethean defiance is not common to human experience.[6] How many people consciously set out to live in rebellion against God? Nowadays, people are much more likely to be apathetic than defiant.

Theologians also struggle to explain how all people incur Adam's guilt. Will the human genome project discover that sin is encoded in human DNA? Does the whole race incur Adam's guilt by juridical imputation—that is, does Adam represent the entire race in some legal transaction? Does sin adhere to Adam's offspring like a substance? Is Adam to be understood as subsuming the entire genus in a single corporate personality? As James Connor has recently observed, none of the explanations offered to date fully satisfies.[7]

From the perspective of the contemporary worldview, common cultural and scientific assumptions are difficult to reconcile with the traditional doctrine. Contemporary culture, with its almost axiomatic assertion of the autonomy of the individual, finds the connection between original sin and original guilt asserted by Augustine, the idea that a newborn child is guilty of Adam's sin, to be fundamentally unjust.[8] Similarly, the modern scientific perspective presents a serious obstacle. Because the Augustinian formulation depends on the theory of a biological heritage common to all humanity, discoveries in the field of anthropology deal an apparently fatal blow. In order for Augustine to have been right, Gen 3 must be historically accurate in the sense that the entire race descends from one original pair. Anthropological evidence strongly suggests, however, that modern human beings descended from a number of individuals who evolved into modern humans (polygenism) or a number of groups of individuals who made the transition in various times and at various places (polyphyletism).[9]

Perhaps the most fundamental flaw in the traditional formulation involves its misreading of the key biblical texts. In short, the doctrine cannot be found in Scripture.[10] According to the doctrine, Adam and Eve "fell" from an original state of innocent perfection in an act that significantly or totally damaged the divine image given them at creation. Their original godlikeness was at least scarred, if not lost entirely. The text, however, does not support this contention.

According to Gen 3, the first pair, already bearing the stamp of godlikeness, sought to become even more like God by eating of the tree of the knowledge of good and evil. Rather than perfection, any definition of which would surely include moral self-awareness, the first pair enjoyed a state of naiveté. Moreover, rather than losing godlikeness, the text suggests that their quest for increased wisdom succeeded, after a fashion. As God admits, "[the humans] have become like one of us, knowing good and evil" (Gen 3:22). Further, according to the traditional formulation, the fallen state in which the image of God in humankind is lost or corrupted becomes human nature. Yet the text employs the same language used to describe humankind's created godlikeness to describe the generation born *after* the "fall": "When Adam had lived one hundred thirty years, he became the father of a son *in his likeness, according to his image* . . . " (Gen 5:3, emphasis added).

In another instance of misreading biblical texts, proponents of the traditional doctrine based their interpretation of an essential text, Rom 5:12, on a *mistranslation* promulgated in the Latin Vulgate: " . . . just as sin came into the world through one man, *in whom* all have sinned, and death came through sin, and so death spread to all. . . . " The modern NSRV translates accurately: " . . . just as sin came into the world through one man, and death came through sin, and so death spread to all *because* all have sinned . . . " (emphasis added).[11] Romans 5:12 does not assert that Adam's sin automatically constituted all his descendants as sinners: "In Adam's fall we sinnéd all." Instead, it attributes the universality of death to the universality of sin. Just as death followed in the wake of Adam's sin, it follows in the wake of the sins of every individual member of the race. All die because all sin.

Alternative Readings of the Key Texts

At root, the traditional formulation erroneously attempts to derive propositional theology from a narrative text with mythic features (God walking in the cool of the day, scooping up clay, experimenting in the creation of Adam's companion, and so forth).[12] As contemporary narratological approaches to literature and theology have demonstrated, narrative texts resist reduction to propositional assertions. Genesis 3 is the *story* of the human condition, complex and paradoxical. Because any narrative, especially a mythic story, is amenable to a variety of interpretations, theologians and philosophers have offered a number of alternative readings of Gen 3, some quite ancient, as the basis for their divergent formulations of the doctrine of "original sin." The traditional formulation seeks rightly to underscore the notion that God did not create humans in a fundamentally flawed condition from the outset and yet to account for the self-evident phenomenon of the universality of human sin. In contrast, each of the alternative versions of the doctrine addresses key issues omitted or slighted in the traditional formulation. In order to broaden further the palette of interpretive possibilities before turning to the biblical texts for a fresh look, it will be useful to outline several of the major options.

Perhaps the most ancient of these alternative interpretations actually predates Augustine and has been the dominant perspective in the Eastern Orthodox tradition all along. Surprisingly, it finds a contemporary parallel in theologians who attempt to take seriously the implications of modern scientific anthropology for theological anthropology. Both see Gen 3 and the history of human sinfulness in the context, not of a "fall" from a state of perfection, but of interrupted or perverted maturation.

The teaching of the early Greek father Irenaeus exemplifies the Orthodox approach. He understood the double phrase "image and likeness" as a reference to humanity's nature, on the one hand, and its maturation, brought about by the outpouring of the Spirit, into the full likeness of God's Son, on the other. The "fall" interrupted this process of maturation so that "humanity's fallen state represents a kind of arrested development."[13] Noting that moral awareness is a characteristic of full maturity, St. Gregory the Theologian argued that God intended for human beings to acquire that knowledge in due course. The first pair tasted of the tree of the knowledge of good and evil prematurely. They were not yet mature enough for the knowledge.[14]

The goal of this process of maturation is Christ, the Alpha and the Omega: "Since man is an image, his real *being* is not defined by the created element with which the image is constructed, in spite of the iconic character which created 'matter' itself possesses, but by his uncreated Archetype."[15] The fact that Adam was created in the image of Christ for the purpose of maturing into greater Christlikeness means that "prior to the hypostatic union of the divine nature with the human, man even before the fall was anterior to Christ, a fact which means that even then, in spite of not having sinned, man had need of salvation, since he was an imperfect and incomplete 'child.'"[16]

The Greek view avoids certain difficulties inherent in the Western view. Panayiotis Nellas argues, for example, that Augustine's assertion that "if man had not perished, the Son of Man would not have come"[17] effectively

> trapped Christ, and by extension the Christian life and the realities of the Church, the sacraments, faith and the rest, within the bounds defined by sin. Christ in this perspective is not so much the creator and recapitulator of all things, the Alpha and Omega as Scripture says, but simply the redeemer from sin. The Christian life is regarded not so much as the realization of Adam's original destiny, as a dynamic transformation of man and the world and as union with God, but as a simple escape from sin.[18]

In sum, the Greek view contributes two very useful statements to Christian doctrines of Christ and of humankind. First, preventing any notion that the incarnation of Christ was merely God's *response* to human sin, it underscores the centrality of Christ as God's Word "through whom all things were made" (John 1:3). Second, it affirms Christlikeness as humanity's true and *original* goal.

A number of contemporary Western theologians have returned to the basic insights of the Eastern view. Like Irenaeus, Ansfried Hulsbosch, for example, argues that sin is to be measured, not against the norm of a presumed paradisiacal innocent perfection, but against the full maturity of Christ. Humans cannot lose what they have never had. Salvation, then, is the completion of creation and, at the same time, reconciliation, because human beings interrupt the process of maturation by refusing it in an act of free will: "What was at the start purely not-yet-possessing has become a sinful absence, because man has affirmed his incompleteness as a positive condition, in conflict with God's creative will."[19]

Whereas the Orthodox tradition speaks of "maturation," a number of modern Western theologians and philosophers, principally and especially the French anthropologist and theologian Teilhard de Chardin, have attempted to reconcile Christian doctrines of creation and man with the scientific theory of evolution. They argue that the process of evolution toward personhood capable of self-transcendence results "from fifteen billion years of persuasive divine creativity and the co-creative response of all entities of our universe." The will-to-live—self-interest, the instinct for survival—characterizes the stage just before emergence into full personhood. In this form, such egotism is not itself sin, but a first-order biological necessity. All human beings are born into this instinctual state. Sin is defiance of God's pervasive and persuasive call to transcend selfishness and evolve in loving relationship with God and others.[20]

James Gaffney describes the basic perspective of theologians who attempt to redefine "original sin" in light of historical-criticism and evolutionary science as follows:

> . . . original sin precisely means the condition of humanity insofar as it lacks salvation in Christ. Sin is accordingly measured rather against that salvation to which it looks forward, than against a state of blessed innocence to which it looks back. What sin represents is, from this point of view, not the forfeiture of life's original quality, but the unaccomplishment of its ultimate destiny: not paradise lost, but, as it were, paradise ungained. Reinterpreted along these lines, it is evident that the doctrine of original sin becomes virtually detached from the doctrine of the fall.

Or, again, these approaches

> involve . . . a tendency to regard basic human defectiveness as an unformed or underdeveloped, rather than a deformed or degenerate state. Accordingly, they situate human sinfulness within a process and understand it primarily with reference to the ultimate goal of that process. Human evil is thus measured in the first place as a distance between present unfulfillment and future fulfillment.[21]

The Eastern tradition addresses a weakness in the Western concept of the "fall" by rejecting the notion that the first humans were "perfect" (human perfection would surely include moral awareness), arguing instead that the first pair failed properly to negotiate the process of maturation intended for them. In other words, there was no "fall" from original essential humanity, but a failure to develop into the fullness of being human. A modern branch of Western theology, taking its starting point from an analysis of the condition of being human in the world, not primarily from a reading of the biblical texts, goes a step further than the Eastern tradition to address implications of the fact that the anxiety arising from the free but finite duality of human nature characterizes human existence. "Existentialism," as it is now generally termed, has roots in the thought of the Danish theologian-philosopher S. Kierkegaard, whose influence can be discerned in the work of M. Heidegger, P. Tillich, and a host of others.[22] Existentialists employ the terms "finitude" and "freedom" to denote the conflict that arises between any and all human limitations, including but not restricted to mortality, the ultimate limit, and the human capacity and urge to transcend, to grow, to create, to mean. Existentialists note that this finitude is a given reality in human existence, not the consequence of the fall. The tension between human finitude and freedom inevitably produces a fundamental anxiety regarding authentic being, an "ontological insecurity."[23]

The individual's task is to struggle for authentic being. The individual is free to fashion his or her personhood; the individual is also free to fail to do so. This freedom cannot be refused or escaped. An individual chooses to act authentically or not. Inaction is itself inauthentic. For theistic existentialists, this dilemma is not itself sin. Instead, the dilemma constitutes the precondition for sin. It gives rise to sin when human beings inevitably resolve it incorrectly by seeking to secure their own existence, by seeking *to be apart from God*.[24] The effort to be apart from the Ground of Being is inauthentic; it is sin.

Freudian psychology confirms Kierkegaard's insights into the fundamental predicament at the center of the human psyche. According to Freud, the human mind is a morass of dualities. The unconscious cloaks "the *id* driven by its 'pleasure principle' struggling against the rational *ego*."[25] Conscious and subconscious vie with each other for control. Neither psychoanalysis nor existentialism considers this duality and self-alienation to be "sin." It is natural, the inevitable consequence of the duality of human freedom and finitude. In biblical terms, human beings are *creatures* bearing the *image of the Creator*. Human freedom is not absolute. It is inherently limited by human creatureliness.

In addition to naturally inherent limitations on human freedom, human beings also suffer the consequences of *being-situated* in history and society. *Being-situated* means that sin precedes human beings, who inevitably encounter it and are inescapably shaped and conditioned by it.[26] The question of the transmission of original sin, from the perspective of existentialism, cannot be resolved by appeal to genetics, nor, indeed, any single mechanism. Human beings deal

Missing the Mark

with an innate dilemma by virtue of their dual nature. Human freedom to attain authenticity is frustrated from the outset by the heritage of inauthenticity (sin) into which they are thrust by virtue of birth into human society.[27]

Significantly, existentialists do not regard the human predicament to be itself evil. Most see the dilemma of limited freedom not as sin, but as the precondition for human choice. The dilemma may be resolved either authentically or inauthentically. Others, however, view the predicament, including the self-alienation and inauthentic efforts at self-security, as a necessary stage in the process of maturation: the "awakening of spirit in the development of human maturity." When the biblical narrative is seen as an archetypal myth describing the development of all human individuals, the "fall" becomes the analogy for the moment of adolescent rebellion against parental authority necessary for successful individuation.[28] The rebellion may be unpleasant, but to remain in a state of innocence and naïveté, to obey uncritically and without question, is unhealthy. Surely, proponents of this reading of the text argue, it is better to know right and wrong, even when the knowledge brings painful responsibility and introduces undesirable possibilities, than to continue in naïve bliss.[29]

Some Questions for the Text

This review of the conventional Western doctrine of original sin, of its shortcomings as perceived by certain contemporary theologians, and of major alternative readings of the biblical narrative raises a number of questions that can now be put to the biblical text. Chiefly, they involve three major constellations of issues. First, what was the state of humanity prior to the consumption of the fruit of the tree of the knowledge of good and evil? Second, how should the act itself be characterized? Third, what changed and what remains the same?

Original Perfection?

According to the conventional doctrine, God created the first pair in a state of perfection, bearing the image of God intact and undiminished. Eastern Orthodoxy and certain contemporary theologians prefer to think of an original state of immature innocence. The intended process of maturation was interrupted by the consumption of the forbidden fruit. The image of God in the first pair took the form of potential to be realized through a process of learning and growth. Existentialists and theologians who attempt to account for anthropological data look not to some primal moment of origination, but to the common experience of all humanity, to the phenomenon of "being-situated" and the related anxiety associated with being as free but limited creatures. In short, the idea of "sin" implies a norm or standard—humanity as it should be, a perfect humanity or an authentic humanity. The definition of that norm will obviously impact every aspect of how the church undertakes its ministries of discipleship, kerygmatic preaching, pastoral ministry, marriage counseling, religious education, and social action.

Rebellion?

The conventional doctrine requires that at least the first pair of human beings sinned by willfully and intentionally transgressing a divine command. A clear and clearly stated expectation or expectations and the human agent's considered decision to defy the commandment are the definitive components of sin in this understanding. One of the most significant problems the conventional doctrine seeks to explain is the universality of human sin. The question is whether its explanation succeeds. How, it might be asked, can an individual who has no knowledge of any divine commandment—a Papua New Guinean tribeswoman, perhaps—be guilty of sin? How can a toddler, incapable of intention with respect to a God of whom he has no concept as of yet, be guilty of rebellion? In both cases, the conventional doctrine would assign Adam's guilt to the individuals in question. Existentialists, perhaps perceiving the threat of unfairness in this explanation, attribute the universality of human sin, rather, to the universality of the human anxiety arising from the dilemma of limited freedom. It arises from human existence itself, not from an externally imposed commandment. The conventional doctrine, then, must impose guilt for the transgression of an explicit commandment where no such transgression has yet taken place—in fact, where no such transgression may ever take place. Nonetheless, the toddler does exhibit a growing selfishness, which his parents must teach him to curb. The tribeswoman may steal or kill or lie, entirely without regard to the expectations of a Creator deity. Must human wrongdoing be categorized as sin only when it is manifests a specific intent to defy God? Can it be judged against the norms of human decency or authenticity?

Fallen?

The issue over which the traditional understanding of the human predicament and alternative conceptions disagree perhaps most concerns the question of the change in status resulting from the consumption of the forbidden fruit. Was the original perfect divine image marred or even destroyed by transgression? Was the acquisition of the knowledge of good and evil, rather, a bittersweet, angst-ridden step toward greater maturity?

Observations Regarding Often Overlooked Elements of Genesis 3

Alternatives to the doctrine of original sin prevalent in the West and its reading of the biblical narrative bear witness to the dynamics of narrative interpretation. Stories yield multiple interpretive possibilities depending upon which motifs and elements the interpreter finds significant. With the various options explored by theologians as background, and aware that the dominant perspective tends to be treated as an absolute despite the richness of the biblical vocabulary and thematics of sin, a reexamination of often overlooked elements of the narrative in Gen 1–3 may yield motifs that are developed into themes elsewhere in Scripture. Six moments in the Eden narrative are particularly noteworthy and will become the basis for the chapters to follow.

Human Imagination and the Burden of Imperfection

The Genesis account juxtaposes the priestly portrayal of humankind created by God's word in the image of God (Latin *imago dei*) with the Yahwistic story of God scooping dust from the earth to fashion Adam, animating the first man with a puff of breath. Genesis 1 emphasizes the *imago dei* notion. Human beings represent the apex of God's creative activity. They were charged with continuing and cooperating with God in populating and ordering creation. But even the *imago dei* notion, as noble as it is, implies human imperfection and incompleteness. To speak of the "image and likeness" attests to an analogy between humanity and the deity. Human beings bear similarity to God in some way and to some degree, but there is no equality. Full and complete godlikeness is deity itself. Genesis 2 expresses the notion of humanity's incomplete godlikeness in narrative fashion. First, it emphasizes that human beings are creatures fashioned from clay. In fact, human beings resemble other creatures at least as much as they resemble God. After all, God apparently created the animals in a fashion similar to that employed for the creation of humankind, although the text says nothing of their inspiration. Indeed, God created the animals in an effort to seek a companion, a counterpart, an equal, for the man who was lonely. Only a being created from the man himself proved suitable, however. Just as the animals, although created to be his companions, were not Adam's equals, so the degree of Adam's godlikeness was not such that Adam and God were equal partners.

Second, Gen 2 accentuates the limitations on Adam and Eve's godlikeness by means of the central motif, the knowledge of good and evil. God had planted a lush garden for the man. Two trees were particularly significant, the tree of knowledge and the tree of life. For unspecified reasons, to be inferred only partially from subsequent events, God prohibited access to the tree of knowledge with the warning that the consumption of its fruit brings death. The first pair was intelligent, knowledgeable and capable of knowing, and free to act on their choices. Adam named things. The first pair spoke with one another, with the serpent, with God. They could contemplate possibilities and make choices. They could imagine new futures. They were not forbidden knowledge itself, only the fruit of the tree of the knowledge of good and evil. Whatever this knowledge represented, it was not knowledge in general; it was a specific category of knowledge. The serpent said that on the day the first pair were to eat of it, they would become like God, indicating both that, although wise, the first pair's knowledge and wisdom had definite limits and that the knowledge they lacked was a category of knowledge reserved for God alone.[30] In fact, the encounter between the serpent and Eve intimates that the serpent, the most cunning of all the creatures of the field, knew more than the humans! Adam and Eve could, nonetheless, entertain the notion of acquiring this forbidden knowledge. They could imagine even greater godlikeness.

Third, although very ambiguous on this point, the account seems to suggest that human beings were also mortal from the outset. Genesis 2 mentions the tree of life, but it plays no significant role in events until God's decision to bar humanity's access to it. There is no prohibition pertaining to its fruit, but after Adam and Eve gain the forbidden knowledge, God, acknowledging that they have, indeed, become more godlike, chooses to prevent them from gaining yet another degree of deity by means of the tree of life. Now, since, by barring Adam and Eve access to this tree, God prevents them from gaining immortality, the account seems to suggest that the first pair were not created immortal. It is entirely unclear whether they had been consuming the fruits of this tree before their expulsion from the garden. Nor is it clear whether one taste was sufficient to convey immortality. The account leaves it unstated. Regardless of whether they had been sustaining themselves through its nourishment and now, cut off from it, would lose its benefits, or they had yet to discover it, the first pair differed from God in their need of this fruit for indefinite life. They were godlike before and after consuming the forbidden fruit. In neither state, however, was this similarity complete, full, perfect.

What was it like to imagine greater, even total, godlikeness? They could imagine, but they could not comprehend! The first pair attempted more than they were capable of accomplishing. Even with the forbidden knowledge, their godlikeness was limited by their finitude. They ate, and their finitude became obvious even to them. Their effort to attain godlikeness became a pratfall. They overreached and the consequences were serious. In order to ensure that they would not overreach even further by grasping for immortality, God banished them from Eden after reminding them that, fundamentally, they were animated dirtballs! Any attempt to transcend human finitude is clownish. Humans must be satisfied to remain within the bounds of their category: finite creatures able to imagine infinity but not fully to comprehend it. Humans are at their most foolish when they aim for perfection. Clearly, the conventional definition of the primal sin as pride accentuates quite accurately one major element of the biblical narrative.

Human Ignorance and the Burden of Responsibility

The conventional definition misses a great deal of the story, however. As liberation theologian Justo González observes:

> The usual interpretation of the passage in Genesis 3 regarding the temptation is that the serpent tempted the human creatures by declaring that they would be "like God." Seen in this light, the primal sin is pride. But as the story now stands, after the two creation narratives of Genesis 1 and 2, it would seem that the serpent was not promising them anything new. They were already "like God" (Gen. 1:26–27). Perhaps then we ought not to interpret this passage as pointing to inordinate pride—to what the Greeks called *hybris*—but rather to inordinate humility based in a lack of trust. They were already like God. They were to have dominion over all the beasts, and therefore presumably also over the serpent. And yet they refused to stand up as "others" before the tempter. In listening to the serpent and refusing to claim their godlikeness, they denied their for-otherness. . . . The result is not only their undoing but also that of the serpent and of all creation over against which they had denied their for-otherness.[31]

Liberation and feminist theologians[32] frequently refer to this refusal to claim the full stature of humanity in an *appropriate* godlikeness as the sin of sloth. It is evident in the first pair's failure to consider the unforeseen and unforeseeable consequences of their decision. It is evident in Adam's silent and immediate acquiescence to Eve's decision to consume the fruit. It is evident in the first pair's efforts to "hide" from God during God's next visit to the garden.[33] It is evident in the blame game played by the first pair when called to account for their actions. It is evident in any human unwillingness to fulfill the possibilities inherent in being authentically human, in responsibly exercising human freedom, in following a path toward maturity.

Basic (Mis)Trust

How can the elements of pride and sloth, both manifest in the one act of consuming the forbidden fruit, be reconciled? Was there some underlying feature, some even more basic "sin"? The biblical narrative reveals that the *seed* of the first sin was neither sloth nor defiance, but mistrust. The serpent said to Eve, "Did God say, 'Do not eat of any tree of the garden'?" Eve replied, "We may eat the fruit of the trees in the garden, but God said, 'Do not eat the fruit of the tree in the middle of the garden or touch it, lest you die.'" The serpent replied, "You won't die. God knows that when you eat it, your eyes will be opened and you will be like God, knowing good and evil" (Gen 3:1b-5, excerpted). Thus, the serpent insinuated that the God who had created them, who had planted the rich and luxuriant garden to provide for them, and who walked with them daily had intentionally and deceptively withheld from them the best gift of all. Adam and Eve disobeyed God because, in their *mistrust*, they *feared* that God might not have provided the best.

Significantly, the New Testament claims that the fundamental problem in human existence is lack of faith, a faulty sense of trust in God. This claim—mirrored in Jesus' teaching on prayer, his sayings on the fatherhood of God, and his admonition against anxiety—can be traced back through the Deuteronomistic Historian's portrayal of Israel's continual murmuring against God to the Genesis account of the first pair's decision to supplement God's provision for their well-being. At root, the human compulsions either to supplant God or to acquiesce to less than full humanity arise from the human fear that God has not, cannot, or will not do for humanity what is best.

Human Intentions and Actual Outcomes

The dynamics and rhetoric of the interchange between Adam and Eve[34] and the serpent are particularly fruitful regarding the Bible's perspectives on sin. Significantly, the serpent tells no lies. Adam and Eve did not die—at least not immediately. Eating the fruit did, in fact, open their eyes, making them more like God; even God admits that this is so later in the account. But the serpent does not tell the whole truth either. The first pair does not die immediately, but their relationships with one another and with God suffer serious injury, and they are banned from the garden and prohibited access to the tree of life. This is the serpent's responsibility. Key for the story of human sin, however, is the fact that Eve extended the serpent's logic on her own, enumerating only the potential benefits to be gained from the forbidden fruit: it appeared to be nourishing, it was aesthetically pleasing, and it promised to make her and her husband wise like the very deity. Surely, this fruit brings only benefits! Who could deny the wisdom of tasting it? In that moment of deliberation, Eve expresses not even a hint that a spirit of rebellion motivates her. Her intentions are only good, however ill-conceived. As far as she is able to anticipate the consequences of her actions, they too will be only good. But she simply is not wise enough to recognize her folly.

Prevalent definitions of sin require that the agent intend to rebel, however. The first pair intended to attain a good. Surely to be more perfect, to be like God, to know—surely this attainment would be good. Unfortunately, however, Eve and Adam had been duped into complicity in a scheme of partial truth. They could not claim, as they later tried to do, that they were merely victims of the serpent's deceit. They had participated in the serpent's system of half-truths, even amplifying it before taking action on its false promises. And, regardless of their intentions to achieve a benefit, their action introduced selfishness, irresponsibility, guilt, pain, and death into the world.

Elsewhere, in harmony with the elements suggested in the dialogue between Eve and the serpent, the Bible contends that sin has an objective component entirely unrelated to the intentions of the agents of sin. Sin is sin, whether intended or accidental. In fact, perhaps the most common avenue into sin is misdirected motivation, uncritical complicity in a system of half-truth.

Human Sins and Sensibilities

The "crime" model of sin treats the guilt of sin as a juridical matter requiring either punishment or acquittal. It is, in essence, a record-keeping category, a notation on the books that a crime has been committed. For contemporary popular culture, influenced largely by the psychoanalytical category of "repression," guilt is the unhealthy and unnecessary product of societal and parental "hang-ups," usually concerning sexual behavior. In this view, guilt must simply be laid aside. There is no reason, it is argued, to feel guilty for natural drives and instincts or for expressing them. Guilt is a vestige of childhood.

The biblical narrative paints a different picture altogether. As soon as Adam and Eve consumed the fruit of the tree of knowledge, their eyes opened, they became aware of their nakedness, they felt shame, and they sought to cover themselves. They hid from God because they were afraid and ashamed. Their sense of guilt and shame was immediate and independent of any juridical context. In fact, according to the internal logic of the narrative, God does not yet know of their actions, so no court records have been made. Their guilt was not an external representation of their debt to justice. It was internal, personal, immanent, and imminent. It was a reality directly, organically linked to the wrong they had done. They had sought superiority over their created status. In effect, they sought independence from God and by extension independence from one another. Each had sought to be independent deity. Now, each was aware of his or her nakedness in the other's presence; each felt exposed and vulnerable to a partner who had sought advantage and who knows that he or she had done likewise.

Within the Bible, the Genesis understanding of guilt as an organic outcome of a sinful act dominates. For biblical writers, God does not impose artificial penalties for crimes. Sin produces its own consequences because God's revealed will is not an arbitrary set of rules. God established the moral order in accordance with the nature of human beings as a means for giving and guiding life ("man was not made for the Sabbath, the Sabbath was made for man"; Mark 2:27). To violate the moral order is to injure, first of all, oneself and simultaneously one's environment and relationships. The sinner need not await a day of judgment; the guilt of sin begins to exact its price immediately.

Humans Sin and the Cosmos Suffers

Read as the foundational text in support of the traditional doctrine of original sin, Gen 3 deals with ultimate matters of salvation. Simply put, human beings have sinned and lost eternal life. Notably, however, the text actually makes no mention of heaven and hell, damnation and salvation. Instead, the focus is on the much more mundane consequences of human sin. God had created a cosmos, a well-ordered system, harmonious and functional. God planted the garden to sustain and occupy humanity. The plants gave their fruits freely. Humanity need only tend and harvest. There was work, but no toil. God created animals as companions for humanity and as its charge. God created Eve from Adam to be his partner, companion, and equal. Adam and Eve, however, were satisfied neither with this harmonious balance nor their place in it. They wanted superiority and their actions threw the whole cosmos into disarray.

Clearing the Deck

God's summary statement describes the organic nature of the relationship between humanity's action and the consequences for the cosmos. In the place of harmonious relations between the animal world and its apex, there will now be enmity and fear. Serpent-kind and humankind will no longer trust one another. Fittingly, because the serpent instigated humanity's dissatisfaction with its assigned place in the cosmos, God fated serpent-kind to crawl on its belly, eating dust. It must spend its life in the dust from which all animal life was created as a constant reminder of its status as creature. It cannot look heavenward. Instead of equality and partnership, hierarchy and imbalance of power, not as part of God's intention, but as the result of humanity's desire for status and power, will now characterize relations between the sexes. Of necessity, the quest for superiority is an attempt to subjugate, after all. Instead of simple, satisfying work, Adam must now toil. The ground from which he was made, the origin of his creatureliness, will resist him. Adam has sought to deny his creatureliness, his kinship with the ground (Hebrew *'adamah*); now the ground will resist his efforts to sustain himself in his creatureliness and mortality. Finally, God reminds Adam and Eve of the basic reality, unchanged by events, that they had sought to overcome: "You are dust, and to dust you shall return" (Gen 3:19). No matter how godlike, humanity's kinship with the dirt can never be altered.

The church tends to think of sin and salvation as issues impinging primarily, if not entirely, on eternity. Not so the Bible. Not so everyday life. Toil, struggles, power structures, hierarchies and inequalities, family strife, enmity, and death— these are the everyday, organic, systemic manifestations of human sin. The actions of the individual occur in the context of a cosmos. Sin lives on in its effects on nature, society, and family.

CHAPTER TWO

Sin: To Be More Than Human

"Men [sic] have rashly undertaken to probe into nature as if there were some proportion between themselves and her."[1]

Parents watch the development of their children with anticipation and joy. They record in "baby books" the precise date and time when the infant rolls over without assistance. Crawling and walking are major milestones in the growth of the toddler, symbol and substance of the child's increasing autonomy, foreshadowing the teenager with a new driver's license. Sounds evolve under parental tutelage into language. If all goes according to schedule, and especially if in advance of it, parents delight in their child's progress. Then, somewhere toward the end of the second year of the child's life, he or she learns that most powerful of words—"No!" "It's naptime," Mom says. "No!" is the response. "Let's put the toys away, we're going to the store," Dad says. "No!" comes the reply. "Have another spoonful of carrots," pleads Grandma. "No!"

On the journey toward autonomy, children who develop normally not only acquire the physical skills necessary to move freely and independently and to manipulate objects and the language skills necessary to communicate and conceptualize, they also manifest, as a healthy matter of course, the autonomy and will that is the common characteristic of all humankind. Usually, in rapid succession, children can exhibit what appears, when judged by criteria appropriate for a morally mature individual, to be selfishness, deceitfulness, and violence. Measured against standards of mature personhood, beautiful, cherubic babes can also seem to be egocentric savages. From the standpoint of empirical evidence concerning the nature of sin and the human condition, however, such an evaluation of infant and toddler behavior—namely, as evidence of humanity's fundamental selfishness/sinfulness—overlooks both the healthiness of developing autonomy and the paradox of holding a toddler morally accountable for actions that are integral to the process of *developing* moral sensibility. Clearly, as any parent can attest, the traditional understanding of original sin as the universal heritage of human egocentrism describes some aspect of fundamental truth about humanity, but it must not be pressed too far or taken too simplistically.

As the introductory chapter argues, in fact, this description does not exhaust the truth with the result that it has limited pastoral usefulness. Even with respect to human rebelliousness and defiance, the phenomena of everyday life and the witness of Scripture call for a much more nuanced and detailed analysis. For example, the traditional doctrine speaks of open, willful rebellion against God and God's will. Very few of us, however, choose the defiance expressed by Milton's Lucifer, "Better to reign in Hell, than serve in Heav'n" (*Paradise Lost* I, 263). Rather than defiance, the most common attitude toward God nowadays is confused indifference. How can the church speak about sin as willful rebellion against God to people who lead substantially moral but spiritually indifferent lives?

The problem of the pastoral utility of the juridical understanding of sin is even more acute from the perspective of personality development. How can the toddler, whose vocabulary does not yet contain the words "selfish" and "rebellion," who does not yet have anything approaching a conception of "God," be considered to be in open, willful rebellion? How can the child—who must learn what it means to share with others, who must learn that others have needs and feelings analogous to his or her own, who must learn, gradually but inexorably, that he or she is not the center of the universe—be accused of rebelling against something she or he has yet to understand? In common human experience, selfishness precedes any conscious capacity for empathy. In relation to the problem of sin, the questions concern when a developing personality may be said to be able to "rebel" and whether the rebellion possible for a mature will may be understood as an expression of some more fundamental human capacity or condition.

Students of personality development[2] examine the stages in the development of infants as they move toward mature personhood. The early stages in typical human development, from infancy to early adulthood, have special bearing for an examination of sin as rebellion.

There is general agreement that, at first, infants are completely unaware of any boundary between subjective self and the objective environment, and certainly of any subjects other than themselves. Their needs and hungers, the persons and means of meeting those needs and hungers, the stimuli present in their environment—in short, the entirety of their experiences—are one. Their actions are purely instinctive, in a real sense, unwilled. Does this infantile egocentricity provide an analog to the *hubris* and arrogance identified by traditional theologies as the essence of human sin? Although he does not draw the analogy explicitly, Reinhold Niebuhr, one of the most eloquent and insightful students of the human condition from a theological perspective in the modern era, describes the essence of human sin, "egoism," in a manner that closely parallels the chief features of the infantile personality. "Egoism" is:

the will to power . . . evident in the human's encounter with creation. The will to power is the inclination of the human creature to try to subjugate its environment (including other persons) . . . to place itself at the center of its existence and, in so doing, to arrogate to its personal reality the false status of ultimate reality.[3]

The analogy is imperfect. One difficulty with this understanding, of course, involves the fact that, according to it, the human propensity for egocentricity first appears at a precognitive stage in personality development. Before the infant can perceive "mother" as an independent subject, and certainly before it can conceive an idea of a personal God, it has already been rewarded by selfishness as a natural condition. Indeed, this infantile egoism, and its survival into later life as the impulse for self-preservation, is necessary. Clinicians observe that without such a drive to live, reinforced by an environment and caregivers that meet the infant's needs quickly and consistently, infants often fail to "thrive." Eric Erikson and James Fowler view events during this stage of development as essential for the development of what they call "basic trust" or "undifferentiated faith," respectively, that the universe welcomes and values the infant.[4] In short, the needy infant can hardly be described as greedy; it is merely and utterly dependent. This is not to deny Niebuhr's insight altogether, but to suggest that, like the traditional formulation of sin as *hubris*, it fails as a fundamental description of the human dilemma.

With the acquisition of language, the development of motor control, and the development of initial cognitive abilities, children begin to evidence awareness of self and others. As yet, however, they have not acquired any real degree of moral understanding, self-control, or ability to deal with abstract concepts. They are supremely impulsive. The cognitive and moral development of early schoolchildren brings them to a point where they can begin to understand cause-and-effect relations: they can tell stories; they can anticipate consequences and can understand that misbehavior will result in correction; and they can conceptualize God in terms of the parental role of enforcer of the rules. Perhaps, in the strictly limited sense of the violation of rules, children at this stage in their development may "rebel" against authority. Since, however, they cannot yet "reflect upon the self as a personality"[5] or identify themes in their own lives, such disobedience can hardly be equated with an act of the mature will. They cannot examine their own inner lives or imagine the inner lives of others. They understand the world only at a surface level.

Rebellion, in the sense of the conscious reallocation to one's self of authority for shaping one's own life, comes to be characteristic of human development only in late adolescence/young adulthood. To this point, the individual has defined himself or herself in relation to parental and peer expectations. Now it is time to evaluate the values, beliefs, and meaning systems one has been given from a critical perspective and to take true ownership of those elements one chooses. Personality theory and common human experience consider this process of individuation, of taking responsibility for the shaping of one's own life, to be necessary for healthy maturation. It can be uncomfortable both for the individual, who can feel a sense of separation and guilt, and for the family and support systems over against which the individual seeks to redefine herself or himself. As a result, some individuals postpone the process and remain abnormally identified by family and community. It can also be a dangerous period, when the individual's impulse to reevaluate can result in the outright rejection of the system of values, meaning, and identity offered by his or her community of origin. In this case, healthy individuation can become an unhealthy individualism.

Clearly, the crises and challenges facing the individual in this stage of personality development more nearly parallel the situation accompanying the rebellion against God and God's will envisioned in the *hubris*/juridical model of sin. Especially when it culminates in an artificial individualism, the erroneous choices one can make at this stage of life recall Paul Tillich's definition of sin or, to use his favored term, *alienation*, as "our act of turning away from participation in the divine Ground from which we come and to which we go [and] the turning towards ourselves . . . making ourselves the center of our world and of ourselves."[6] In many ways, post-Enlightenment Western culture makes a virtue of such rebellious individualism. Existentialist philosophy, with which Tillich engaged in conscious dialogue, for example, argues that although human existence is a polarity of finitude and freedom, and that it is foolish to fail to recognize the limits given in being human, one must nonetheless exercise one's freedom to create one's own authentic existence. The meaning of one's life is one's own to define.[7]

In short, the complexity inherent in the development of human personality even in the early stages is not consonant with the assumption that sin can be defined exhaustively and fundamentally as egocentric "rebellion against God and God's will." Dangers other than willfulness threaten persons. The necessary will to live can become egomaniacal. One can continue to define oneself only or primarily in terms of how others value one, abdicating responsibility and short-stopping authenticity. Humans are complicated creatures.

The Bible on Rebellion and Egocentricity

The Bible is also aware of the complexity of human nature. It addresses the problem of human selfishness and defiance in a variety of traditions and from a number of perspectives. Old Testament prophetic literature excoriates Israel and Judah for rebelling against YHWH in the context of the Mosaic covenant. Here the issue is Israel's conscious choice to violate the terms of the covenant—that is, Israel's rebellion is predicated on an existing relationship with YHWH. These texts do not deal with the fundamental nature of human arrogance. A very few New Testament texts deal with the analogous situation of Christian apostasy, arguing in a fashion very similar to the prophetic claim that such willful abandonment of covenant relationship merits severe treatment. In contrast, a number of wisdom and wisdom-influenced texts, many of them in the form of exegeses of motifs found in the Genesis narrative, examine the issue of human arrogance in relation to the deity but quite apart from any covenantal context. For these texts, the fundamental issue is not the violation of an established relationship, but the universality of human egocentricity. Paul, specifically in the first half of his Roman correspondence, attempts to harmonize the covenantal and the universal perspectives, arguing that pagan idolatry and Israelite covenant disloyalty both manifest humanity's universal rejection of its proper status before God. The teachings of Jesus recorded in the Gospels focus attention on the everyday manifestations of human selfishness, especially in futile attempts to attain absolute self-sufficiency.

The Hebrew Bible on the Violation of Covenant Relationships

The semantic range of a key term for sin in the Hebrew Bible, פשׁע *psh'*,[8] coincides almost precisely with the idea of rebellion against God called for in the conventional definition of basic sin. The Hebrew term is very interesting in relation to the question of the basic nature of human sin for at least two reasons. First, apart from usages of the term in which its semantic distinctive has been largely obscured,[9] the term addresses the actuality of a *breach*.[10] Common to "property crime" and "political rebellion" is the basic idea of "breaking with." Psychologically, פשׁע *psh'* assumes intention on the part of the one who commits פשׁע *psh'*, but it is *not* restricted to attitude only. Sociologically, it describes separation, but is not limited to the effects only. פשׁע *psh'* is "the breaking away of a thing or person from an owner . . . the breaking away of one's self from a community."[11]

Second, the root is notably concentrated in deuteronomistic and prophetic texts dating from the period of the late monarchy (there are no instances of the verb in the Torah, for example, and only nine occurrences of the noun), a distribution suggesting that the deuteronomistic/prophetic movement appropriated—whence and wherefore are unclear and for current purposes probably insignificant—the term as a designation for Israel's breaches of covenant. For this movement, the central flaw demonstrated at the core of the history of Israel and Judah was the violation of the basis and substance of God's covenant with God's people, namely, that YHWH would be Israel's God and Israel YHWH's people. Just as Moab had revolted against Israel's political dominion, the people of Israel, the texts charge, had repeatedly turned to worship idols or to seek security in political alliances. For this movement, Israel's basic sin, its "rebellion," does not consist in ethical transgressions or moral failings but in fundamental rejection of its exclusive covenant relationship with YHWH.

The prophets describe this fundamental rejection explicitly as breach of covenant, apostasy, often employing language that alludes to the account of the establishment of covenant on Mt. Sinai. Ezekiel narrates YHWH's promise to redeem Israel so that "the house of Israel may go no more astray from me, nor defile themselves any more with all their transgressions (*psh'*), but that they may be my people and I may be their God . . . " (Ezek 14:11; cf. 37:23; Hos 8:1; Jer 5:6). Since the Sinai covenant defines the relationship between YHWH and Israel in exclusive terms (Exod 20:3 || Deut 5:7) and, consequently, prohibits the worship of idols (Exod 20:4-6), the prophets and the deuteronomistic literature regard the worship of other deities to be the quintessential expression of Israel's rebellion. As a result, they invoke particularly harsh language to condemn it. Joshua warns the people that their decision to renew the covenant with YHWH must be understood in terms of radical exclusivity; YHWH will accept no less than total devotion (Josh 24:19-20; cf. Jer 2:8; Amos 4:4; Mic 1:5).[12] The prophets describe the act of turning to other gods, "who are no gods" (Jer 2:8), despite YHWH's demonstrated devotion to the covenant people, as Israel's abandonment (Isa 1:28; etc.) or denial of God (Isa 59:13), as treachery and deceit (Isa 48:8; 57:4; Hos 7:13; etc.), and as entirely unfounded (Jer 2:29).

Clearly, the backgrounds of this term in covenant and legal contexts shape its metaphorical use in discussions of Israel's sin against YHWH. The prophets and the Deuteronomistic Historian did not engage in discussions of the origins of universal human sin. Their focus was on the historical idolatry and the related political entanglements of the nation of Israel.[13] The horror of Israel's disloyalty to YHWH lay in Israel's conscious and deliberate abandonment of their God. The term functioned for the prophets and the Deuteronomistic Historian(s) as an expression of their conviction that Israel/Judah had violated a covenant relationship. Israel had freely and consciously entered into exclusive relationship with YHWH only to freely and consciously betray the God who had delivered them from Egyptian bondage. Hosea (Hos 1–3), Jeremiah (3:6-10, 13), and Ezekiel (16; 23), in particular, found the marital metaphor a suitable vehicle for conveying the "voluntary" nature of the relationship, binding once established. Israel/Judah had behaved shamelessly and to its own hurt.

The covenant character of this sin concept, while stressing willful rebellion, is not equivalent to the traditional Christian doctrine of sin as *hubris*. The prophetic concept is predicated on a relationship entered into as a conscious choice. The traditional doctrine describes a universal human predilection present in all human beings and manifest in overt action prior to conscious participation in any covenant; it attempts to account for the universality of human sin. In contrast, rather than offering a mythopoeic or psychological explanation for Israel's behavior, the prophets confessed their dismay. Hosea voices YHWH's lament, now not in the vehicle of the marital metaphor, but in the context of a parental analogy, that Israel had forsaken its divine parent (Hos 11:1-2). Isaiah, too, describes the unfathomability of Judah's behavior in terms of the folly of errant children who behave worse than stupid animals (Isa 1:2-3). Jeremiah expresses God's dismay at Israel's futile decision. They have preferred death to life (Jer 2:12-13). In sum, for the prophets, whose purpose was constructive critique of the behaviors of a specific society, the central assertion did not concern universal human nature, but rather addressed Israel's conscious rebellion against its God in the context of their covenant relationship.

One stream of biblical tradition, perhaps with origins in an important text in Deuteronomy (30:1-20), struggles with the question of why Israel should behave in such a foolhardy manner.[14] Deuteronomy makes several key assertions: first, that it is *not* humanly impossible to keep the terms of the Sinai covenant ("Surely, this commandment that I am commanding you today is not too hard for you," v. 11); second, that the requirements of covenant relationship with YHWH are not obscure or mysterious, but plainly revealed (" . . . nor is [this commandment] too far away . . . it is very near to you . . . ," vv. 11, 14); and third, given that the covenant is knowable and doable, that the only feasible explanation for Israel's failure to observe the covenant must lie in Israel's *will* (" . . . YHWH your God will circumcise your heart and the heart of your descendants, so that you will love YHWH your God with all your heart and with all your soul, in order that you may live," v. 6). Deuteronomy suggests that circumcision can correct the heart, the seat of the will (cf. also Jer 4:4); that is, it needs to be opened, laid bare, in order to be receptive to YHWH's will. Ezekiel (36:26) promises a heart transplant. YHWH will replace Israel's dead and unresponsive heart of stone with a living heart of flesh.

Perhaps the most influential text related to this theme is found in Jer 31:31-34, Jeremiah's promise of a "new covenant." In it, the prophet predicts a day when the law, formerly written on stone tablets (cf. Jer 17:1), will be written directly in human hearts. No longer will it be necessary for experts in the law to teach it to and interpret it for the people; everyone will have immediate and direct knowledge of YHWH's will. Since it will be written in their hearts, the seat of decision-making, their former intransigence will be remedied. Significantly, the prophet's promise of a new covenant focuses, not on the novelty of its content—YHWH's will for Israel does not change—but on the new mode of its mediation. Nowhere does the Old Testament see Torah as a problem; the problem lies in the human will. Of equal significance is the fact that the prophets deal exclusively with the problem of the human will in relation to fidelity to the Sinai covenant established with Israel after the exodus. Nowhere do the prophets engage in discussions about primal human sin. They deal only with historical Israel's fundamental breach of covenant. They do not examine the universal human propensity for arrogance and egocentrism. The prophets do not confront an Israel seeking to establish itself as its own god, but an Israel willing to abandon the God who delivered from bondage in favor of idols.

New Testament "Sin unto Death" Traditions

The Old Testament characterizes Israel's history prior to the fall of Samaria, and Judah's before the Babylonian exile, as a history of wanton violation of the exclusive nature of the covenant relationship between God and God's people. Does the New Testament anywhere extend and develop this understanding of sin? The analogous situation for New Testament Christianity, of course, would not be breach of the Sinai covenant but denial of one's relationship with Christ. In fact, this issue arises in two spheres of New Testament discussion: in the Johannine discussion of a difficult to identify early Christian heresy, and, especially, in Hebrews, one example of the so-called "persecution literature" in the New Testament.

The "Sin unto Death" in the Johannine Epistles

The Johannine correspondence—in particular, the first epistle—reflects a situation of upheaval and discord in the Johannine community. The author seeks to correct a number of misperceptions that are difficult to reconcile into an overarching picture of the party or parties at the source of the disagreement. From one perspective, the letter addresses an issue often characterized as "perfectionism." Are Christians above sin? On its face, the letter seems to contradict itself, arguing both that everyone sins and that those "born of God" cannot sin. From another perspective, the author expresses concern that there seems to be fraternal discord in the community. He warns that those who do not love their brothers and sisters cannot claim to love God. Finally, a viewpoint akin to that held by Gnosticism seems to underlie the author's urgent admonition that confession of Jesus Christ "come in the flesh" is essential to Christianity. The task of forming a coherent image of the argument on the basis of only one side of the discussion hinges on three central texts, 1 John 1:8-10; 3:4-10; and 5:16-18.

1 John 1:8-10. After reminding his readers that his teaching is based on eyewitness experience, the author turns to the first major issue to be treated in the epistle: the assurance that God, through "the blood of Jesus his Son," cleanses those who "walk in the light" and "fellowship with one another" (v. 7). This cleansing from sin is necessary because all sin. From the perspective of the sum of the biblical witness, the claim that everyone needs to be cleansed from sin because everyone is a sinner might seem almost unnecessary. The hypothetical form of verses 8-10, however, can be understood as evidence that some in the Johannine community claim to be sinless: "If we say that we have no sin, we deceive ourselves . . . if we say that we have not sinned, we make him a liar, and his word is not in us." Although this seems to be a rather straightforward declaration of the universality of human sinfulness, subtleties in the diction may be important indications of the nature of the contention between the author and his opponents in the community. The author distinguishes between having "sin" and committing "sins."[15] The expression "to have sin" occurs in the Gospel of John (9:41; 15:22, 24; 19:11) in the sense of "to be guilty of sin." The author differentiates between specific acts, which God forgives and cleans away, and the propensity that abides. Apparently, then, some in the Johannine community have claimed that God's forgiveness through the blood of Jesus Christ takes away not only the guilt of specific sins but also the very propensity to sin, which the author of 1 John recognizes as a continued reality in the lives of Christian disciples.

This distinction between propensity and actions will be central to the argument advanced subsequently. It underlies the paradox inherent in the author's claim to be writing his readers "so that [they] may not sin" coupled with the assurance that "if anyone does sin, however, we have an advocate with the Father, Jesus Christ the righteous" (2:1). To further undermine the claims of the perfectionists, the author turns again to a hypothetical series of statements that presumably represent the position of his opponents. "If" one truly knows God, one obeys God's commandments: "In such a person, the love of God has truly been *perfected*" (2:5). Evidently, some in the Johannine community claim this perfection while "hating a brother" (2:9), despite the fact that such hatred violates Jesus' basic commandment to his disciples to "love one another, as I have loved you" (John 13:34). Claiming that God's love has been perfected in them, they nonetheless hate.

1 John 3:4-10. So far, the author's argument is clear and pointed: Everyone sins; those in the community who claim otherwise demonstrate their sinfulness in their attitudes toward and mistreatment of their fellow believers. It comes as a shock to many readers when, a few paragraphs later, the author makes the statements that "no one who abides in him sins" (v. 6) and that "all those who have been born of God do not commit sin because God's seed abides in them; they are not able to sin, because they have been born of God" (v. 9). On their face, these statements contradict 1 John 1:8-10 and seem, rather, to support the position of the author's perfectionist opponents. Not surprisingly, many interpreters consider the tension between 1 John 1:8-10 and 3:4-10 to be the central problem in reading the epistle. Nor is it surprising that they have suggested a wide range of possible solutions. Stephen Smalley has conveniently catalogued the scholarly attempts to explain this apparent contradiction:[16]

The grammatical explanation hinges on the continuative force of the present tense in 3:6. The problem thus becomes one of translation. Proponents of this view translate 3:6, "no one who abides in him *keeps on* sinning," and 3:9, "all those who have been born of God do not *keep on* committing sin because God's seed abides in them; they are not able to sin *habitually*, because they have been born of God." In this understanding, the author does not claim that believers can be sinless—everyone will occasionally err—but that believers can avoid sin to the degree they maintain intimate fellowship with God. This explanation finds support in the author's choice of the term "abide" to describe the nature of the relationship between God and the believer. It is a favorite term in the Johannine literature for the enduring, intimate, almost organic (John 15:1-11) fellowship with God of the true disciple (John 1:38-39; 4:40; 6:27, 56; 8:31, 35; 14:10, 17; 15:4-7, 9-10; 1 John 2:6, 10, 14, 17, 19, 24, 27-28; 3:15, 17, 24; 4:12, 15-16; 2 John 1:2, 9).[17]

Nonetheless, this solution fails on two key counts. First, 1 John 1:8 also employs the present tense. If translated consistently—"If we say that we do not *continue* to have sin, we deceive ourselves"—the apparent contradiction between the two texts remains unresolved. Second, while it is true that the Greek present tense can have a continuative or durative force, linguists have demonstrated the danger inherent in requiring that it do so. In order to be justified in deriving theology from verb tenses, it is necessary first to demonstrate linguistically that in a specific case the subtleties of the verb system are operative. This observation returns the discussion to the first objection against the grammatical explanation, namely that there is no obvious distinction between the uses of the verb tenses in 1 John 1:8 and 3:6, 9.

Situational explanations view the statement either as hyperbole common to polemic or as evidence of two varieties of *perfectionism* held by members of the Johannine community. According to one view (that of the Johannine author), perfection is an obligation toward which one must strive; according to the other (rejected in 1 John 1:8-10), perfection is a realized truth. Both of these explanations fail, however, to account for the absolute character of the author's language: "in him there is no sin" (3:5); "no one who abides in him sins; no one who sins has either seen him or known him" (3:6); "the one who commits sin is a child of the devil" (3:8); "[those born of God] are not *able* to sin" (3:9). The author offers no clue that the language is to be understood hyperbolically. If such were his intention, he has certainly left himself open—quite unnecessarily—to misapprehension.

Theological explanations that take into account the development of the entire argument of the epistle offer the best possibilities for clarifying the apparent contradiction. These explanations typically regard 3:6 as a reference to a special *kind* of sin. Some argue that it refers to "conscious" sins (cf. Lev 4:2, 13, 22, 27, 5.15, 17-18; Num 15:27-31; Deut 17:12; Ps 19:13; 1QS; 5:11-12; 8:21–9:2; CD 3:14-15). This solution, however, overlooks the impression given by the language in verse 4 that the author has in mind not a category of "sins" but a particular "sin"—indeed, *the* sin. In fact, the author equates this sin with "*the* lawlessness," indicating that the author does not refer to conscious violations of specific requirements of the law, as treated in the Old Testament and Qumran texts cited, but to a total disregard for the will of God.

Others think that 1 John 3:6 describes the *ideal*, placing emphasis on the term μένω (*menō*, "to abide, remain") so that the text would argue that, to the extent that the Christian abides in Christ, he or she can be sinless. Georg Strecker, for example, regards the reference in verse 9 to be the "eschatological" reality in which the community can and should live in contrast to the existential reality facing the community.[18] This solution, however, depends upon a misreading of the obscure expression in verse 9: "his [God's] seed." To whom or what does this expression refer? Does it suggest that the Johannine author subscribed to an anthropology similar to the Stoic theory of the *logos*, the divine spark resident in every human being? There is no definite article as would be required were the expression to stand in apposition to "anyone born of God" and, furthermore, such an apposition would be tautological. The more likely interpretation regards the "divine seed" as a reference to the Spirit of God/Christ who indwells the believer (cf. Rom 8:9). The point is not, then, that the believer abides in Christ, but that the Spirit of Christ inhabits the life of the believer.

In addition to the significant clues in verse 4, namely, the use of the definite article to specify a particular sin, lawlessness—which leads the reader to expect that the author will expand upon this motif elsewhere—the summary statement in verse 10 encourages the reader to locate 1 John 3:4-10 in the context of the entire letter. In this regard, two companion passages provide background and explication of the content of 3:4-10. The passage immediately preceding, especially 2:18-29, adumbrates many of the themes treated in 3:4-10. The believer must abide in the Son and the Father (2:24, 28; cf. 3:6, 9) just as the anointing of the "Holy One" will abide in the believer (2:27; cf. 3:9). Behavior reveals character. The one who does right is the one born of God; the one who does not do right is a child of the devil (2:29; cf. 3:7, 10). In the role filled by "the sin"/"the lawlessness" in the argument of 3:4-10, one finds in 2:18-29 a discussion of the antichrist (v. 18) who denies the incarnation of the Son of God (vv. 22-23). Here the author seems to rely on a tradition that also underlies Paul's discussion of the Parousia in 2 Thess 2:3-12. Both Paul and the Johannine author associate the appearance of the antichrist with the eschaton (1 John 2:18; 2 Thess 2:1) and the work of Satan (1 John 3:8; 2 Thess 2:9). Both identify the defining characteristic of the antichrist as denial/apostasy (1 John 2:22-23; 2 Thess 2:4). In fact, Paul equates this apostasy with lawlessness (ἀνομία, *anomia*), the term employed by the Johannine author to define "the" sin that marks one as a child of the devil. All of this contextual evidence leads to the conclusion that the discussion of antichrist begun in 1 John 2:18 *continues* in 1 John 3. In this view, *the* sin, *the* lawlessness that a believer is entirely incapable of committing is the antichrist's denial of the incarnation.

Similarly, 1 John 4:1-21, the passage that follows an explication of the theme of Christian love in 3:11-24, returns to the discussion of antichrist, making it explicit that the denial of Jesus as the Christ is a denial of the incarnation. One can distinguish between true and false spirits on the basis of whether they confess Jesus Christ come "in the flesh" (4:2, 14-15) or deny (4:3). Denial of the incarnation is the province of the "spirit of antichrist" (4:3).

Thus, it seems almost self-evident that, sandwiched between two passages devoted to warnings concerning the antichrist's denial of the incarnation of the Son of God, the discussion of *the* sin that the true believer simply cannot commit must refer to this denial. In fact, this conclusion finds further support in the

Johannine author's culminating admonition to his readers in which he ties together the various themes running throughout the letter: sin, antichrist, the incarnation, and Christian love.

1 John 5:16-18. This passage also marks out some sin as unique. Harking back to 1 John 1:8-10, this text distinguishes between sins, wrongs done, and "sin unto death," *the sin* which is ultimate, beyond forgiveness. Here the apparent contradiction between 1 John 1:8-10 and 1 John 3:6, 9 is explicitly resolved. Believers can and do sin in the more mundane sense of committing error and even transgression against some aspect of the will of God. Believers cannot, however, violate the very basis of their faith and remain believers. Mere wrongdoing can be corrected and forgiven. The Johannine author encourages believers to intercede in prayer for fellow believers observed to be involved in such sins. He almost forbids such intercession on behalf of those who commit *the* sin, however. For them, correction and forgiveness are impossible.

What could merit such harsh condemnation? The context suggests (5:1-12) that it involves the (docetic?)[19] denial of the incarnation (see 2:18-24; 4:1-3; 5:1, 5-12). The issue apparently concerns the genuine humanity of Jesus. The author has already condemned the denial that Jesus is the Christ come "in the flesh" (4:2-3). Now he amplifies the claim made in the confession that Jesus is the Christ by calling on the testimony of the blood (5:6), the supreme evidence of Jesus' humanity, his death, and his redemptive sacrifice. In true Johannine fashion, the author insists that the believer must embrace the humanity of Christ, that the believer must "gnaw on [Jesus'] flesh" (cf. John 6:48-58).

Taken as a whole, the association of this denial of the incarnation with the antichrist, "lawlessness" (3:4), and the "sin unto death" (5:16-18) seems to confirm the notion that in 3:4-10 and 5:16-18 the author has in mind "the sin" of denying the incarnation as *the* sin, supreme and unforgivable (cf. Num 15:30-31 LXX; Isa 22:14; *T. Iss.* 7:1; *T. Gad* 6:3-7; 1QS 8:17, 21–9:2; *Jub.* 21:22; 26:34).[20] Although it is difficult to reconstruct from only one side of the conversation the complete position held by the opponents of the Johannine author, the outlines of their argument resemble the teachings of a number of groups throughout Christian history. The incarnation has always been scandalous. Apparently there were those in the Johannine community who espoused a Christology similar to what is today called "docetic Gnosticism." That is, they denied that Jesus was the Son of God incarnate as an authentic human being. Presumably, they would have regarded the material world as inferior and would have emphasized the spiritual in a fashion similar to Greek idealistic philosophy. In turn, they would have claimed for themselves a spiritual superiority and perfection. Again presumably, they would have based this claim on the irrelevance of the material world. As superior spiritual beings, their behaviors in the shadow world of matter, they would have argued, were insignificant. In fact, they did not even feel that community with other believers was necessary. In short, their denial of the true personhood, authentic humanity, and actual death of Jesus Christ led them away from the essence of the gospel, in the Johannine author's view. It led them to deny their own authentic humanity as Christ revealed it and made it possible (1 John 3:2); it led them to deny the love of God (1 John 4:7-12).

The gospel contends that God values authentic humanity enough to be willing to identify with human beings. In Christ, God calls humanity to become *more human, fully human*, as God had always intended. The Johannine dissidents considered material human existence to be inherently inferior and, seemingly, could not comprehend how or why God would be willing to take on inferiority. They looked for salvation in the possibility of becoming *more than human*. In essence, their hope reproduced the error of the first pair, who were dissatisfied with their station, who undervalued authentic human existence, and who therefore sought to become their own gods.

"Spurning the Son of God": The Book of Hebrews on Ultimate Apostasy

The Synoptic Gospels describe the failure to recognize God's presence and power in the person of Jesus Christ as the unpardonable sin against the Holy Spirit. First John speaks of the denial of the incarnation, a rejection of the value God places on authentic human existence, as the "sin unto death." The book of Hebrews addresses a very specific problem that Christians periodically confronted throughout roughly the first two centuries of church history. Originally, Christianity was illegal in the Roman Empire and from time to time and place to place, Roman officials persecuted Christians in the effort to squelch the movement. Christians were called upon to renounce their loyalty to Christ, to swear allegiance to the emperor as lord, and to expose fellow Christians. Consequences of the refusal to recant could include the confiscation of property, subjection of one's self and one's family members to slavery, and even martyrdom. While the date of the book of Hebrews is far from certain and the persecution to which it refers cannot be easily identified with any known campaign against Christians, ample evidence in the book itself makes it clear that the author writes to a group of Christians who face hardships because of their faith.

Twice, the author refers explicitly to the persecution of the faithful (Heb 10:32-34, 39; 13:3). More commonly, the author's repeated exhortations to hold fast to hope and faith imply a situation in which the readers are hard pressed to abandon their confession. Given the testimony of the very angels to Jesus' glory and authority, the readers must take care not to "neglect such a great salvation" (2:1-3), because "[one] share[s] in Christ, if only [one] hold[s one's] first confidence firm to the end" (3:14), "without wavering, for he who promised is faithful" (10:23). This perseverance in the face of suffering and oppression is possible, first, because Jesus' suffering and death was the means of salvation and the prelude to Jesus' glory and honor (2:9-10). In fact, since Jesus endured suffering and death in order to bring salvation, he is supremely suited to minister to those facing persecution. Believers can endure suffering with absolute confidence in the consolation of Christ.

> Since then we have a great high priest who has passed through the heavens, Jesus, the Son of God, let us hold fast our confession. For we have not a high priest who is unable to sympathize with our weaknesses, but one who in every respect has been tempted as we are, yet without sin. (Heb 4:14-15; cf. 2:18)

Furthermore, Jesus was not the readers' only predecessor able to withstand persecution, endure suffering, and persevere in faith. The great catalog of the faithful in Heb 11 reassures its readers that faith, hope in the unseen fulfillment of the promise of rest, can prevail, as it did for Abel, Enoch, Sarah, Abraham, Moses, and a host of others, who suffered deeply for their faith, yet persevered (Heb 11:33-38). In the course of this lengthy (thirteen chapters) encouragement to persevere, the author adds warning to exhortation on only three occasions. In the author's view, clearly, the danger of apostasy far exceeds the threat posed by any persecution at human hands.

Heb 3:12-19. The first of these three admonitions appeals to a passage in the Psalms. Just as Old Testament heroes of faith can serve as examples of courage and endurance, Old Testament figures can also serve as warnings. Psalm 95:7-8 [= 94:7-8 LXX] refers to Israel's objections to Moses' leadership and YHWH's providence because of a shortage of water, voiced at Meribah ("contention"). The tradition of this dispute between the people, as one party, and their prophet and their God, as the other, occurs twice in the Hebrew Bible (Exod 17:1-7; Num 20:1-13; cf. other references to the incident in Num 27:14; Pss 81:7; 106:32). The two references, appearing early in the account of Israel's migration from Egypt to the promised land and again very near the end of that account, form a parenthesis around the whole story of Israel's mistrust of God's leadership as exercised through Moses, of its reluctance to endure the hardships of the journey in order to attain the rest and plenty awaiting them in the land, and of its downright disobedience. As a result of this pattern of mistrust and resistance, God had prohibited the contentious generation from finally entering the promised land. The author of Hebrews concludes from the Old Testament that even God's people can, by rebellion, provoke God to exclude them from "entering into rest." The readers of Hebrews must be willing to endure the hardships they face because of their faith in order finally to attain the promised rest. God has not abandoned them or deceived them, nor is God unable to deliver. While the author does not yet draw the full implications of the analogy between his readers and the ancient Israelite murmurers, the terms employed here are strikingly ominous: apostasy, obduracy, fraud, provocation, contention, unbelief, and disobedience. Subsequent passages will make explicit the nature and degree of the danger of Christian apostasy.

Heb 6:4-6. The author of Hebrews finds it repugnant that a believer, who has been "enlightened, having tasted the heavenly gift, shared in the Holy Spirit, tasted the goodness of God's word, the power of the coming age," should then renounce the experience. The circumstance in view does not involve a person who has yet to become convinced of the gospel, but someone with rich personal experience of relationship with God, someone who has already sampled the goodness and power of the eschatological kingdom of God. To spurn this knowledge, turning away from the kingdom of God itself, from God God's-self, is virtually unthinkable. It is to spurn and deride Jesus Christ crucified. Such a decision, in the view of the author of Hebrews, is irrevocable.

The chief issue, of course, concerns the precise definition of apostasy, of "falling away." What would constitute apostasy for the readers of Hebrews? The immediate context does not provide content (cf. *Aboth* v. 26; *Sanh* 107b). It must be sought in the final of these three passages.

Heb 10:26-31. The first word (= the levitical notion of sinning "with a high hand")[21] is the keynote. Does the author mean to suggest that any violation of God's will committed consciously renders one unfit for the kingdom of God? Is he advocating a moral perfectionism? No, for elsewhere the author has expressed sympathy for human weakness and the tendency to err. In fact, he argues, Jesus' high-priestly ministry is effective precisely "because he himself has suffered and been tempted; he is able to help those who are tempted" (2:18). That is, "we have not a high priest who is unable to sympathize with our weaknesses, but one who in every respect has been tempted as we are, yet without sin" (Heb 4:15). Human beings need such a sympathetic priest because humans are "ignorant and wayward" (Heb 5:2). So the author of Hebrews, like the author of 1 John, distinguishes between the errors and failings to which all human beings, even believers, are prone, on the one hand, and a particular sin which is grievous, repugnant, and unforgivable, on the other.

This particular sin is defined in the threefold description found in verse 29 (cf. Zech 12:3, 10): "trampling under foot the son of God," "regarding as common the blood," and "insulting the Spirit of grace." Now this is serious business, not some mistake committed inadvertently, nor even some willful violation of one of the commandments, for example. This is willful, intentional breach of the foundation of the believer's relationship with God through Jesus Christ. It is rejection of the Christ and of his self-sacrifice. It is difficult to imagine who would commit such an act. The early Christians, however, often faced death unless they were willing to deny Christ. Western Christians have little or no point of contact in their experience.

The Bible on Arrogance: O! To Be More Than Human

To this point, the focus has been an examination of biblical discussions of human violations of an established relationship with God, as in Israel's transgression against the fundamental provision of the Mosaic covenant, exclusive loyalty to YHWH, or as in the recanted faith of persecuted first-century Christians. The traditional doctrine of sin, however, claims to be valid as a definition of the sin, not just of those in covenant relationship, but also of all humanity, regardless of age, station, gender, ethnicity, or knowledge of God's revelation. Not surprisingly, the Bible, which was written in the covenant community and to address its needs, deals extensively with the violation of covenant relationship. There are, however, a number of texts, especially in Israel's so-called "Wisdom" literature, that raise the broader question of universal sin.

Dust to Dust: Ecclesiastes on the Human Condition

Biblical covenant traditions, including the New Testament concept of personal relationship with God through Jesus Christ, deal with sin as violation of the parameters of committed relationship: violation of the first commandment, denial of the incarnation, rejection of the kingdom of God. Biblical wisdom traditions ask more fundamental questions concerning the universals of human nature. They value the human capacity for knowledge and wisdom as a component of the image of God stamped on all human beings. They stress the importance of fulfilling the human potential for gaining wisdom. As the next chapter will explore, the failure to strive for this fulfillment is, itself, a manifestation of sin. In relation to the idea of rebellion against God, however, Israel's wisdom tradition does not suggest, as did classical liberalism, that education, the attainment of knowledge, alone provides the solution to the problem of human sin and suffering. The human capacity for learning is limited by the fundamental limitation of being human. The book of Ecclesiastes expounds the warning inherent in portions of Israel's primal history concerning the limitation of humanity's capacity for wisdom, a limitation inherent in human nature and a limitation dangerous to disregard. In short, human beings are responsible for the proper exercise of their minds in relation both to their wonderful godlikeness *and* to their creaturely finitude.

Commentators often puzzle over apparent contradictions[22] in the thought of the Teacher who speaks in the book of Ecclesiastes. Did this Teacher share the wisdom school's confidence in the benefits of learning, as a number of passages indicate *prima facie* ("I saw that wisdom excels folly as light excels darkness," 2:13; cf. 1:16; 7:11-12, 19; 8:1; 9:16a, 18a; 10:2, 10, 12)? Contrariwise, was he fundamentally skeptical of the human capacity for understanding, as a number of other texts seem clearly to suggest ("Then I said to myself, 'What happens to the fool will happen to me also; why then have I been so very wise?' And I said to myself that this is also vanity," 2:15; cf. 2:21; 7:23; 8:7)?

If the Teacher intended either of these perspectives to be absolute positions, his thinking is irreparably incoherent. On the other hand, a number of texts suggest that the Teacher meant them rather as boundary statements defining the limits of humanity's capacity for wisdom. Within the boundaries lies an arena in which wisdom is both possible to attain and profitable to exercise. Only beyond these boundaries does wisdom become futile. The Teacher who speaks in Ecclesiastes agreed with Israel's wisdom tradition that the failure to exceed the lower boundary—that is, to remain in folly—is a great disadvantage, even sin. But the upper boundary represents a danger, as well. Specifically, humans encounter the upper limit of human wisdom, according to the Teacher, in the attempt to discern knowledge properly reserved to God alone: the future course of one's life (10:14), or more generally, the pattern of God's activity in human history (8:16-17; 11:5). Significantly, the Teacher does not dispute the value of wisdom applied to "practical" matters, only the possibility for the human mind to discern ultimacy. His position finds its most whimsical statement in 7:16-18: "Do not be too righteous, and do not make yourself too wise. . . . Do not be too wicked and do not be a fool. . . . It is good to take hold of the one without releasing the other; for the one who fears God will avoid both extremes."[23]

Human Creatureliness and Finitude. In a midrash on the tradition recorded in Gen 3, Eccl 3 traces this human limitation to humanity's origins.[24] Noteworthy are the elements of this tradition that the Teacher chose to emphasize and the manner in which he did so. First, the Teacher observes that "[God] has put עלם ['lm] into their hearts/minds . . . yet they cannot find out what God has done from beginning to end" (Eccl 3:11). Owing to its elasticity, the Hebrew vocable עלם, often translated "eternity" (although linguistic evidence suggests that Hebrew thought did not include notions of infinity), here presents a challenge to translators and interpreters. Has the Teacher been influenced by Greek philosophy? At least one commentator has suggested emending the term to עמל ('ml), the Teacher's favorite expression for "toil," the common lot of humanity, noting its occurrence in the immediate context (v. 9).[25] The occurrence of עלם ('lm) in verse 14 and the several other expressions for various dimensions of time in the context (עת 't, "time," vv. 1-8, 11; מראש ועד־סוף, *mero'sh we'ad-sof*, "from first to last," v. 11; מה־שהיה כבד הוא, *mah-shehayah kebad hu'*, "what will be after him," v. 15), however, assure the text and suggest the parameters for understanding the key phrase. Diethelm Michel has noted that together *'t* and *'lm* establish a semantic field in which the two terms represent alternatives: *'t* is time as occasion; *'lm* is time in duration. He observes: "In every human being resides the impulse to inquire beyond the given moment and thus to perceive 'meaning'. . . ."[26] In contrast to human beings, who can imagine/conceive of *'lm* but who cannot fill the category with content, God knows past and future as though they were present (v. 15). This distinction between human knowledge/wisdom and divine is that between a *formal category* and *content*.

Although vocabulary explicitly linking Eccl 3 with the tradition found in Gen 2–3 does not appear until verses 19-20, the Teacher's discussion of the human capacity for ultimate knowledge/wisdom in terms of the similarities and distinctions between human and divine capacities for comprehending *'lm* can be regarded as a paraphrase of one of two interrelated issues in the Genesis tradition: the degree to which human godlikeness is limited by human creatureliness.

Second, the Teacher reports, "I said in my heart with regard to human beings that God is testing them to show that they are but animals" (3:18). For the Teacher, the incontrovertible reality, both attested by experience and taught by the creation tradition, is the absolute boundary represented by human mortality. Notwithstanding the human capacity for imagining the ultimate, human beings share both origin and destiny with the animal world: "from dust to dust" (v. 20). The Teacher insists that evidence and tradition offer no clear indication whether the human advantage over the animal world in terms of wisdom signifies some advantage in an afterlife. Who knows—has empirical knowledge of—what lies beyond the grave?

Qoheleth's Agnosticism. Many interpreters find the Teacher's agnosticism discomfiting. T. Longman objects to R. Norman Whybray's characterization of the Teacher's position as "completely in accordance with traditional Israelite belief,"[27] arguing from Gen 1:27 and 2:7 that the Teacher is not entirely orthodox since "Gen 2 teaches . . . in a context that shows not only human kinship with creation . . . but also its special and distinct relationship with God."[28] Ulrich Kellermann, on the other hand, sees the Teacher's statement as polemic against an emerging doctrine of the afterlife such as one finds expressed in Sir 40:11.[29] Both of these arguments push the Teacher's position too far. He denies neither the human advantage over the animals manifest in superior human wisdom nor the possibility that this advantage extends in some way beyond the grave.[30] Instead, he affirms simply and definitely that the grave stands as an absolute limit on human knowledge. He is absolutely agnostic concerning *'lm*.[31]

In the end, the Teacher offers a sobering view of reality, a reminder of the precarious status of humanity balanced between the animals and the angels.[32] Humans can and should attain an appropriate degree of wisdom. They can and should find "good" in their work and their family life. They can and should enjoy the life God has given. The ability to know and to create testifies to human godlikeness. But humans must not overreach. Even though created in God's image, they are still *creatures*. The category of perfection should not be applied to human beings. Humans must be happy with their station. Ecclesiastes reminds us that humans have *'lm* in their hearts. Naturally, they would like to fill that category with content, but absolute knowledge is reserved for God.

Covenant Disloyalty and Basic Arrogance: Paul's Synthesis

Both Testaments of the Bible discuss sin as rebellion against God in the context of covenant traditions. Israel rebels against its God; Christian apostates deny the humanity of Jesus or recant their confession of his lordship. This type of rebellion presupposes that the rebel is party to the "special revelation" entrusted to the community of faith and that the rebel has entered into the relationship with God offered in that revelation. Old Testament wisdom and creation traditions explore the nature of human rebellion in more universal terms, apart from the Mosaic covenant. If Israelites can willfully transgress the first commandment, denying the exclusive loyalty owed to Israel's deliverer, how can the "sin" of non-Israelites, who have no knowledge of the exodus or Mt. Sinai, be defined? The Teacher answers that all human beings are aware of the possibilities beyond themselves and seek, uselessly, to appropriate for themselves capabilities that are God's alone.

In the New Testament, these streams are integrated, especially in Paul's analysis of sin in Rom 1–7 and, to a degree, in James's statement of the homogeneity of sin. Both rely heavily on exegesis of the account of the first human transgression recorded in Gen 3.

Paul on Sin

Paul enjoys pride of place in the New Testament as the only writer to offer a "systematic" analysis of sin from the perspective of its significance in relation to the gospel. As an increasing body of scholarship recognizes, this was a problem for Paul. He had confessed Jesus as the Christ, the key to human history, the Messiah of the Jews and the Savior of the Gentiles. As someone has put it, however, if Jesus is the answer for Paul, what is the question? In anticipation of a proposed journey to Rome, the capital of the Empire and, presumably, the seat of what must have already been one of the most influential congregations in early Christianity, Paul wrote a letter of introduction. He had not founded this church, so he took the opportunity to detail his theology systematically. Although it is unclear what, if any, conclusions can be drawn from the prominence of the Gentile/Jewish problem as to the nature of the church in Rome, it is important to note that Paul's apostleship was defined in these terms, both by Paul himself and by his enemies. He obviously thought it important to address the issue in his own words rather than risk his reputation to hearsay. As a means of reconciling his mission to the Gentiles with Israel's status as the covenant people and of accounting for the centrality of the gospel, Paul insists on the "righteousness of God" as the central, consistent, and abiding truth. Both Jews and Gentiles are sinners—this has always been true; both Jews and Gentiles must come to salvation by faith—this, too, has always been true. God is fair and just.

Paul's analysis of the human condition in Rom 1–7 plays an important role as the scriptural basis for the conventional definition of "original sin." Proponents of this doctrine have rightly recognized that, like the Teacher of Ecclesiastes, the apostle Paul based his only systematic analysis of the human condition in part on a midrashic exegesis of the Genesis account of Adam and Eve. Exegetes have long noted echoes of Gen 1–3 in Rom 1–7, especially Rom 1.[33] Indeed, Paul appeals specifically to Adam as the author of the sinful human condition. The conventional reading of Romans looks especially to Rom 5:12-21 as scriptural warrant for the notion that Adam's sin and guilt have been automatically transmitted to all of humanity as a heritage. Additionally, Paul's frequent use of the term "law" seems to support an understanding of sin primarily as transgression against divine commandments.

Paul's very complex and nuanced argument with its frequently shifting metaphors deserves fresh consideration, however. If only because it is healthy periodically to compare anew historically held interpretations of the text with the text itself, it will serve us well to try to set aside what the tradition has taught us to find in Romans in order potentially to hear emphases and assertions that tradition may be overpowering. Read, to the extent that it is possible to do so, with ears attentive to themes otherwise unnoted, at least three central emphases of the traditional doctrine of "original sin" seem to be unsupported, even contradicted, by Paul's statements in Rom 1–7. First, one can dispense with the notion that Paul is concerned primarily with describing the process whereby sin is *transmitted* from generation to generation. Instead, his principle concern, in service of the overarching theme of God's righteousness, is to demonstrate the universality of sin. Second, one can dispense with the traditional tendency to understand Paul's use of the term "law" unequivocally as a reference to the Mosaic covenant. Understood in this limited sense, the term gives rise to understandings of Paul's argument in Rom 1–7 as a diatribe against Judaism and, at the same time, ironically, as scriptural warrant for juridical concepts of sin and salvation. Instead, Paul employs the term in a variety of ways, ranging from references to the law of Moses to designations of the law manifest in every human conscience. Unifying the range of Paul's usage of the term is the notion that God's revelation of God's-self is a fundamental principle of creation available in some form to all humanity. Third, arguments concerning whether Paul engages in so called "natural theology," especially in Rom 1—arguments that have raged since the Second World War in Protestant circles—typically fail to discern the impact of Paul's argument in Rom 1 on the whole question of Paul's stance on "natural theology." The argument usually hinges on the question of whether Paul means to propose the idea that human beings, relying solely on their powers of observation and deduction, can come to "saving knowledge" of God. Romans 1 deals, however, not with salvation, but with universal human behaviors that necessitate salvation in the first place. Romans 1 corresponds to Gen 3, not John 3. With ears better attuned to the logic of Paul's argument, one can now listen for Paul's position on the basic nature of human sin.

The Universality of Sin

As noted briefly above and in the introduction,[34] Rom 5:12-21 is a very important text for the conventional doctrine of original sin. Since it is key to

Paul's argument, it is essential to interpret it as carefully as possible. For present purposes, the core of Paul's argument can be found in verses 12-14 and 18-19.

> Therefore, *just as* sin came into the world through one man and through sin (came) death, *so also* death spread to all men **because** everyone sinned. For, before the law, sin was in the world, but sin was not recorded, there being no law, but death ruled from Adam to Moses, even over those who did not sin in the same way that Adam, who is the type of the one to come, transgressed.

> Thus, *just as* one transgression resulted in the condemnation of all, *so also* one righteous act results in the justification of life for all. For, *just as* through the disobedience of one man, many were made sinners, *so also* through the obedience of one, many will be made righteous.

Several features of Paul's argument should be noted. First, the translation above offers the correct reading of the conjunction ἐφ' ᾧ, *eph hō* ("because" in bold typeface above, not "in whom"; cf. 2 Cor 5:4; Phil 3:12; 4:10), introducing the second clause in the verse. Augustine and his followers argued on the basis of the mistranslation "in whom" that all of Adam's descendants became guilty when Adam sinned: " . . . just as sin came into the world through one man, *in whom* all have sinned. . . . " Properly understood, the text does not describe an automatic, mechanical transmission of guilt, but emphasizes the analogy between the consequences of Adam's sin and the sin of each of his descendants.

Second, Paul's purpose here, in fact, is not to describe how all human beings are sinners, but to develop the analogy between Adam and Christ. For example, verses 12-14 do not seek to account for the universality of sin—it is treated as a given—but for the universality of death attributable to the universality of sin. Neither death nor sin is described as characteristic of persons, but as related realities present in the world as a consequence of Adam's actions.[35] The chiastic structure of the argument and the supporting explanation in verses 13-14 (introduced by the conjunction "for") are significant in this regard. Just as Adam's sin (A) brought death (B), so death (B') spreads to all because all sin (A'). Death occupies the central position. Furthermore, the explication—somewhat surprisingly[36]—relativizes the role of sin itself prior to the advent of the Mosaic law. To be sure, sin was in the world in the period between Adam and Moses, but its primary consequence was not its impact on the sinner's status in the age to come, but its immediate fruit: death. In short, verses 12-14 argue that the universality of death is linked directly to the universality of sin, even when sin is present but not "booked." Similarly, verses 18-19 do not explicate the etiology of sin, but compare the ways in which sin brings condemnation and Christ's death brings salvation.[37] Both consequences result through the actions of individuals, Adam and Christ, respectively.

Third, the logic of these analogies is paramount. Christ's death has an effect on the human race analogous ("just as . . . so also," vv. 12, 18, 19) to the manner in which Adam's sin had an effect on the human race. The issue is the precise nature of this analogy. If one maintains, as do proponents of the traditional doctrine of original sin, that Paul's purpose here is to describe the manner in which Adam's sin is *automatically* transmitted to his descendants, then the logic of the analogy would require that one also understand Paul to be propounding universalism: "Just as Adam automatically made us all sinners, so also Christ automatically made us all saints." Proponents of the traditional doctrine are rarely—if ever—universalists, however, and, more importantly, judging from the whole of his correspondence, Paul was not either. In contrast to the traditional interpretation, the logic of this passage, in fact, negates the notion that Adam's act necessarily and automatically made his descendants sinners. Bruce J. Malina notes that Paul argues in typically rabbinic fashion *from the lesser to the greater*. In this approach, Adam, as the lesser case, is used to illustrate an even greater truth. Malina concludes: ". . . if the causality ascribed to Adam is equal to or greater than the causality ascribed to Christ, we certainly do violence to what Paul intends. Thus I believe we can safely say that for Paul if the life given by Christ does not reach all automatically, neither does the death brought by Adam."[38]

Still, Paul draws the analogy. Something about the way in which Adam's actions resulted in sin and death for humanity and the way in which Christ's actions result in salvation and life for humanity is the same or very similar. What is this something? Since, for Paul, the most fundamental theological truth involves God's righteous provision of salvation through faith in Jesus Christ, it is reasonable to derive Paul's position regarding the relationship between Adam's sin and universal sinfulness from Paul's understanding of salvation. Christ's saving act, in Paul's view, does not automatically bring salvation to every individual human being. Instead, it establishes salvation as a potential for all. Individuals appropriate this salvation through faith.

Paul frequently describes both this potentiality and the universality of human sin in terms of participation in one of two "realms." One is either *in* Adam, participating in sin and death, or *in* Christ, participating in Christ's death to sin and in Christ's newness of life. The most extensive treatment of these realms appears in Paul's discussion of baptism in Rom 6:3-11.

> Do you not know that we who have been baptized *into* Christ Jesus have been baptized into his death? We were buried therefore *together with* him though baptism *into* death so that, just as Christ arose from the dead through the glory of the Father, so also we too might walk in newness of life. For if we have become *participants* in the likeness of his death, we shall surely also be participants in the likeness of his resurrection. Knowing this, that our old self was crucified *together with* him in order that the body of sin might be destroyed so that we might no longer serve sin. For death justifies one from sin.

Now, if we have died *together with* Christ, we believe that we shall also live *together with* him, knowing that Christ, having been raised from the death, will never die again: death no longer rules over him. For the death he died was death to sin once for all; but the life he lives is life to God. So also we, too, consider ourselves to be dead to sin, but alive to God *in* Christ Jesus.

Here Paul treats sin and death as a "realm" juxtaposed to new life in Christ. Baptism *into* Christ is participation in his death.[39] Once "dead," one is no longer in the realm of sin. Significantly, the imagery here does not involve substitution (Christ died *instead of* sinners), but participation. The believer dies *together with* him, *participating in* his death in order to *participate also* in Christ's life. Throughout this discussion, as elsewhere,[40] Paul relies heavily on the prepositions and related prefixes "in" (ἐν, *en*), "into" (ἐις, *eis*), and "together with" (σύν, *sun*) to convey his thought. One is justified, then, in understanding these prepositions/prefixes analogously in statements concerning the relationship between Adam and universal human sin. One is a sinner, not because Adam's sin automatically made one so, but because one actively *participates* in Adam. Faith in Christ, pictured in baptism, effects the shift from one realm to the other.[41] It is participation in the death and life of Christ. This realm-concept underlies Paul's discussion of the church as the body of Christ. Believers, baptized *into* Christ's death and resurrection, live *in* Christ as Christ's "body." In the same way, unfaith is participation in the sin of Adam.[42] As Paul put it summarily in 1 Cor 15:21-22, "For, since death [came] through a man, so resurrection [came] through a man. For just as *in* Adam all die, so also *in* Christ shall all be made alive."[43]

The Universality of "Law"

Paul's purpose in Romans was to outline a description of God's righteousness, manifest in the gospel, as it applies uniformly to both Jew and Gentile. In order to do so, he appealed to the Adam/Christ typology, demonstrating that, just as the sin of Adam, the common ancestor of Jew and Gentile, created a realm of sin and death in which all of humanity participates, so did the redemptive death of Christ create a realm of salvation and life in which all of humanity may participate. Paul found it necessary also to address the problem posed by the historical specificity of God's revelation to and relationship with a particular people. If sin is rebellion against God's will and God's will is known in God's revelation as contained in the Torah/Sinai covenant, how can Gentiles, or for that matter, Israel's pre-Sinai ancestors, be said to have been in rebellion? Paul addresses this problem by means of an expanded concept of the law, a concept that incorporates both the Sinai revelation and what might now be termed the human conscience. In other words, Paul relates the specific revelation of God's will contained in the Sinai covenant to the general revelation of God's will evident in the created order, arguing that they are fundamentally uniform and universally available to human beings. Except for a few idiosyncratic or unclear usages,[44] Paul employs the term νόμος, usually translated "law," in two principal, but ultimately related, senses.

In a number of passages in Romans, Paul clearly employs the term "law" in reference to the Mosaic Torah.[45] He speaks of being "instructed in the law" (2:18) and to those, who, therefore, "know the law" (7:1), a codified document ("written code," 2:27; "the old written code," 7:6), which is "the form of knowledge and truth" (2:20). In the service of his overall purpose to demonstrate God's absolutely evenhanded righteousness toward all humanity, Jew and Gentile alike, Paul makes three basic points concerning the written Torah. First, the possession of the Sinai covenant does not advantage the Jew because the law's objective is obedience: not hearing but doing (2:13, 17-25). Second, God's special relationship with Israel was not based upon the law in the first place, but upon faithful response to God's unconditional promise (3:28, 31; and, especially, 4:13-16). Third, the law affords no power for keeping its standards. It establishes the criterion of righteousness but cannot make one righteous (7:1-25). In fact, knowledge of the law entices one to sin (7:5, 7-11, 13). Even when one agrees with the requirements of the law, apart from some reconfiguration of one's will, one finds oneself mysteriously incapable of obedience (7:15-25).

In another usage, however, Paul expands the concept of the written law to include the principles universally available to humankind. He probably does so in keeping with a tradition of exegesis growing out of the wisdom school that identified the written Torah with the unwritten principle of Wisdom (חָכְמָה, *hokmah*), according to which God created the world and which is the common heritage of humankind (Prov 8). Here Paul stands in the tradition of the prophets, especially Amos,[46] and the Teacher of Ecclesiastes. Like other New Testament writers (John's *logos* doctrine, for example), Paul was also probably influenced by Greek thought, especially, perhaps, Stoicism.[47] At any rate, just as he demonstrated that, despite their possession of the written Torah, Jews stand in need of salvation offered as a gift of God through faith, Paul took pains to establish that Gentiles are on equal footing with Israel. Gentiles, too, are sinners without excuse to whom God offers salvation through faith.

Paul develops this element of his overall argument that God is absolutely fair and just in chapters 2 and 3. He establishes, first, that Jews enjoy no advantage over Gentiles by virtue of their access to the law because God's law, a principle of the created order, is somehow[48] imprinted on the human conscience.

> For, when Gentiles who do not have the law do by nature the requirements of the law [lit., "the things of the law"], they are law to themselves even though they do not have the law. They manifest the works of the law written on their hearts, their conscience bears witness and their internal conflict accuses or excuses [them] on the day when God judges the secrets of men according to my gospel through Jesus Christ. (2:14-16)

In fact, the importance of the law lies not in the having, but in the doing. Gentiles, then, who obey the law "written on their hearts" qualify as members of the covenant community, and their obedience stands as an accusation against disobedient Jews (2:26-27).

Paul's chief point, however, is not the status of obedient Gentiles, but the establishment of the fact that, because knowledge of God's law either written on tablets or on the heart is universally accessible, everyone is guilty before the law of God, on an equal par as sinners. God, therefore, cannot be charged with partisanship toward Israel or with caprice for holding Gentiles accountable for their sin.

> . . . I have already accused all, both Jew and Greek, with being in sin . . . (3:9)

> We know that whatever the law says it speaks to those in the law in order that every mouth may be silenced and the whole world become accountable to God. (3:19)

This much seems straightforward. God's will has been made known to all people, to Jews through the covenant and to Gentiles through the universal law written on the human conscience. Elsewhere, Paul makes a number of statements that, at least at first blush, seem inconsistent with each other and with the main line of his argument. Preliminary to the discussion of the responsibility of Gentiles to the requirements of the law "written on their hearts" (2:15), Paul announces a principle to which he returns at several points subsequently, namely, that "whoever sins without the law dies without the law, and whoever sins in the law will be condemned by the law" (2:12). A few chapters later, he affirms that "before the law, sin was in the world, but sin is not recorded when there is no law" (5:13). Indeed, death, the immediate consequence of sin, "ruled from Adam to Moses" (5:14), but the sins of the people in that period of time were somehow unlike those of Adam himself (5:14), since for these sins God showed a measure of forbearance (3:25). The difference made by the coming of the law is to make the sin already present in the world evident (7:7, 13) and egregious (5:20; 7:5, 8-11).

Yet Paul can also assert that "if there is no law, neither is there transgression ($\pi\alpha\rho\acute{\alpha}\beta\alpha\sigma\iota\varsigma$, *parabasis*)" (4:15), which seems to contradict the notion that there can be sin "apart from the law" and, even more basically, that knowledge of the law is universally accessible to both Jew and Gentile (3:19). Either Paul speaks of an entirely hypothetical situation in 4:15—"if there were ever a situation in which a human being was unaware of the law, there would be no trespass"—or, in light of the discussion in Rom 7, in which Paul seems to have in mind the process of personal maturation, of the situation of immature individuals who have not yet attained moral accountability.[49] Alternatively, the key to resolving this apparent inconsistency may lie in the choice of the term "transgression" in 4:15 and 5:14. In this case, Paul would be distinguishing between sin, wrong done ignorantly, and trespass/transgression, wrong done despite full knowledge of divine expectations. The former results in death; the latter in condemnation.

Explicitly, then, Paul addresses the possibility of sinning without willfully rebelling against God's law. The greater difficulty, however, involves situating this line of thinking in Paul's overall argument. Does Paul's analysis of the Gentile situation conclude that all human beings have some familiarity with divine "law" and are, therefore, transgressors? Or does Paul allow for the existence of Gentiles (and Jewish children?) who have no such innate acquaintance with the principles of divine order and who, although sinners, remain in a state of innocence comparable to that discussed in Rom 7? On balance, the apparently intentional choice of the term "transgression" instead of the more general "sin" and the context of the discussion of personal maturation in Rom 7 support the conclusion that Paul distinguished between the levels of responsibility attributable to naïve or mature consciences. If so, Paul must have worked on the basis of a definition of sin that was more fundamental than "transgression against specific criteria."

Sin: "Claiming to be wise, they became fools . . ."

Paul stated this fundamental understanding of sin in Rom 1:18-32, in which he seems to argue rather straightforwardly that *all people* know God, but that *all of them* deceive themselves, exchanging the true God for a mere replica (cf. Jer 2:11). Interpretation of this passage has become controversial in recent decades, especially for Protestant theologians, because of its role in the dispute over so-called "natural theology."[50] The issue, brought to prominence by the influential theologian Karl Barth, involves whether and to what degree it is possible, apart from the special forms of God's revelation in God's relationship with Israel, in the Bible, and, uniquely, in Jesus Christ, for human beings to know anything of God. Proponents of natural theology argue that the Creator reveals something of the Creator's self in the creation and that, through this evidence, any human being can infer something significant about the Creator. Opponents argue that such knowledge is not generally available and that, even if it were, it would be insufficient as a grounds for relationship with the deity.

While this is not the place to undertake a full examination of the argument or to offer a fresh assessment of the problem,[51] it is so closely linked to the interpretation of Rom 1:18-32 that a few comments concerning the debate, particularly as they impinge on Rom 1, are necessary. First, as J. Barr has helpfully pointed out, it is important not to impose the terms of the contemporary debate on the biblical text. That is, Rom 1 may not espouse natural theology as defined by its opponents, but Rom 1 does involve ideas that could be best described as a natural theology of sorts. The objective, then, would be to adopt a definition consonant with the text. For example, opponents of natural theology often define it in terms of the efforts of "pure reason" to make deductions about God or in terms of the program of "proving" the existence of God. Opponents reject the possibility of the former on the grounds of the marred state of fallen human reason and of the latter as contrary to the nature of faith, which cannot be proven. Those who see elements of natural theology in Rom 1, however, do not find there support for the effectiveness of "pure reason" nor any attempt to prove the existence of the deity. Rather, the emphasis in Rom 1 is on the failure of human beings to properly acknowledge God's revelation of God's-self in the created order, not on the possibility of deducing God from first principles. God reveals God's-self in nature as God reveals God's-self in Jesus Christ. Human beings respond to the revelation. The adjective "natural" refers, then, to the arena in which God reveals God's-self and, thus, to the arena in which human beings encounter God.[52]

Second, as Barr also notes, Paul's argument—that some knowledge of God is available to all human beings because God has made God's-self known in creation—is consistent with biblical teaching. As noted above, the fact that the prophets addressed significant oracles to non-Israelite nations implicitly asserts that even those outside the covenant have some knowledge of God's will for humanity. Wisdom literature predicates its teaching on the idea that human beings can pursue wisdom, the principle by which God created (Prov 8), by studying the created order. The psalmist celebrates components of the created order as the "honor and majesty" with which God clothes God's-self (Ps 104:1-4). Creation bears speechless testimony throughout the whole world to the glory of God (Ps 19:1-4; cf. Rom 1:23). Even the great celebration of God's Torah in Ps 119 (vv. 89-90) acknowledges that God's will is embedded within the created order.

Third, as the discussion of Paul's position on the universality of law has shown, Paul needed to be able to appeal to a general revelation of God and God's will in nature for the sake of his argument that God is universally just. Barr summarizes this aspect of Paul's argument in Romans as follows:

> . . . the plan of Romans . . . is to compare the status of Jews and Gentiles in relation to God's justice. Both, according to Paul, are under the wrath of God for their failings. Why so? For the Jews, it is easy enough to explain: they had the Law of Moses, but did not obey it. But what about the Gentiles? This was more complicated. They had known that which was knowable of God but failed to honour him accordingly and devoted the veneration proper to him to images of humans or, worse, of animals . . . [J]ust as Jews, who had the law, had disobeyed the law, so Gentiles, who did not have it, might in effect have obeyed it. . . . [T]he Gentiles were at fault because the realities of God had indeed been revealed to them through his works of creation, and . . . that means that the structures and elements of the created world form in themselves a testimony from which the reality of the creator God could have been and should have been inferred. Not only so, but it *was* inferred: they *did know* God, but did not honour him as God. This is why they are inexcusable.[53]

Finally, much of the recent "natural theology" debate has been fueled by concerns over whether the knowledge of God presumed to be universally available by observation is sufficient grounds for salvation. Protestant theologians, especially those influenced by Karl Barth, have argued on the basis of a strictly delimited understanding of the notion that salvation is only possible "through grace by faith in Jesus Christ" and that, therefore, any knowledge of God inferred by observation of nature is necessarily deficient. Contrariwise, attention to the structure of Paul's argument in Romans suggests that his discussion of God's revelation in nature does not address the question of the means to salvation but establishes the universal need for salvation. Paul begins at the beginning, showing that every human being, even Gentiles, has first rejected God in some fashion. Paul does not assert that sinful humanity can come to "saving knowledge" of God/Christ by observing nature and inferring the truth—although he does not deny the possibility either. Instead, Paul asserts that human beings are sinners simply because, "knowing God, they did not honor God as God" (Rom 1:21).

In Paul's understanding of the nature of the Gentiles' sin, therefore, they are without excuse, not because they have violated the will of God expressed in the special revelation on Mt. Sinai, but because they have responded improperly to the revelation of God universally available to human beings through creation. In this regard, it is no doubt significant that Paul shapes his discussion in dialogue with Gen 1–3 (see above). As he understood it, that is, Gentiles replicate the error committed by Adam and Eve in the garden.

In summary, Paul's argument follows a very straightforward logic. He first establishes that all human beings stand on an equal footing in terms of the opportunity to relate to God. In so doing, Paul asserts: (1) that some knowledge of God is universally available because God has revealed God's-self universally, 1:19; (2) that the observable creation points clearly beyond itself to its Creator, 1:20; (3) and that, therefore, all human beings are accountable for their relationship to God; they are "without excuse," 1:20. The human problem lies, then, not in some limitation on access to revelation, but in the human response to this revelation. Paul describes this problem in a second sequence of premises. (1) Knowing God is insufficient. Humans do not honor God as God, acknowledging in thanksgiving their creatureliness (1:21). (2) This failure manifests human arrogance. Like Adam and Eve, who sought wisdom, human beings only demonstrate their folly (1:21-22). (3) In essence, again like Adam and Eve, all human beings choose to elevate creatures—indeed, mere "images" of creatures—to the status of Creator (1:23).

Parallels with Gen 3 are unmistakable. Paul effectively argues that all human beings undergo the same process that Adam and Eve underwent in the garden. All human beings choose to disregard God and to magnify some aspect of creation. For reasons that not even Ecclesiastes or Paul seem to understand, human beings are uncomfortable with the boundary between finite creatureliness and infinite deity, between image that can be seen and immortal glory that cannot, between the eternity in our hearts and the mind of God. Inevitably, human beings foolishly try to erase or obscure the boundary, assuming undeserved authority and status.

Summary of the Bible's Position Regarding Sin as Disobedience

Because two elements seem to unify the Bible's discussion of sin as disobedience, they merit reiteration. First, the most important aspect of sin is not disobedience to some precept of the law, but the violation of the basic relationship to God. Even in Gen 3, the focus is on the nature of the first pair's disobedience, not the mere fact. God had not pronounced an arbitrary rule—"Do not cross your fingers before lunch"—to test humanity's obedience. The substance of the commandment was significant in itself. Fundamentally, neither of the two major interpretations of Gen 3 found within the Bible place major emphasis on the act of disobedience, per se. Instead, both find the substance and quality of the act paramount. According to the Hebrew Bible's covenant traditions, Israel sinned by betraying the most fundamental principle of its life as the covenant people: YHWH will be Israel's God and they his people. New Testament covenant traditions focus similarly on the question of relationship to God, now in terms of the presence of God in the person of Jesus Christ. The Synoptic Gospels insist that the most fundamental sin involves the failure to relate to God in Jesus Christ. Sin is not the violation of some moral code, but the inability or unwillingness to recognize the presence of God. The author of Hebrews was appalled that some, facing persecution and oppression, could publicly deny their confession of faith.

Second, biblical texts that deal with sin in non-covenantal contexts explore the fundamental nature of humanity's failure of relationship. Genesis 3 establishes the parameters of the discussion continued in Eccl 3 and Rom 1–7. Adam and Eve did not disobey for disobedience's sake, but because they desired the enhanced godlikeness to be gained by disobedience. In their view, the wonder of bearing the image of God was not enough to counterbalance the limitations of human finitude. They wanted to be more than human. The Teacher of Ecclesiastes reflects on the manner in which the descendants of the first pair continue to strive futilely for knowledge and wisdom beyond their reach. He counsels acceptance of the human station. Paul, too, observes that human beings are universally accountable for their sin because, knowing God through God's revelation in creation, they seek their own wisdom, exchanging Creator for creature. The Johannine literature specifies further that the presence of God incarnate in Jesus Christ is key. Some who sought to transcend their own humanity rejected the notion that God could or would identify with human beings. In their view, humanity was unworthy of the deity's involvement on such an intimate level. They pursued and claimed *perfection*.

Implications for Ministry

The results of the examination of biblical and theological dimensions of the notion that all human beings rebel, in some sense, against God reveal that the concept is much more highly nuanced than is often indicated in the preaching and theology of the church. Commentators on contemporary society from a theological perspective often note the eclipse of the doctrine of sin in the ministry of the church and in the thinking of the people in the pews. Could it be that many people, Christian or otherwise, simply do not find the idea that they are wanton rebels against God to be true to their experience? Is it true that the most interesting Christian testimony is that of the converted drug addict/murderer/sex worker/spouse abuser? From what does Jesus redeem the absolutely normal, unremarkably well-behaved adolescent? Must she first sin greatly that grace may abound? Could it be that the confusion concerning the gospel's role in the world and in the lives of individuals arises from the sense that dealing with sin, understood as outright rebellion, simply does not apply in the lives of most people today? How is the message that Jesus brings salvation to rebels against God good news for the Sunday school teacher and father of three who loves his wife and works hard—too hard, perhaps—to support his family, and who now faces a crisis of meaning at midlife? Is he rebelling against God? Is his depression the penalty for his wantonness?

The key lies in unpacking the statement that all human beings rebel, *in some sense*, against God—or better, that all human beings find it impossible to fully accept and embrace their proper place in relation to God and in the created order. Human beings want to be *more than human*. The image of God is not enough. The gospel message, however, affirms that being authentically human is valuable enough to God that God was willing to *become human* in order to redeem our humanity. Humans *need not* be more than authentically human; indeed, one *cannot* be more than authentically human. What are the implications of this simple affirmation as they relate to the ministry of the church to people and to the culture today? Where does this sin manifest itself and what is the gospel message in these situations?

Over-optimism, the Post-Enlightenment "Rebellion"

Perhaps the most endemic form of "rebellion" in post-Enlightenment Western culture—to which the church is not immune—is unbridled optimism in the potential for human achievement. "Man is the measure of all things." Science will unlock all the mysteries of the universe. Technology will provide the tools for solving all problems facing humankind. Education will lift the race from darkness and sin. Medicine will eliminate disease and death. Humanity will "build a tower to heaven" and "make a name" for itself (Gen 11:4).

Progress is a myth, however. The church can speak a word to a society marked by an arrogant overconfidence in human capabilities. Historically, every economic revolution (industrial, electronic) has meant opportunity and wealth for some and displacement and disadvantage for many. Automobiles are convenient, but they are also dangerous. Airplanes are marvels, until terrorists use them as guided missiles. In the realm of science and technology in recent history alone, sinners confident of the effectiveness of thalidomide, DDT, nuclear power, and a score of other inventions and techniques and their unintended by-products have only demonstrated that the human capacity to imagine far outstrips its ability to foresee. For every advance in medicine, a new disease or illness arises. The very drugs meant to cure often bring unintended consequences, as well. Overuse of antibiotics is producing strains of resistant "super-bugs." Efficient atomic energy and deadly, persistent nuclear waste are inseparable. Almost every technology useful in commerce, manufacturing, and communications has military applications. Many of these technologies are in the hands of people who do not share Judeo-Christian convictions about the sanctity of life. While today's weapons are more efficient than ever before in human history, arrogant, egocentric, ethnocentric human beings still wield them. Wars are still fought. Fewer people can kill more of the enemy (and the innocent) more quickly and with less danger to themselves than ever before. Progress! Strip away all the technology and gadgetry and one finds that the users are the same human beings who thought to ascend to heaven via a tower made of bricks with pitch for mortar. Christianity does not offer a utopian vision of perfected human society; it issues a call to the kingdom of God.

A perfected human society would consist of "perfect" human beings, but the notion of a "perfect" human being is nonsense. Currently, self-help guides, the "human potential movement," and pervasive pop psychology point to a widely held "open-ended optimism about the possibilities of human growth,"[54] more evidence that human beings find it difficult to be satisfied with being authentically human. A human being cannot be "perfect." Authenticity is possible, but not perfection. Even the first pair lacked the knowledge of good and evil. Attaining this knowledge, they encountered their limited capacity for it. Apples cannot see because they were not meant for sight. Human beings, created in the image of God, are destined nonetheless to remain creatures, less than God. Ironically, true wisdom includes the acknowledgment of one's limits. Sinners overreach, missing marks at which they should never have aimed. While humans can and should pursue wisdom, in the end it is attainable only in part. The church can speak a word to individuals burdened by false expectations of human perfection and unrealistic drives for control. Despite the pessimism of Ecclesiastes' admonitions, they hold the promise of liberation, as well. People ought not to hold themselves to artificial standards of absolute perfection. By nature, human beings are limited, less than God. Freedom can only be found by living within the limits. Human limitations, human finitude, is not sin. Much that human beings cannot do, they were never meant to do.

Neo-Gnosticism, a Modern Paradox

Why do human beings find it difficult to accept the limits of their humanity? The desire to be *more than human* implies a devaluation of humanness. In the New Testament era, the gnostic heresy argued that material existence is inherently impure. True reality, real being, can only be found in the spiritual realm. Gnostics even denied the incarnation on the grounds that God, whom they defined as perfection and pure spirit, simply could not have taken on full humanity. Human fleshly existence is, by their definition, profane. Sadly, a strain of this gnostic denigration of the material world survives in many forms today. Christians fascinated with "spiritual warfare," churches that seem by their message to emphasize that this life is *only* a waiting room for heaven, and Christian young people who lead libertine lives, contending that what they do with their bodies is unimportant so long as their "heart is right," would have fit seamlessly into first-century gnostic communities. The Bible consistently and clearly maintains, in contrast, that, although human beings are limited creatures, they bear the image of God—now, in this world, in all finitude and physicality. Indeed, despite the gnostic denial, the New Testament insists that *God was incarnate in Jesus Christ*. God valued humanity and embraced it into God's person. No one need strive to be *more than human; authentic humanity is God's intention*. Self-esteem need not be earned. No one need transcend humanity. The need is to fulfill it. There is no shame in being human. In fact, sin is, in part, the unwillingness to embrace being human.

Fulfilling the Proper Role, Bearing the Image of God Boldly

Human beings are like God, but not God. If one accepts one's place, embracing authentic humanity as made possible and modeled by Jesus Christ, one can fulfill one's role as God's representative in creation. The struggle to escape being human, to attain wisdom beyond one's capacity to manage, perverts one's relationship with the created order. Human beings are out of place and the whole of creation suffers for it. Relationships with family, friends, and community suffer. The opponents in the Johannine community thought that they had attained a status beyond humanity and, as a result, they disdained other members of their community. The arrogance of Adam and Eve brought them into conflict with one another, each distrusting the other's motives and intentions. Humans are creatures alongside the rest of creation; but they are creatures with the responsibility of stewardship. Every member of the human race bears the image of God. Every one deserves the respect due a child of God.

In essence, then, "rebellion against God," or the underlying principle that motivates such rebellion, can take the form of disrespect for creation, for fellow creatures, and especially for other human beings created in God's image. To misuse, disdain, abuse, or dishonor another human being is to rebel against God's orderly creation.

So, worshipers at Sunday morning services may never have shaken a rebellious fist in the face of God, but if they are tyrannized by the need to determine their own lives, to overcome all limitations; if they invest more of themselves in the tools for living than in being authentically human; if they are uneasy with being merely human; or if they doubt their own inherent worth and call the worth of others into question, they participate fully in the sin of the first pair, nonetheless.

CHAPTER THREE

Sin: Failure to Embrace Authentic Freedom

> *"Surely, I am too stupid to be a human being;*
> *I do not have the understanding of a human being."*
> Prov 30:2

Some sin can be defined in terms of the individual's dissatisfaction with or denial of the limitations of human existence. People sometimes act on the sense that *being (merely) human* in healthy, balanced relation to God, other human beings, and the created order *is not enough*. In these cases, an individual may behave as though he or she were of central importance to the universe, as though his or her will were primary, as though everyone and everything else has no other usefulness than to meet his or her wishes. One can observe this phenomenon in the demands of a self-absorbed teenager, the recklessness of the aggressive driver, and the tyranny of history's most infamous dictators.

Even the casual observer of the human condition, however, will recognize that much, even most, of what is wrong with human beings does not stem from such egocentrism, but from its polar opposite: behaviors that manifest the conviction that *one is not or cannot or dare not be good enough to be authentically human*. Teenage boys accept the culture's message that superior academic performance characterizes "nerds" and "geeks," that to be truly masculine one may only pursue athletics, or gang involvement, or social popularity. Teenage girls join the flocks of Britney Spears and Christina Aguilera clones, eager to conform to popular culture's definition of the bad good girl. Many young people forsake commitment in relationship in favor of the practice of "hooking up." Children of both sexes assimilate the negative message communicated by parental abuse and neglect and, convinced at some level that they do not deserve to be nurtured and respected, go on in adult life to seek out partners who will continue the pattern of abuse and neglect. As parents themselves, these victims become victimizers, perpetuating the cycle of rearing children who will not lay claim to their own intrinsic value as human beings.

Considered from a theological perspective, the lives of addicts, of victims of the many varieties of abuse and oppression, of "failures" of all sorts, surely represent some manifestation of sin. It is difficult, however, to accuse the child of a single alcoholic parent—who has been conditioned throughout childhood to expect neglect, to bear responsibility for his mother's drinking, to compensate for her mother's incompetence—with willful rebellion against God. Sin must be more complicated than the simple "pride" definition often forwarded by traditional theology.

In fact, a number of contemporary theological enterprises argue that treating "pride" as the essential definition of all human sin not only discounts the experience of a significant proportion of humanity, but is also inherently limited and therefore even dangerous if treated as the sole paradigm. As early as 1964, Harvey Cox observed, "I believe a careful examination of the biblical sources will indicate that man's [sic] most debilitating proclivity is not his pride. It is not his attempt to be more than man. Rather it is his sloth, his unwillingness to be everything man was intended to be."[1] L. Mercadante and others have termed this surrender to human finitude the "sin of self-loss."[2] Criticism of the *hubris* definition of sin comes, especially, from feminist quarters, although the scope of this criticism can easily be expanded to reflect the situations of any individuals or groups who find themselves in the inferior status in over-under relationships. S. Dunfee argues, for example, that this definition perpetuates injustice toward women (and, it may be added, toward oppressed minorities, socioeconomically dominated classes, abused and neglected children, etc.): " . . . by encouraging woman to confess the wrong sin, and by failing to judge her in her actual sin, Christianity has both added to woman's guilt and failed to call her into her full humanity."[3] In essence, the "pride" definition of sin reduces women, the oppressed, and the abused to victims of sin; they are not sinners themselves.[4] In Dunfee's view, Reinhold Niebuhr, one of the leading proponents of the "pride" definition in the modern era, sensed that the basic nature of sin is more complicated than his analysis suggests, but failed fully to develop the insight. He argued that sin can take the form of immersion into finitude, the sin of "sensuality."[5] Dunfee points out that he goes no further in the analysis of "sensuality," a term she finds particularly unfortunate due to its implication that this variety of sin is limited to the pursuit of physical pleasures. She argues that areas of escape "need not be only aspects of one's own physical cravings, but may also be loss of one's self in other finite persons, institutions, or causes."[6] Niebuhr's analysis also produces a dangerous conclusion regarding the highest good for human existence. Since, he argues, prideful egoism is the primary sin, its opposite, self-sacrifice, is the *bonum ultimatum*. Passivity and submission, heteronomy not autonomy, is the objective of human existence.[7] This risks elevating the sin of hiding into a virtue.[8] Thus, the argument that pride is the fundamental human sin reinforces the status quo in any hierarchical relationship: those who seek liberation are guilty of exercising self-assertion rooted in pride.[9] We will return to many of the issues raised by this critique of the adequacy of the "pride" understanding of sin below, especially to the paradoxical relationship between the status of victim and the status of sinner.

The task of this chapter, then, is to explore areas in which the Bible, a growing trend in various contemporary approaches to theology, and the insights of modern psychology and psychotherapy agree that, in addition to the *hubris*, the overreaching characteristic of *some* human sin, human beings also often fail to attain authentic autonomy—they underachieve.

The Bible on Sin as Falling Short of Humanity

Significantly, the most commonly employed terms usually translated "sin" in the two portions of the Bible (Hebrew חטא, *ht'*; Greek ἁμαρτ-, *hamart-*) do not denote "willful rebellion/transgression," as the "pride" definition might expect. Very close equivalents, both convey instead the image of "missing the mark," that is, they assume the intention on the part of the actor to hit the target and describe the *failure* to do so. In the Hebrew Bible, the Hebrew root can describe without moral judgment a failure or error, "missing the mark," a significance most clearly evident in Judg 20:16, which refers to skilled archers who do not miss their targets, but also apparent in Exod 5:16 ("stumbling" under oppression),[10] Isa 65:20 ("falling short" in reference to a foreshortened lifespan), Job 5:24 ("missing nothing" in the context of personal safety and security), and Job 41:17 (= 41:25 English; "faltering" before Leviathan[11]). This usage establishes the fact that the root does not inherently address the question of intentionality. Archers miss the target unintentionally. The root describes the act as error, as shortcoming, not the flawed intentions of the actor. Like Hebrew *ht'*, the Greek root ἁμαρτ- (*hamart-*) "originally" denoted "missing the mark," although in common usage the specific idea gave rise to a broader use in the sense of "to do wrong." The translators of the LXX, the early Greek translation of the Hebrew Bible, employed it somewhat indiscriminately to translate all the principle Hebrew terms for "sin" in its various aspects, a circumstance that indicates that the LXX failed consistently to render Hebrew with technical equivalents. On the other hand, the frequency with which *hamart-* translates Hebrew *ht'* suggests some awareness of the correspondence. Outside Romans and 1 John, the verb occurs once in its "original" sense of "to err, make a mistake" (1 Pet 2:20) and in a roughly equal distribution with either of the connotations "to offend against (someone; once, something)" (Matt 18:15, 21; Luke 15:18, 21; 17:3, 4; Acts 25:8; 1 Cor 6:18; 8:12; 15:34) or "to transgress" (Matt 27:4; John 5:14; 8:11; 9:2-3; 1 Cor 7:28, 36; Eph 4:26; 1 Tim 5:20; Titus 3:11; Heb 3:17; 10:26; 2 Pet 2:4).

One can "miss the mark" in a number of ways and for a number of reasons. Perhaps one's equipment is substandard, the bow poorly strung, the arrow bent;

perhaps the wind gusts during the arrow's flight; perhaps one is not skilled, or one's vision blurred, or one's grip on the string tentative. Not surprisingly, the Bible deals with a number of elements that characterize the human tendency to sin by "falling short" of the target, true and full humanity. Apparently, the Bible nowhere offers a systematic analysis of this tendency in terms of causal relationships or sequence of events. The Bible does offer, however, fundamental insights that can serve as grist for the theological mill.

Complicitous Acceptance of the Lie

Basic to sin as failure to accept the value of one's humanity and, therefore, to exercise authentic human autonomy is the lie: "I am not enough; I am intrinsically insufficient." Eve and Adam present the first example of this complicity with the lie. Although created in the image of God as part of God's good creation and given responsibility as God's partners for managing creation as its paramount specimen, the first pair comes to doubt their sufficiency. Rather than valuing the godlikeness inherent in being human, they sought to supplement it. More importantly, however, in so doing they paradoxically allow themselves to be duped by an inferior creature—the serpent, one of the "beasts of the field"—over whom they were to exercise dominion. The text describes the serpent as "crafty," but not as wise. In other words, despite the serpent's claim to have superior knowledge regarding God's motivations and the fruit's properties, in truth, the serpent cannot exceed the first pair, who bear the image of God. They accept the serpent's lie and its implication that the serpent can rightfully advise them. They abdicate their role and their responsibility, subjecting themselves to a crafty beast.[12]

One might also add that, in terms of the exercise of responsible autonomy, Adam failed to meet the standard of authentic humanity to an even greater degree than did Eve. At least Eve deliberated before acting. Adam, who was "with her" throughout the conversation with the serpent, simply complied with Eve's decision and "ate" (Gen 3:6).

Fearful Avoidance of Human Potential

Adam and Eve believed the serpent's lie. The Bible describes a number of others who prefer inertia and passivity to the effort required by God's call to fulfill their humanity. Moses, called to be God's representative in liberating the people of Israel from slavery, resisted. He objected, among other things, that he did not have the talent and skill necessary for the task ("I am not eloquent," Exod 4:10). Similarly, Gideon, called upon to deliver Israel from Midianite oppression, offered the excuse that "my clan is the weakest in Manasseh, and I am the least in my family" (Judg 6:15), and Jeremiah, called to be a prophet to the nations, that "I do not know how to speak, for I am only a youth" (Jer 1:6). Initially, these three champions of faith, convinced of their own inadequacy, would have chosen obscurity over the challenge of answering God's call.

Sin: Failure to Embrace Authentic Freedom

Even the people Moses freed from slavery preferred the certainty of bondage to the challenges of autonomy. If freedom meant risk, change, and struggle, they longed for the "comforts" of subservience. Weary of a steady diet of manna in the wilderness, they remembered wistfully the bounties afforded them by their masters.

> Now the rabble that was among them had a strong craving; and the people of Israel also wept again, and said, "O that we had meat to eat! We remember the fish we ate in Egypt for nothing, the cucumbers, the melons, the leeks, the onions, and the garlic; but now our strength is dried up, and there is nothing at all but this manna to look at." (Num 11:4-6 RSV)

Disheartened by the report of the spies sent into the promised land while they were encamped at Kadesh-barnea, a report that brought news of the giant race of Nephilim in the land and of fortified cities and well-equipped armies, the people of Israel rejected God's call to take possession of the land promised them. Even with the assurance of God's presence and assistance, they felt unequal to the task, too afraid of failure to try for success.

> And all the people of Israel murmured against Moses and Aaron; the whole congregation said to them, "Would that we had died in the land of Egypt! Or would that we had died in this wilderness! Why does the LORD bring us into this land, to fall by the sword? Our wives and our little ones will become a prey; would it not be better for us to go back to Egypt?" And they said to one another, "Let us choose a captain, and go back to Egypt." (Num 14:2-4 RSV)

Jesus seems to have been keenly aware that sometimes people prefer to remain incomplete rather than face the challenges and responsibilities that come with competence and freedom. The Gospels report that, on at least two occasions when Jesus encountered infirm individuals, he did not simply assume that they wished to be made whole. John (5:2-9) reports Jesus' exchange with an apparently lame or paralytic man at the pool by the Sheep Gate, known for its curative properties, who had suffered his affliction for thirty-eight years. Jesus "knew that he had been lying there a long time." Given this long period in which there would have been many opportunities to bathe in the pool "when the water was troubled," Jesus could rightly wonder whether the man had become so accustomed to his lifestyle—indeed, it may have been that he had been infirm his entire life and knew no other—that he feared the uncertainty of a future in which he could no longer rely on the pity and charity of others. Did he prefer the limited but familiar life of a beggar to the challenges of learning a trade at his age and earning his own living? Therefore, Jesus did not assume, as many might, that the man wished to be made well. Instead, he asked him, pointedly, "Do you want to be healed?" (John 5:6). Similarly, even though Bartimaeus, a blind beggar, the son of Timaeus, cried out loudly for Jesus to show him mercy, Jesus did not assume that Bartimaeus sought healing. The call for mercy could as easily have been a call for alms. Jesus summoned Bartimaeus and put to him the knowing question, "What do you want me to do for you?" (Mark 10:51).

Stunted Maturation

Perhaps not surprisingly, Hebrew Wisdom literature (Psalms, Proverbs, Job, Ecclesiastes, for example) focuses systematic attention on the human willingness to stop short of full, authentic humanity. It contains by far the highest concentration of the usage of the root *ht'* in the sense of the "failure" of those who refuse to seek wisdom. Indeed, scholars now generally recognize that Wisdom literature employs a form[13] of the root in a specialized fashion, "emptied" of moral connotations,[14] to describe the "bumbler, the loser, the one who is always making mistakes."[15] People are "bumblers" limited in ability and understanding, although this need not be the case, since God makes wisdom available to any who will seek it. People often "miss the mark" because they have not taken training and developed their skill as "archers."

Consequently, Wisdom literature urges the acquisition of wisdom. Understanding is key not only to limiting error but also to being authentically human. To choose ignorance of God's will and way is folly, even sin. In relation to this concept, usage of the root *ht'* in Israel's Wisdom literature exhibits the transition from the more concrete, basic sense of physically missing a target to the more abstract characterization of human behavior. Ignorance—lack of wisdom—leads to error.[16] In terms of the metaphor employed in the previous chapter of this study to describe one aspect of sin as the *dissatisfaction with being (merely) human*, Wisdom literature explores the consequences of the *failure to be fully human*.

Apart from the book of Ecclesiastes,[17] Israel's Wisdom literature does not explicitly relate the human capacity for gaining wisdom to the notion that human beings are created in the image of God, the Bible's most potent statement of the value of being human. It nonetheless maintains that God incorporated wisdom, personified as Lady Wisdom, as the principle of order and justice into the fabric of creation and, most importantly, that human beings have the *capacity* and *responsibility* for acquiring this wisdom and living according to it. The well-known hymn in praise of wisdom in Prov 8 includes a speech by the personified Lady Wisdom describing herself as the first of God's creations, the ordering principle God chose to follow in the rest of God's creative activity.

> The LORD created me at the beginning of his work,
>   the first of his acts of old.
> Ages ago I was set up,
>   at the first, before the beginning of the earth.
> When there were no depths I was brought forth,
>   when there were no springs abounding with water.

> Before the mountains had been shaped,
> > before the hills, I was brought forth;
> before he had made the earth with its fields,
> > or the first of the dust of the world.
> When he established the heavens, I was there,
> > when he drew a circle on the face of the deep,
> when he made firm the skies above,
> > when he established the fountains of the deep,
> when he assigned to the sea its limit,
> > so that the waters might not transgress his command,
> when he marked out the foundations of the earth,
> > then I was beside him, like a master workman;
> and I was daily his delight,
> > rejoicing before him always,
> rejoicing in his inhabited world
> > and delighting in the sons of men. (8:22-31 RSV; cf. 3:19-20)

Outside Israel's Wisdom literature, the Hebrew term for wisdom applies to a wide range of competencies and bodies of knowledge, including technical expertise in various crafts and skills (Exod 28:3; 31:6; Isa 3:3; 40:20; Jer 9:17; 1 Chr 22:15; 2 Chr 2:7, etc.) and everyday common sense (2 Sam 13:3; 1 Kgs 2:9). By elevating the concept to describe God's plan for creation, Wisdom literature expanded the scope of knowledge and competency meant by the term. Now it describes the most fundamental understanding of and skill in God's purposes and objectives in creation. Just as wisdom manifests the order and balance in the natural world, with the seas in their proper limits and the foundation of the earth rightly laid out, so it encompasses "every good path" for human life (Prov 2:9). Lady Wisdom speaks only of "noble things," "what is right," "truth." Her words "are all straight to him who understands, and right to those find knowledge" (Prov 8:9). To know wisdom is to understand righteousness, justice, equity (cf. "the rights of the poor," Prov 29:7), and discretion (Prov 8:6-9). Wisdom leads one in the straight paths of uprightness, in ways of light. The wise "walk in the way of good men and keep to the paths of the righteous" (2:9-16, 20-22; cf. 8:20).

As understood in Proverbs, this wisdom "is always prudential, conducive to the individual's well-being," as indicated by the fact that the bulk of the book is devoted to the many maxims for living daily life successfully, but it is not limited to pragmatic dimensions. For the book of Proverbs, everyday wisdom is a species of understanding related to the overarching principle of order according to the will of God. In this regard, wisdom "is also a quality of character, for it entails not only the knowledge of the right ends, but also the will to pursue them." It is expertise in "right living and good character."[18]

Consequently, the proper objective of being human is to live in accordance with this principle of order and justice. The teacher/father who speaks in Proverbs repeatedly beseeches the student/son, above all else, to get wisdom.

> My son, keep sound wisdom and discretion;
> > let them not escape from your sight,
> and they will be life for your soul
> > and adornment for your neck.
> Then you will walk on your way securely
> > and your foot will not stumble.
> If you sit down, you will not be afraid;
> > when you lie down, your sleep will be sweet.
> > > (3:21-24 RSV; cf. 4:4-9; 8:10-11)

Wisdom is "a fountain of life" (Prov 16:22), honey for the soul, the source of a hopeful future (24:13-14). "He who gets wisdom loves himself" (19:8).

Obviously, the appeal to pursue wisdom indicates that Israel's wisdom teachers did not assume that human beings possess this wisdom innately. In terms of the categories found in the Genesis account of primal humanity, the wisdom teachers might well have agreed with the Teacher of Ecclesiastes that, as creatures in the image of God, human beings have the capacity for a degree of wisdom, but that the substance of that wisdom must be acquired through a process of experience, education, and maturation. Indeed, Prov 2:1-22 outlines the pedagogical theory of the ancient Israelite wisdom thinkers responsible for the book. Motivated by the fear of God (1:7), one seeks wisdom (2:1-4) and God grants it (2:6). Wisdom enhances one's moral sensibility (2:5a) and brings the knowledge of God (2:5b). As a result, one is better attuned to the will of God, better equipped to enact it, and has the will to do so (2:9; 3:6).[19]

Notably, despite the apparent emphasis on empirical and pedagogical methods, ancient Israel's wisdom teachers did not understand the acquisition of wisdom to be a human achievement. Instead, wisdom is accessible to whoever seeks it (Prov 8:17) because God makes it abundantly available (Prov 18:4) as God's gift (2:1-8). In fact, Wisdom seeks disciples even before they become interested in her. In this sense, Wisdom's longing for adherents exemplifies God's "prevenient grace."

> Wisdom cries aloud in the street;
> > in the markets she raises her voice;
> on the top of the walls she cries out;
> > at the entrance of the city gates she speaks:
> "How long, O simple ones, will you love being simple?
> How long will scoffers delight in their scoffing
> > and fools hate knowledge?
> Give heed to my reproof;
> behold, I will pour out my thoughts to you;
> > I will make my words known to you."
> > > (1:20-23 RSV; cf. 8:1-5; 9:4-6)

Sin: Failure to Embrace Authentic Freedom

If wisdom is God's ordering principle for all God's creation, failure to live wisely is failure to live in accordance with the will of God; it is sin. Since it is so readily available, failure to seek wisdom, then, is also sin. In fact, Prov 8:36 describes wisdom as the very "mark" that to miss is to cause oneself harm ("the one who misses [*ht'*] me does violence to himself"). Not even zeal substitutes for competence, nor eagerness for accuracy ("Indeed, without knowledge desire is not good and the one who hurries afoot misses [*ht'*]," Prov 19:2). Wisdom, not passion, guides one in the right path. Wisdom warns that the harm possible from a leader's[20] failure to attain wisdom can be as destructive as war (Eccl 9:18).[21] In the presence of power, incompetence can be self-destructive ("the one who crosses [the king] misses [*ht'*] life," Prov 20:2). Ignorance renders one vulnerable to the snares of that dangerous woman so feared by Israel's wisdom teachers (Eccl 7:26).[22]

Here, Israelite wisdom offers a view of human sin quite at odds with the legal/intentional paradigm. Like Job's angry question, "If I sin, what do I do to you?" (7:20), theology often seems to envision the category of "error" as outside God's jurisdiction. Indeed, almost by definition, Israel's wisdom focused on everyday life to the degree that scholarship has struggled to incorporate so-called "practical wisdom" into a scheme of biblical theology. Similarly, the teaching, preaching, and practice of the church typically ignores the common sense message of these texts, probably because it lacks the theological luster of themes such as love, grace, and atonement. An honest contemporary observer of the human condition, however, would surely agree with the Teacher that a great proportion of human suffering proceeds not from the evil hearts of fallen humanity, but from the avoidable ignorance and unnecessary incompetence of human beings who have failed to actualize the potential of their humanity. Willful ignorance and immaturity is the abdication of one's authentic humanity. It is sin.

> Because I have called and you refused to listen,
>   have stretched out my hand and no one has heeded,
> and you have ignored all my counsel
>   and would have none of my reproof. . . .
> Because they hated knowledge
>   and did not choose the fear of the LORD,
> would have none of my counsel,
>   and despised all my reproof,
> therefore they shall eat the fruit of their way
>   and be sated with their own devices.
> For the simple are killed by their turning away,
>   and the complacence of fools destroys them;
> but he who listens to me will dwell secure
>   and will be at ease, without dread of evil.
>   (Prov 1:24-25, 29-33 RSV; cf. 21:16; 24:9; 27:12)

Slavery and Sub-humanity

In its refutation of what seems to have been an early form of docetic Gnosticism, Johannine literature focuses on the gnostics' contention that they had attained a spiritual, superhuman perfection. Paradoxically, the same attitude concerning the inherent inferiority of fleshly existence can also promote carnality and licentiousness. Early libertine Gnosticism was characterized by the argument that, since the flesh is inherently evil, there is no reason even to attempt to live according to any moral or ethical standard. Salvation, in this view, consists in freeing the (spiritual and therefore superior) soul from bondage to the (material and therefore evil) body. Desires of the body, which is to be discarded, can be indulged freely without fear of tainting the spiritual and immortal soul.[23]

Both major varieties of Gnosticism seem to have developed very late in the New Testament period, as reflected in the fact that the church's struggle with them is reflected only briefly and only in the latest literature in the New Testament. This late New Testament literature is lesser known to readers of the Bible and, precisely because it reflects the doctrinal and institutional struggles of the period of transition at the close of the apostolic era, it is sometimes obscure. Developments, documents, and ideas not widely known to readers of Scripture—some of which biblical scholars have known only in the modern era—provide the proper context against which to read these texts. Their complexity notwithstanding, portions of these late biblical era texts portray a striking view of sin as inauthentic, sub-human slavery to the animal components of human nature. That is, the following discussion may be intricate and will deal with material that will be foreign to many readers. Still, it will be fruitful to decode the logic of early Christian struggles with ideas that impugn the goodness of God's creation.

Specifically, in polemical denunciations of "false teachers" from the late New Testament period, the epistles of Jude (5-16, 18) and 2 Peter (2:4-22) offer related[24] analyses of the dynamics of sin as captivity to the drives characteristic of the animal dimension of being human. While the precise identity of these heretics and the nature of their doctrine can only be partially reconstructed from the accusations leveled against them by the New Testament authors, their manner of life clearly represented to the biblical authors a failure to fulfill the gospel's promise of authentic humanity.[25] Jude 4 describes them as "ungodly" and "licentious" "intruders" who "deny our only Master and Lord, Jesus Christ." Second Peter 2 echoes the charges ("ungodly," vv. 5, 6; "licentious," v. 2, cf. vv. 7, 18; denial of the Master, v. 1). The introduction to 2 Peter (1:3-15), stating the author's purposes in writing, provides additional clues concerning the nature of the danger that these heretics and their doctrine represented for the church. He intends to remind his readers, no doubt fearing the influence of the false teachers, that through Jesus God has provided everything necessary "for life and godliness" (1:3), namely, "virtue," "knowledge," "self-control" ($\dot{\varepsilon}\gamma\kappa\rho\acute{\alpha}\tau\varepsilon\iota\alpha\nu$ *egkrateian*, lit., "being in power, control"), "perseverance," "godliness," "fraternal love," and finally "sacrificial love" (1:5-7). The goal is "participation in the divine nature" (1:4). In contrast to these characteristics of life in Christ, the author warns against the alternative, "corruption [inherent] in desire" (1:4), "ineffectiveness and unfruitfulness" (1:8), "blindness" and "forgetfulness of the cleansing of past sins" (1:9).

The author of 2 Peter then turns attention directly to the false teachers, as does the author of Jude following a much more concise introduction. Because of the close relationship between the two texts, they may be examined together. Both begin by citing a series of events described in Scripture as analogies to the behaviors of the false teachers (Jude 5-8; 2 Pet 2:4-10*a*), continue with a direct denunciation of these behaviors, including additional scriptural precedents (Jude 9-13; 2 Pet 2:10*b*-16), and conclude with a pronouncement concerning the horrible fate of these false teachers (Jude 14-18; 2 Pet 2:17-22).

Scriptural Analogies to the Behaviors of the "False Teachers." Jude (unbelieving Israelites, corrupt angels, Sodom and Gomorrah) and 2 Peter (angels, Noah, Sodom and Gomorrah) cite three scriptural analogies each, of which two are in common, in order to establish the biblical precedent for their denunciation of the false teachers.[26] On the assumption that Jude served as the source for 2 Peter, the latter seems to have substituted Noah for the unbelieving Israelites among those delivered from Egypt and supplemented the discussion of Sodom and Gomorrah with a reference to the deliverance of Lot in order to support the contention that God is able both to punish the deserving and to deliver the faithful. The common core analogies address the fundamental issues with respect to the heretical teachers. The reference to the angels, abbreviated in 2 Peter, seems to have in mind the episode recorded in Gen 6:1-4 concerning the "sons of God" who marry "daughters of men" and beget the Nephilim, a race of giants.

In the intertestamental period, this story fascinated Jewish apocalypticists who saw in it something of an alternative explanation for the universality of sin, and especially for the universality of God's judgment on Noah's generation.[27] It appears in substantially the same form[28] in *1 Enoch* (6–11; 12:4; 15:3-4; 64:1-2; 69:4-6; 106:12-16), *Jubilees* (4:21-24; 5:1-7; 7:21-25; cf. 8:3-4; 10:5), the *Testaments of the Twelve Patriarchs* (Reuben 5:6; Naphtali 3), and *2 Enoch* (18).[29] *First Enoch* 7:1-6 contains a brief—but complete in most essentials—version of the intertestamental tradition:

> [The angels] took unto themselves wives, and each chose for himself one, and they began to go in unto them and to defile themselves with them, and they taught them charms and enchantments, and the cutting of roots, and made them acquainted with plants. And they became pregnant, and they bare great giants, whose height was three thousand ells: Who consumed all the acquisitions of men. And when men could no longer sustain them, the giants turned against them and devoured mankind. And they began to sin against birds, and beasts, and reptiles, and fish, and to devour one another's flesh, and drink the blood. Then the earth laid accusation against the lawless ones.[30]

Typically for apocalyptic and midrashic literature, the non-canonical "Watchers/Grigori" tradition amplifies the biblical story, filling in perceived gaps and providing explanations for details unexplained in the original. The Genesis account says only that, in the period just before the flood, the "sons of God" took interest in, married, and begot children (the Nephilim) by the "daughters of man." Immediately following this account, Genesis reports that violent sin multiplied rampantly among humankind, prompting God to send the flood as cleansing judgment. The "Watchers/Grigori" tradition connects the behaviors of the biblical "sons of God," now the "Watchers/Grigori," to the increase of sin as its cause and supplies a more complete narrative. A group of angels became interested in human women. Leaving their proper station, they "defiled themselves" (*1 En.* 7:1; 9:9; etc.) with women. In so doing, they, who "were formerly spiritual, living the eternal life, and immortal for all generations of the world" (*1 En.* 15:6-7), acted "against the laws of their ordinances" (*Jub.* 7:21); they "departed from nature's order" (*T. Naph.* 3:5). As a consequence, they introduced disorder into all creation: "And lawlessness increased on the earth and all flesh corrupted its way, alike men and cattle and beasts and birds and everything that walks on the earth—all of them corrupted their ways and their orders . . . " (*Jub.* 5:2). God responded in a two-fold manner: (1) by sending the flood against humankind's corruption of the divinely established order of creation; and (2) by binding the offending angels until the final judgment (*1 En.* 10:4-7, 11-15; 64:1–69:1; *Jub.* 5:6-7).

A number of observations suggest that Jude and 2 Peter rely heavily on the tradition preserved especially in the Enoch literature, if not, in fact, on the book of *Enoch* itself. First, Jude describes the sin of the angels in question as failure to "keep themselves to their own station" (v. 6). As noted, in contrast to the extrabiblical emphasis on the angels' violation of the proper order, the biblical account makes no judgment on the "sons of God" who married human women. Second, the analogy with the sin of the inhabitants of Sodom and Gomorrah—fornication, going after "strange flesh," as Jude puts it—establishes that, in the view of Jude and 2 Peter, the Sodomites' sin, like that of the angels, was a violation of the proper order of creation, a crossing of the boundaries between the human and the divine. In fact, in summary statements concluding the opening sections, Peter and Jude agree that the corrupt angels, the inhabitants of Sodom and Gomorrah, and the false teachers all "defile the flesh" and "deny authority" (Jude 7-8; 2 Pet 2:10*a*), for the biblical authors the chief elements of violations of the divinely established order of creation. Third, whereas the Genesis account is mute with respect to the fate of the "sons of God," Jude and 2 Peter agree with the pseudepigraphal tradition that God bound the defiled angels in "gloom" until the day of judgment. Finally, Jude explicitly cites the Enoch literature, probably *1 Enoch*, later in the context.

Although somewhat cryptically from the perspective of a modern reader, the opening section of the denunciations of the false teachers vexing the church when Jude and 2 Peter were written argues forcefully that the false teachers are guilty of violations of the proper order of creation on the order of the Watchers' willing abandonment of their station in heaven in order to procreate with human women—in short, a willing condescension from the divine to the human. Like that of the inhabitants of Sodom and Gomorrah, these heretics' error is not primarily doctrinal, but a denial in their behaviors of their proper humanity. They go "after strange flesh," defiling themselves by animalistic, sub-human behaviors tantamount to a descent from the human to the animal.

Scriptural Analogies to the False Teachers as Teachers.[31] After likening the errors of the false teachers with the sins of three groups of exemplary biblical characters, Jude and 2 Peter turn attention to the heretics' activities *as teachers*, once again employing three biblical examples by way of analogy. Jude's argument here unfolds in three phases. First, he reiterates the basic character of the false teachers' error, appealing, as he did in reference to the fallen angels tradition, to extra-biblical sources.[32] Jude's citation of the precedent focuses on Michael's reticence to charge the devil with the blasphemy expressed in the dispute over Moses' body. Even though he knew well the devil's culpability, Michael did not overstep the boundaries of the established order. Such condemnations are God's province. What, however, was the nature of the devil's blasphemy? The contention concerned the body of Moses, the lawgiver, which the devil attempted to claim by some supposed right. In context, the dispute between Michael and the devil can be understood as a foreshadowing of the false teachers' disregard for the order of creation in the specific form of disdain for the law, the statement of the principles of that order. Just as the devil blasphemously claimed rights to Moses' body, the false teachers claim that the law is "devilish." Second Peter 2:10*b* refrains from the extra-biblical allusion in favor of an abstract statement. The false teachers have no qualms about despising authority or denigrating "the holy ones."[33] R. Bauckham points to the extra-biblical understanding of the angels as administrators of the order of creation on God's behalf, a responsibility the Watchers abandoned, as the interpretive key for this passage. The false teachers "[slandered] the angels as givers and guardians of the Law of Moses . . . the angels as guardians of the created order." In this view, the accusation made in Jude 8 stands as a coherent statement not of three distinct errors but of three expressions of the single sin. The false teachers, like their predecessors, defiled themselves by disdaining the divine principle of order in creation and slandering the angels appointed to administrate it.[34]

Second, Jude and 2 Peter offer an assessment of the true state of the false teachers. They must have claimed freedom from moral constraint. "In Christ," they must have said, "we are free to do as we please." In reality, however, principles and values—the Petrine author's "virtue, knowledge, self-control, perseverance, godliness, fraternal love, and sacrificial love" (2 Pet 1:5-7)—distinguish humans from animals. The false teachers' "freedom" from the hallmarks of humanity leaves them little more than "irrational animals . . . born to be caught and killed" (2 Pet 2:12; cf. Jude 10). Brazenly self-indulgent, adulterous, greedy, and deceived, they pervert even table fellowship into an opportunity for "carousing." This portrayal of the animalistic behavior of the false teachers resurfaces later in 2 Peter's description of their efforts to "entice" their students "with indecent desires of the flesh," "promising them freedom" (2:18-19). Similarly, the Petrine author's designation of Balaam—known elsewhere in the Bible as "the son of Beor"—as "the son of Bosor" may be an intentional play on words. Hebrew *basar* (בשׂר) means "flesh."

Third, Jude and 2 Peter conclude that these would-be teachers of the church have nothing to offer. Jude lists three biblical figures who became examples of "false teachers" in intertestamental and extra-biblical tradition. All of the Targums except *Onkelos* add midrash at Gen 4:8 describing Cain as the first heretical teacher. Post-biblical Jewish tradition emphasizes Balaam's greed. According to Pseudo-Philo, Balaam, unable to curse Israel as he had been asked to do, advised Balak regarding a means to entice Israel into sin and thereby accomplish the same result as the curse would have. "Select the most beautiful women among you and in Midian, and set them before them naked, adorned with gold and jewels. And it shall come to pass that when they see them, they will sin against the Lord their God and they will fall into your hands, for otherwise you cannot overcome them."[35] Thus the false teachers, like Balaam, were enticing members of the church into indecency, and they were being paid to do so. Korah, the chief antinomian in Jewish tradition, disputed Moses' authority as giver and interpreter of the law. Teachers who know no more than the irrational animals have nothing to teach. They are "dry clouds carried along by the wind," unable to produce life-giving rain and without direction. They are fruitless autumn trees, producing no fruit and bearing no leaves, "twice dead." They are froth, wandering planets, so insanely mistaken that even a dumb animal can teach them wisdom.

Not Freedom! Slavery! Jude concludes with assurances to his readers that the false teachers and their destruction have been anticipated in prophecy. Both Enoch and the apostles foretold their appearance. God can be trusted to administer justice. Second Peter 2:19-22, in contrast, offers a final summary analysis of the false teachers' condition. Although they think themselves free, their behaviors demonstrate that they have, in fact, become slaves to their animal desires. They are entangled in "the defilements of the world" (cf. Gal 4:8; 5:1). Like the wisdom teacher, they are "too stupid to be human" (Prov 30:2). They are no better than animals. Notably, the Petrine author does not engage here in a spiritualist denunciation of bodily existence. Instead, the argument focuses on the false teachers' rejection of the nobler principles of living as a rational creature. Ironically, the false teachers, who have claimed freedom by rejecting the notion that in order to be authentic, human life must be structured according to the principles by which God created and for the purposes to which God created, have become captives to their physical urges. "Their gods are their bellies" (Phil 3:19).[36]

Christlikeness: True Humanity

Israelite wisdom, Jude, and 2 Peter define sin as the failure to fulfill the potential of human existence measured by the standards of wisdom revealed in the creation or by the authority of the Torah revealed to Moses and entrusted to angelic administrators. The task of New Testament authors was to incorporate Christ into a theology of creation. Unless the incarnation, death, and resurrection of Jesus were to be viewed as an afterthought, God's reaction to human sin, Christ must be rooted more firmly in God's intention and nature. The solution involves the insight that God not only created humankind in God's image, but that God chose to reveal God's-self and to redeem humankind by coming into the world in the person of Jesus of Nazareth. From the perspective of an understanding of sin, Jesus as the supreme image-bearer corresponds to the creation of humankind in God's image. Jesus is the prototype and goal of true humanity. Sin, then, cannot be reduced to violation of rules; sin must include the failure, for whatever reason and by whatever modality, to manifest God's image. Sin is not solely the prideful effort to transcend humanity, it is also living a less than fully human life as exemplified and made possible in Jesus Christ.

John's Gospel seizes on the vocabulary available in Greek thought, the wisdom tradition's affirmation that the structure of creation reflects and incorporates God's purposes, and the Mosaic tradition of God's will revealed verbally to claim boldly that, in fact, this principle of creation, this Word of God, manifests God's very personhood, is God, and most shockingly and essentially, became the person Jesus of Nazareth. A human being, John claimed, incarnates the Word and personhood of God, the creator and the plan of creation. To know this particular human being is to know God. The glory of God is a human being. There can be no greater affirmation of the value of being truly human. In fact, John's Jesus affirms that human authenticity consists in the human capacity to reflect the glory of God, to bear God's image, in analogy to the incarnation of God's glory: "The glory that you have given me I have given them . . . " (John 17:22).

In similar fashion, Pauline literature extends a trend already evident *in nuce* in Old Testament wisdom (Prov 3:19, 8:22-31; Ezra 7:14, 26-27; Prov 7:1-4; etc.) and culminating in intertestamental texts such as Sir 24, which identifies Wisdom with Torah. Pauline literature adds Christ, "the image of God, the firstborn of creation" (Col 1:15), to this equation. Early in his greatest systematic explication of sin and salvation, as we have seen, Paul appeals to the language of the Genesis creation account of the *imago dei* for his argument that human beings seem to prefer imitations to authenticity. They have willingly "exchanged the glory of God for [mere] images" (Rom 1:23).

Later, in a very familiar passage nestled at the center of a section devoted to his central point concerning God's impartial righteousness (Rom 3:21-26), Paul restates the claim that every human being fails to live authentically: "For all sin and fall short of the glory of God." Although Paul's central purpose is to demonstrate the universality of human sinfulness, the subtleties of Rom 3:23 prove to be key for understanding Paul's view of the character of human sin. The significant issues involve the text's grammatical and semantical nuances. Paul employs the standard, general term for "to sin" (ἁμαρτάνω, hamartanō), which, as noted above, need not connote a prideful act of transgression but can refer in the broadest sense to sin as error, as "missing the mark." Does Paul mean to argue that every human being intentionally violates God's express will, or that every human being fails in some way and at some point to live an authentic human life? In the larger context, Paul argues that knowledge of the law brings awareness of sin (3:20), that is, "sin" in the sense of "transgression," and that God exercises forbearance with respect to sin committed apart from knowledge (3:25). Paul's assertion of the universality of sin applies both to those for whom knowledge of the law brings awareness of sin and to those who, although ignorant of the law, sin nonetheless. Apparently, then, Rom 3:23 does not have in mind transgression against the revealed will of God but refers to a category that can include both groups.

In fact, the parallel phrase "and fallen short" (ὑστεροῦνται, husterountai) seems to confirm the hypothesis that Paul's contention concerns the universality of sin as missing the mark. This phrase is also ambiguous, however, in three respects. First, the second verb in 3:23 may denote a state of want or need (1 Cor 1:7; 8:8; 12:24; 2 Cor 11:9; Phil 4:12; Luke 15:14; 22:35; John 2:3; Heb 11:37) or describe a failure to attain (2 Cor 11:5; Matt 19:20, 21; Heb 4:1; 12:15). If the former, the clause would describe the consequence of sin, the loss of the glory of God; if the latter, it would emphasize failure to attain the objective, "the glory of God," as the substance of sin. Second, the syntax of the conjunction (και, kai) permits three possible translations: (a) as a copulative expressing a hendiadys (all sin and also fall short); (b) as a consecutive introducing the consequence ("Adam sinned *and therefore* lost his glory");[37] or (c) as an epexegetical or appositive stating a definition ("sinned, that is, fallen short"). Third, the syntax of the two verbs, an aorist followed by a present, raises several possibilities. The Greek aorist tense can refer to past time while the Greek present often refers to the present: "all have sinned and are falling short." This construal of the verbs would favor the consequential reading: falling short in the present is the result of having sinned. Yet Greek verb tenses are notoriously flexible. The aorist also often describes a gnomic condition tantamount to a universal present (i.e., "birds fly," "fish swim"). On balance, taking into consideration the context's insistence on the universality of sin even apart from knowledge of the law and the parallel between the notions of "missing" and "falling short" of the object, it seems most reasonable to take the two clauses as true parallels expressing the universal truth that every human being misses the mark and fails to obtain the true objective of human being, namely, "the glory of God."

What does the "glory of God" mean here?[38] It is clearly the object, the standard that defines sin or some aspect of it. To fall short of it, to miss it, is sin. In the New Testament, the expression seems to occur in three senses. In keeping with Hebrew usage, it sometimes refers to God's reputation and honor (John 11:4; 12:43; Rom 15:7; 1 Cor 10:31; 2 Cor 4:15; Phil 1:11; 2:11). In the fundamental biblical sense, it can denote a revelation of God's essence, even, sometimes, "the final eschatological consequence of justification"[39] (John 11:40; Acts 7:55; Rom 1:23; 5:2; 2 Cor 4:6; Titus 2:13; Rev 15:8; 21:11, 23). Less often, but no less significantly, it can function as a near-synonym for "image of God" (1 Cor 11:7). In fact, Paul frequently speaks of Christ as the new Adam, the image (εἰκών, *eikōn*) of God, the glory of God, as though the concepts, all allusions to the creation of humankind in the *imago dei* (Gen 1:26-27), were interchangeable (2 Cor 3:18; 4:4; 1 Cor 15:43, 49; Rom 8:29-30; Phil 3:21; Col 1:15; cf. 2 Cor 4:6). Paul can argue, for example, that "a man ought not to cover his head, since he is the image and glory of God" (1 Cor 11:7), promise that "we all . . . are being changed into [God's] likeness from one degree of glory to another" (2 Cor 3:18), and refer to the "gospel of the glory of Christ, who is the likeness of God" (2 Cor 4:4; cf. 4:6).[40]

In this reading, Rom 3:23 represents an abbreviated statement of a major component of Paul's thought. In more complete form, it involves only two basic but profound assertions. First, for Paul and Pauline literature, Christ is the quintessential image of God, fulfilling the role intended for humanity in the truest and fullest sense, holding priority over Adam in every way. Allusions to Gen 1:26-27 are unmistakable: "Christ . . . is the likeness (εἰκών, *eikōn*) of God" (2 Cor 4:4). Thus, to behold the face of Christ is to see the glory of God (2 Cor 4:6). The eternal Christ did not become the image of God. Instead, in language reminiscent of descriptions of Wisdom's role in creation (Prov 8) and of John's *Logos* doctrine (John 1:1-18), a Pauline author describes Christ, "the image of the invisible God," as "the first-born of all creation, for in him all things were created . . . all things were created through him and for him" (Col 1:15-16). God created humankind in the image of God by, through, and for Christ, the image of God *par excellence*. Christ's personhood is the model for all other persons. Christ is the principle, agent, and goal of creation.

Second, since God intended that humankind bear God's image and since Christ is the quintessence of that image, the proper goal of every human life is to mature into the full stature of Christlikeness. Paul describes salvation as conformity "to the image of [God's] son" (Rom 8:29). He promises that having "borne the image of the man of dust," those who are Christ's will "also bear the image of the man of heaven" in the kingdom of God (1 Cor 15:49; cf. Phil 3:21). The apostle labors so "that we may present every man mature in Christ" (Col 1:28). The new nature imparted to believers involves renewal "after the image of its creator" (Col 3:10). J. Murphy-O'Connor concludes from a consideration of this theme in Paul, especially as expressed in Rom 7:7–8:4; 2 Cor 4:4-6; and

Col 1:15-20, that Paul's anthropology was based on this Christology, in other words, that "Christ . . . was conceived to represent the divine intent which came to historical expression in the creation of Adam," that Christ is the standard for measuring true humanity.[41] He observes that

> If the truly human are those who have actuated the capacity for creative love that is built into their being, then those who fail to actuate this potentiality are non-human, or sub-human. [Against objections that this position sounds like Nazism it may be replied] that this in fact is not the case, because built into their being is the permanent possibility of *becoming* authentically human. . . . It is comforting to think that all who walk upright on two legs and talk are human, and to believe that humanity is a given. It is disconcerting and disturbing to discover that humanity is in fact something to be achieved, and that the only way to this goal is a continuous created effort directed toward others.[42]

The Augustinian-Lutheran tradition holds that, as a consequence of the first sin, humanity either lost the image of God, or, at best, retained only a severely marred likeness. The text of Genesis makes no such claim, however, and Paul seems, rather, to have thought in terms of a process of maturation (Col 1:28; Eph 4:13, 15) and renewal (Col 3:10; Eph 4:23). For him, human beings have not been stripped of godlikeness. They "fall short" of maturity. Maturation into the full stature of Christ involves growth and change "from one degree of glory to another" (2 Cor 3:18). In short, while sin can be manifest as arrogant, prideful dissatisfaction with being merely human, it can also be manifest as fearful, reticent immaturity tantamount to failure to be fully human.[43] To be sure, limitation inheres in being human. As Paul reminds the Corinthians, God created humankind from the earth. By definition and God's design, human beings exist only in relationship—to God, to others, to the rest of creation—such that they cannot act autonomously without risking damage to relationship. Humans are not free to be and do whatever they will. They cannot behave as though they can attain some higher status in the created order. They are mortal animals.

Nonetheless, God created humanity in God's image on the pattern of Christ. The call to maturity in Christ reminds us that humans are not *merely* animals. God has given human beings capacities for creating, for growth, for genuine personhood, for nurturing others, for redemptive engagement. In this sense, the image of God is more a capacity to be realized than an inherent state of being. Human beings can and should grow into full personhood in a process Robert Connor has recently termed "personagenesis."[44] This process is, unfortunately, rife with opportunities to be stunted by perversion and suppression: sin. No view of the human condition that fails to affirm the inherent value of human being or that overlooks the significance of personagenesis, the process of maturation into full humanity, can reflect biblical faith.

Sin: Failure to Embrace Authentic Freedom

Falling Short of Humanity: Examples in Contemporary Life

Does the biblical picture of sin as failure to be fully human, as stunted growth, as lacking wisdom correspond to life as experienced in the contemporary world? As a matter of fact, several problems encountered in the lives of contemporary human beings can best be explained, theologically, by this view of sin. In particular, this view of sin can help clarify a number of categories of wrong and suffering for which the traditional *hubris*/juridical understanding of sin fails woefully, namely, those in which the conventional analyses in terms of nature or nurture, sin or sickness, victim or sinner, or bystander or participant represent false dichotomies. If every situation in which harm has clearly been done *must* be analyzed juridically in terms of intentional wrongdoing, the result can only be a lack of clarity with respect to weakness, evil, and victimization, so that guilt is sometimes assigned without cause, and sometimes excused.[45] If the church is to offer a truly Christian response to all that is wrong in the world, its engagement with the world's pain must reflect a comprehensive understanding of the human capacity for sin. Although the dynamics apply across a wide spectrum of human experience, the problems of addiction, social and economic oppression, child abuse, and benign neglect offer extreme and therefore clear-cut examples of how these phenomena manifest the biblical dynamics of sin as falling short of true humanity.

Complicitous Acceptance of the Lie

Sin as "loss of self" begins with the subject's acceptance of some form of the lie that one's human being is inherently and fundamentally flawed or impotent.[46] This conviction characterizes drug addicts, threatens to overwhelm victims of various kinds of abuse and oppression, and subtly reinforces the passivity necessary for injustice. While emphasizing the polygenetic character of dependency,[47] therapists and researchers who deal with addiction, for example, generally agree that thoughts and feelings of worthlessness, insignificance, unloveliness, and so forth constitute a major factor in generating and sustaining dependencies. L. Jampolsky identifies a three-step process of addictive thinking: (1) I am not OK as I am; (2) I need something external to myself to make me OK; (3) I must find it.[48] According to Howard Clinebell, this thought process typically results from "psychological trauma or deprivation that cause deeply wounded individuals and family systems who experience high anxiety, shame, and alienation, as well as low self-other esteem and general well-being."[49] Addicts typically do not see themselves as worthy persons. Their actions do not express arrogant and willful rebellion, but desperation and emptiness. Similarly, although sexual predators clearly violate religious and moral norms, psychological research indicates that their behavior, too, is a perverted mechanism "for resolving issues of personal identity that reflect distorted identity structures sedimented through histories of distorted interaction. . . . Issues concerning security, trust, worth, vulnerability are resolved through power, domination, humiliation or the semblance of intimacy."[50] At some point, abusers have interiorized from the circumstances of their childhood an identity of unworthiness, of less than full humanity. The status quo works to convince victims of spousal abuse, class and racial injustice, or any other form of the abuse of power that their experience is simply reality: their lot in life, God's will, or even their own fault. Even religion can function to reinforce oppressive and abusive systems: women should be submissive; God blesses the good with prosperity and curses sinners with hardship; one's primary duty is obedience to authority.[51] Sadly, all too often, victims come to believe the lie.

As in Gen 3, the lie usually comes as a message from outside the subject, delivered either directly and explicitly by a "tempter"/abuser, or more insidiously by the subject's environment. H. Clinebell identifies four destructive "parental patterns" common to the overwhelming majority of alcoholics' families of origin that undermine the child's sense of well-being in ways that impede successful personality development: heavy-handed authoritarianism, success-worship, moralism, and overt rejection.[52] The commonality is contingent love that produces low self-esteem. Perpetrators of sexual abuse of children, egregious examples of explicit liars, must create a pseudo-reality in which wrong seems right to the victim and which sustains the necessary secrecy. A. McFadyen's probing and disturbing study of the theological dynamics of childhood sexual abuse details the manner in which predators exploit "the age-related disparities in knowledge and understanding . . . in order to effect a confusion in their victims' willing."[53] The child's desire for rewards and inducements—to take measures to avoid the execution of the predator's threats should the secret become known, for example—becomes confused in the child's mind with willing the abuse. The abuser creates a situation in which the child can come to believe the lie.[54] "The abuser bends the child's willing for non-abusive objects to abusive purposes by eliding the difference between them, so that the child's willing and intentionality is incorporated into those of the abuser. Childhood sexual abuse abuses the child's active willing and intentionality, and this is why it can have such long-term traumatic consequences."[55] A similar process takes place when abuse advances in gradual increments so that the child has difficulty distinguishing the transition from non-abusive to abusive acts.

> The gradient of incrementation is so shallow that it obfuscates, not only the point at which acts become abusive, but the point at which her willing is operative. Even when she becomes aware that she does not want the abusive acts to continue, she may feel pressed to consent because she senses that she has, in a sense, already consented to them by accepting those which now, from this perspective, appear not so different.[56]

Victims of gender, class, or racial oppression are born into systems built on a version of the lie (that women, the poor, or minorities are inferior human beings). As extant reality, the only framework of understanding themselves, the status quo disorients everyone's will and intention.[57] Family systems, dominant cultures, and societies invite their members to accept the proposition that things *should be* as they *are*.[58] Only the widespread acceptance of the framework as the true reality permits its continuation.[59] Victims, victimizers, and "innocent" bystanders cooperate to sustain the lie,[60] and all suffer its consequences. Acceptance of the lie injures even the abuser/oppressor since it does not create the possibility for the abuser to repent or for redemption to come to the system.[61]

The temptation to blame the victim must, of course, be resisted, but the converse error must also be avoided. In the commendable effort not to charge the victim with *causing* the addiction or the victimization, doctrines of sin usually overlook the function of the victim's passivity and complicity in supporting and sustaining the illness or the conditions of abuse.

Feminists have very insightfully clarified this tricky issue of the relationship between victimization and sin. They emphasize "the personal involvement of women in their diminution of selfhood" or "the mode of women's involvement in 'patriarchy.'" A. McFadyen points out the key function of the verbs feminists use to describe sloth: in relation to personal involvement—failing (to make authentic, free choices, to take responsibility, etc.), hiding, refusing, abdicating, abnegating, denying, or fleeing; in relation to participation in patriarchy—participating, being complicit, acquiescing, accepting, consenting to, complying, and cooperating with.[62] This is not to say that the victims are to blame; the distinction between sin and injury must be maintained.[63] "Women do not have the kind of autonomous agency in relation to 'patriarchy' that would render them liable to blame for causing or freely choosing their oppression; *nevertheless*, they participate in it personally, through the exercise of some other form of personal agency."[64]

In effect, then, sin as "loss of self" can be described as complicity in the lie, the false framework of reality. As victim, the sufferer is not responsible for creating the situation. Neither, however, is the victim merely a passive object.[65] Instead, the victim has been induced or coerced into cooperation. The dynamics are clearly evident in child sexual abuse.[66] The abuser has co-opted the child's will as a tool to enable the abuse. Indeed, feminists, in part for therapeutic reasons, eschew the term "victim" in favor of "survivor." In other words, the child is not merely done to, as an object. The child does something, as well: She survives the ordeal; her will operates to ensure her survival, "yet, because the context of will is totalitarian, this achievement may only be a form of accommodation to abuse." The child's very identity "is organised around the reality of abuse, which becomes the prime informant of identity."[67] Still, during the ordeal, she exercised agency and will. Thus, there is some therapeutic basis for reclaiming the narrative of her life as her own.

The contention that this complicity is, indeed, the mechanism of sin as "loss of self" finds substantiation in the victim become victimizer pattern so common in the psychological histories of abusers. The process comes full circle. Abusers fully accept the false framework of reality imposed by their own abusers and perpetuate it for another cycle. Clearly, *as victims*, they are not sinners responsible for creating the false framework; if later, *as victimizers*, however, they accept and perpetuate it, they become responsible for their actions. The fact that numbers of victims go on to become victimizers indicates that something happens to them subjectively during or as a consequence of the abuse.[68] To some degree, victims who become victimizers give assent to the framework of reality established by their abusers and to that extent become complicit in the circumstance. Later, they perpetuate this false framework of reality by abusing as they were abused. Their complicity in their own victimization matures into the perverted will of abusers.[69]

Fearful Avoidance of Human Potential

L. Jampolsky points out that contemporary society inundates everyone with the message that they need something external to themselves in order to be happy and whole: a new pair of jeans, a new job, an ideal spouse and family. At the core, this orientation toward externals rests on fear, fear of one's inadequacy and fear to attempt life without external supports.[70] The cycle of guilt and fear becomes self-reinforcing. Having failed, persons accept the idea that they are failures: "I have done a bad thing, therefore I must be a bad person. I can expect only failure and its consequences." As Earnie Larsen observes, people fulfill their self-definitions. If one feels unlovable, one behaves unlovingly.[71]

These dynamics are clearly evident in the struggles of addicts whose dependence involves, in addition to the chemical component, the need to self-medicate the pain they feel at their own inadequacy and shame. The temptation to despair represents the supreme spiritual and psychological danger for victims of many forms of abuse. All too easily, the victim may falsely accept responsibility for the abuse in the form of a self-image defined by the abuse and, consequently, accept the limited scope of existence prescribed by that self-image: "A bad thing has happened to me, therefore I must have deserved it because I am a bad person. I can expect only failure and its consequences." Many women and minorities in repressive circumstances, children of neglectful parents, adherents to hypermoralistic religions, and to some degree, every human being who has ever felt horrible shame know the steps along this path of fear.

In the end, people become afraid of freedom and love. Persons with negative self-images "are so concerned with their reduced worth (in their eyes), that they refuse to take growth-oriented risks for fear of losing what they have. . . . When they do act, it is more out of fear of offending, rather than the exhilaration of accomplishment." This refusal is tantamount to "failure to accept that they are made in the image and likeness of God."[72]

The distinction between guilt—the acknowledgment that one has done wrong—and shame—the false (by definition) conviction that one is simply a bad person—demands attention here. Rather than celebrating the freedom and potential inherent in the notion that human beings bear the image of God and embracing joyously the gift of God's grace, shamed persons adopt a deterministic stance toward their own unworth. "I'm just an old drunk. What do you expect of me?" Persons dare not attempt to incarnate the image of God in their lives because they are convinced that it has been lost—if it were ever present.

Stunted Maturation

Personagenesis does not perfectly attain its ultimate goal in any human life. Furthermore, the definition of a healthy process of growth will, naturally, vary according to specific characteristics of the individual in question and according to age and phase-appropriate criteria. But, for any number of reasons, ranging from the individual's free and intentional choices to limiting factors and obstacles imposed by the individual's environment, individuals often get off-track in their development toward being authentically human. As defined by Israelite Wisdom literature, especially, this arrested development is sin. It manifests itself in the lives of addicts, abusers, and people suffering from a wide variety of emotional and psychological disturbances in the form of a constant preoccupation, conscious or unconscious, with unmet needs and developmental crises from the past. Addicts typically relive the feelings of worthlessness and abandonment that derive from troubled childhoods, seeking to find comfort and meaning through some external source. Abusers fixate on the experiences of their own traumas. Addicts and abusers alike try to fill holes left from their difficult pasts by seeking, either through substances, overindulgences, or false intimacy, "to self-medicate emotional pain, low self-esteem, sexual guilt and shame, body hatred, spiritual emptiness, and lack of meaning in their lives."[73] To some degree, victims of various forms of abuse and injustice, while not responsible for the abuse and oppression, allow themselves to be defined by the abusive and oppressive other. In this regard, a perspective on sin as stunted maturation points to the dynamics of personality development as outlined by Erik Erikson and others, which will be discussed immediately below in relation to sin as enslavement. For now, let it suffice to endorse N. Ring's definition of this type of sin as "anything which we consciously allow to interfere with the process of self-transcendence. . . . "[74] A comprehensive doctrine of sin will recognize that prideful overreaching alone does not account for ways in which specific approaches to being human can disappoint God's intentions. A comprehensive doctrine of sin will be equally aware of the sinfulness of "deference and dependency."[75]

Slavery and Sub-humanity

Paul's expression of frustration in Rom 7 that the will to do right in agreement with God's Torah cannot break humanity's bondage to its lesser drives gives the lie to any definition of sin limited to willful rebellion. Instead, the ultimate result of sin as failure is a dependency on the lesser and bondage to it that hinders one from any sort of authenticity, autonomy, or responsible exercise of freedom. This slavery can have several dimensions. Victims of abuse and oppression suffer physical and, ultimately much more damaging, psychological coercion.[76] On a broader scale, society often exerts similar coercion, resulting in the subjugation of the individual to the collective, by offering the (false) possibility of transcendence through the divinization of some finite aspect of the culture (ethnicity, das Volk, etc.) and requiring the individual's complete allegiance to the group or its ideology. Addicts of various kinds, bound physiologically and psychologically, are only apparently self-centered; in truth, they are substance-centered; they are slaves to their fears and their urges.[77] They cannot be said to willfully and arrogantly transgress upon divine prerogatives because they have free will in only a limited sense. As H. Clinebell observes:

> If depth psychology has demonstrated anything, it has shown that human behavior, and mental and physical illnesses are never simply a matter of freely choosing between simple alternatives. Every act is conditioned by early life experiences that shaped the personality. Untrammeled free will, in the sense that it is used in much mission thought, does not exist. The concept is especially inapplicable to addictive-compulsive illnesses. The more driven persons are, the more their actions are controlled by inner compulsions, the less freedom of choice they have in the areas of their addictions.[78]

In fact, to the extent that all human beings, as Paul argues, suffer this sort of entrapment resulting from the logic of fear described by Jampolsky and others, the dynamics of addiction correspond analogously to the universal and ubiquitous human need for grace in response to human powerlessness.[79] That is, human beings seem universally bound psychologically by dread, by failure, and by acceptance of the lie that authentic human existence lies beyond reach. Addicts are not alone in accepting "the fallacy of looking outside ourselves for happiness."[80] Human beings regularly abdicate responsibility for their own lives. In fact, a form of this abdication is a normal component of human development. By early adolescence cognitive development enables abstraction and conceptualization to such a degree that it becomes possible, even characteristic, for youths to engage in what the theorists call "mutual interpersonal perspective taking," that is, to become acutely aware of oneself in relation to others and as seen by others. What others think about one becomes very important and motivates, for the first time, the conscious effort to formulate an identity. In fact, E. Erikson refers to the central issue one faces during this period as an "identity crisis."[81] Owing to the powerful influence exerted by the expectations of significant others, a great danger during this phase of development involves surrender to these external expectations. Peer pressure, parental demands, and puppy love may threaten to produce "other-oriented" persons willing to subjugate themselves to an external will. H. Doweiko[82] observes that dependent personalities often struggle with shame/autonomy issues, finding it difficult to distinguish between proper concern for others and responsibility for them.

Significantly, although it clearly threatens to culminate in an abdication of authentic personhood—surely in contradiction to God's will for the developing personality—such "other-orientation" is virtually opposite to the "willful rebellion" described by the traditional doctrine. Early adolescents are driven to conform, not to rebel. It might be argued that "other-orientation" in relation to God would be an appropriate expression of faith. Niebuhr regarded the juxtaposition of the divine will over against the egoism characteristic of human sin as the corrective for sin.[83] Yet Niebuhr did not advocate the subjugation of the individual ego even to God. Most often, however, early adolescents unfortunately displace "other-orientation" onto unworthy "others," whether other persons, material goods, or behaviors, thereby failing to attain the ego strength and individuality of an authentic human being. Adults commit the same sin.

Conclusion
Christlikeness: True Humanity

The gospel asserts that God through Christ reconciles the world to God's-self, accomplishing a new act of creation. God does so by revealing and modeling God's original intention for being human in the person of Jesus Christ. Jesus' life and death not only demonstrate authentic humanity but also, in the mystery of redemption, make it possible for his disciples. God's love for humanity as shown in the life and death of Jesus gives the lie to the idea that "such-a-worm-as-I" theology adequately describes the human condition. Anti-humanist and spiritualist, it emphasizes willful disobedience as the sole form of human sin and directs attention away from the most fundamental character of the Bible's assertion concerning the nature of humankind and its relationship with God. An unequivocally "wholly other," dialectic view of God overlooks the counterbalancing biblical doctrine that God created human beings in the divine image, that God revealed God's-self most clearly *in the human person Jesus Christ*. In short, it devalues humanity. To be sure, human beings can and regularly do overreach. But human beings also can, and even more commonly do, underachieve. The call to surrender one's life to God's lordship does not equate with a call to passivity for fear of affronting God's dignity. God calls every human being to actively represent the image of God in the world, to be God's partner and representative.

Christlikeness—authentic humanity—is not, therefore, an idealized, platonic notion. Maturity in Christ does not involve the negation of one's humanity. One need not fear that to be truly and fully human is insufficient. Jesus did not die to save human beings from their humanity, but to redeem and authenticate it.

Again, the central affirmations of biblical faith—that God made human beings in God's image, that God became incarnate to redeem, to recreate, to enliven the image of God in human beings—assure humanity that in God's purposes, creation, including the human race, is good.

Of course, the human species universally experiences stunted maturation, even, or some might argue, especially among those who profess Christ. The contemporary church's woeful neglect of the practice of "making disciples"—the "what-would-Jesus-do" movement notwithstanding—and of the theological doctrine of sanctification must be addressed. Obviously, Israel's view of the importance of gaining wisdom offers a direct endorsement of education in all forms. Human beings do not come into the world as fully formed persons, nor do believers immediately and instantaneously conform to the image of Christ. Persons must intentionally cooperate with the Spirit of God as God completes God's unique purposes in unique individuals. What would Jesus do? What would Jesus drive? Jesus would die on the cross and probably walk to his execution. The gospel's affirmation of the value of humanity does not envision a human ideal of "perfection." Instead, human "authenticity" is the desideratum. Christlikeness does not consist in the details of hair color, gender, talent sets, or skills. As Niebuhr contends,

> . . . it is only through the self's appropriation of its unique individuality that a person is able to encounter and be in proper relationship to God. Only in the acceptance of responsible freedom, which is accomplished in the self's appropriation of its individuality, does the self realize that the true measure and meaning of its existence cannot be wholly equated with the finite conditions of that existence. This realization causes the individual to seek the meaning of its existence beyond the immediate conditions of its finitude. . . . this search for ultimate meaning inexorably points to God.[84]

In other words, Paul's call to share the mind of Christ (Phil 2:5) is not a call to passivity in relationship. Submission that is coerced and purposeless is not Christlike. Christlikeness is not bondage; it is purposeful self-giving.

The gospel promises a comprehensive salvation. The insidious gnostic tendencies of Western, especially American, evangelical piety deny the value and significance of *this* life, *this* body, *these* relationships, *this* community, *this* creation. To sin is to neglect the profound importance of corporeal and corporate human being. The ideal, then, would be "right relation," the proper balance between being-for-oneself and being-for-others-in-relation. It should be possible to be for others out of a strong and centered self. Indeed, being for others should be more effective in this circumstance. Further, proper being for others should not diminish the self, but enrich and enhance it. Autonomy need not be isolated individualism; relationship need not be subjugation. Salvation is God's gift of full humanity.[85]

CHAPTER FOUR

Sin as Basic Mistrust

"Lord, I believe, help my unbelief." (Mark 9:24)
"All I have seen teaches me to trust the Creator for all I have not seen."[1]

Human beings sin either by overreaching their humanity or by failing in the effort to realize it fully. Their behaviors manifest either an unwarranted and prideful egotism or an equally unwarranted and shame-based passivity. To be authentically human is to fully embrace the two poles of humanity: the image of God in which and for which God created all human beings, and the creaturely finitude that constitutes humanity's kinship with the dust from which it was shaped. Authentic human existence involves living in and for the image of God while fully aware that one comes from the dust. When this polarity becomes imbalanced in either direction, one falls into sin.

Are there, then, two basic categories of sin so that the Christian doctrine of sin proposes a dualism in human nature? Both the Scriptures and the tradition of Christian theology maintain that sin is a universal human phenomenon, that is, that all human beings participate in a common experience. In the most fundamental terms, humanity cannot be divided into two categories of sinners. While the Bible utilizes a number of terms for sin, each emphasizing some aspect of the rather complex phenomenon, neither biblical Hebrew nor biblical Greek speaks of a dichotomy.

The question arises, then, as to whether some common behavior lies behind both *hubris* and self-loss. In fact, the Bible, modern depth psychology—especially insights from the field of personality development and the hybrid field of faith development—and constructive theology all agree to some extent that underlying both forms of sin, human beings abandon authentic existence out of a sense of anxiety rooted in mistrust: as Ecclesiastes expressed it,[2] human beings are existentially uncomfortable with the capacity for imagining in a godlike manner while accepting creaturely limitations and finitude. Humans find it difficult to embrace God's pronouncement that human existence at the boundary between animal and divine is inherently good. At root, this existential discomfort results from a lack of trust that God has, indeed, created a good order. Humans overreach to compensate or underattain in despair.

The Bible says a great deal about this human propensity to mistrust God. From the garden of Eden to Babylonian exile, the Hebrew Bible traces humanity's fear that God has not or will not relate to God's creation faithfully and beneficially. The authors of the New Testament came to see the essence of the human problem, sin, not as rebellious breech of God's express will, nor as underachievement, but as an inability or unwillingness to place ultimate trust in God as revealed in Jesus Christ, the quintessential expression of God's faithfulness and benevolence toward humankind. Not surprisingly, the Bible's contention that misdirected trust constitutes the foundation of all human sin finds a cognate in modern psychological descriptions of the human individual. Human beings, to various degrees, find it difficult to trust, especially to trust a God that cannot be seen. Taken together, these theological and psychological insights into the flawed human capacity for trust raise a number of significant implications for the practice of ministry to an untrusting world.

The Bible on Basic Mistrust

It bears noting that the Bible's fundamental vocabulary points to the necessity of trust in the relationship between God and humanity. Both the Hebrew Bible and the New Testament speak of trust in God as the basis for relationship. As has often been noted,[3] biblical vocabulary (Hebrew *'mn*; Greek *pisteuō*) does not address matters of intellectual assent, a connotation often elicited by the typical English translations "to believe," "to believe in," and "to have faith." As the New Testament author put it, "even the demons believe *that* [God is one]" (James 2:19). In the Bible, the essential question facing human beings involves not whether one can accept the notion that God exists, nor whether one can affirm a particular statement of doctrine. Instead, the Bible understands faith in God as basic confidence in God's trustworthiness, as basic trust that God is good and that God's ways are good. Relatedly, the most basic sin is failure to trust God and God's order. A range of biblical texts, beginning with the Eden narrative and culminating in perhaps the most sublime treatment of the theme in the Gospel of John, underscores this essential insight.

Significantly, the New Testament claims that the fundamental problem in human existence is lack of faith, a faulty sense of trust in God. This claim—mirrored in Jesus' teaching on prayer, his sayings on the fatherhood of God, and his admonition against anxiety—can be traced back through the prophets' analysis of Israel's failure to trust God, manifest in idolatry and political machinations, and the Deuteronomistic Historian's portrayal of Israel's continual murmuring against God, to the Genesis account of the first pair's decision to supplement God's provision for their well-being. At root, the human compulsions either to supplant God or to acquiesce to less than full humanity arise from the human fear that God has not, cannot, or will not do for human beings what is best.

The Prototypical Mistrust in Eden

Traditional theology charges Adam and Eve with willful rebellion in the garden of Eden; but as discussed in the previous chapter, contemporary readings of Gen 3, especially by liberation and feminist theologians, point to the first pair's failure in relation to the serpent-beast to exercise the responsibility over the garden that God had given by means of the autonomy inherent in their godlikeness. Genesis 3, then, is the appropriate starting point and test case for the assertion that the Bible recognizes an even more essential form of sin that gives birth to both pride and self-loss. In other words, Gen 3 suggests that the elements of pride and sloth, both manifest in the one act of consuming the forbidden fruit, actually arise from a common source, an underlying feature, an even more basic "sin."

The biblical narrative reveals that the *seed* of the first sin was neither sloth nor defiance, but mistrust. The serpent said to Eve, "Did God say, 'Do not eat of any tree of the garden'?" Eve replied, "We may eat the fruit of the trees in the garden, but God said, 'Do not eat the fruit of the tree in the middle of the garden or touch it, lest you die.'" The serpent replied, "You won't die. God knows that when you eat it, your eyes will be opened and you will be like God, knowing good and evil" (Gen 3:1b-5, excerpted). The serpent insinuated that the God who had created them in God's own image, who had planted the rich and luxuriant garden to provide for them, who had populated it with all manner of living creatures and had entrusted them into human care, who walked with them daily had intentionally and deceptively withheld from them the best gift of all. Adam and Eve disobeyed God because, in their *mistrust*, they *feared* that God might not have provided the best, after all. They suspected that God's good order was not good enough.[4]

Mistrust in the Wilderness: Murmuring and Suspicion

The first pair's mistrust of God in the garden resurfaces in Israel's experiences in the desert on the way to the promised land. Faced with the variety of hardships encountered on the way from Egypt to Canaan, the Israelites repeatedly, and often disastrously, doubted God's presence, power, and benevolence. The motif known to biblical scholars as the "murmuring" tradition appears in a distinct strand of narrative materials in Exodus, Numbers, and Deuteronomy, in addition to several references outside the Pentateuch texts concentrated in the Psalter.[5] Characteristically, these texts recount occasions when Israel "murmured" (Hebrew לון, *lwn*; RSV/NRSV has "complained," Exod 15:24 [Heb. 15:24]; 16:2, 7-10; 17:3; Num 14:2, 27, 36; 16:11, 41 [Heb. 17:6]; 17:10 [Heb. 17:25]) against God or God's representatives, Moses and Aaron. Sometimes the narratives describe Israel's behavior as "quarreling" (Heb. ריב, *ryb*, Exod 17:2; Num

20:3, 13), "complaining" (Heb. אנן, *'nn*, Num 11:1), "speaking against" (Heb. על דבר, *dbr 'l*, Num 21:5, 7; Ps 78:19), "crying out" (Heb. צעק, *ts'q*, Exod 14:10, 15), "gathering together against" (Heb. יעד על, *y'd 'l*, Num 14:35), "grumbling" (Heb. רגן, *rgn*, Deut 1:27; Ps 106:25), or "weeping" (Heb. בכה, *bkh*, Num 11:4, 10, 13, 18; 14:1). Texts in the Deuteronomic and prophetic traditions equate Israel's murmuring with rebellion (Heb. מרה, *mrh* Deut 1:26, 43; 9:7, 23-24; Pss 78:17, 40, 56; 106:7; Ezek 20:13, 21).[6] As will be demonstrated, however, the act of rebellion culminating the episode of Israel's refusal to enter the promised land as God had instructed, for example, results from Israel's underlying failure to trust God or God's plan and provision. Mistrust is the central component of Israel's propensity to murmur in the biblical narratives. Mistrust gives rise both to rebellion and to indecisive inaction. In Deuteronomy, Moses explicitly describes the relationship between the attitude of mistrust and the overt behavior of rebellion: "You rebelled against the command of the LORD your God, neither trusting ['*mn*] him nor obeying him" (Deut 9:23).

Although the presenting problem varies—lack of water (Exod 15:24; 17:2, 4), food (Exod 16:3; Num 11:4-5; Ps 78:18-20), or both (Num 20:5; 21:5), military hazards (Exod 13:17; 14:11-12; Num 14:2-3; Deut 1:27-28), disputes concerning the authority of Moses and Aaron (Num 16:3, 41), or hardships in general (Num 11:1)—Israel's murmuring involves a common sequence of elements,[7] four of which demonstrate clearly that the tradition deals primarily with Israel's mistrust of God: (1) Israel's accusing questions; (2) characterizations of Israel's behavior as tantamount to an expression of no confidence; (3) comments regarding Israel's failure to remember and properly interpret the history of God's intervention and provision; and (4) God's responses, intended to give evidence that Israel's mistrust is unfounded.

Israel Accuses God. The narrative texts in this tradition relate that Israel "murmured" or the like and, in most cases, go on to report the substance of Israel's grumbling in the form of thinly veiled accusations cast as often sarcastic rhetorical questions. Many of these questions reveal Israel's mistrust of God's intentions in delivering from Egypt:

> "Would that we had died by the hand of the LORD in the land of Egypt, when we sat by the fleshpots and ate bread to the full; for you have brought us out into this wilderness to kill this whole assembly with hunger." (Exod 16:3 RSV)

> "Why did you bring us up out of Egypt, to kill us and our children and our cattle with thirst?" (Exod 17:3 RSV)

> "Would that we had died when our brethren died before the LORD! Why have you brought the assembly of the Lord into this wilderness, that we should die here, both we and our cattle? And why have you made us come up out of Egypt, to bring us to this evil place? It is no place for grain, or figs, or vines, or pomegranates; and there is no water to drink." (Num 20:3-5 RSV)

"Why have you brought us up out of Egypt to die in the wilderness? For there is no food and no water, and we loathe this worthless food." (Num 21:5 RSV)

"Because the LORD hated us he has brought us forth out of the land of Egypt, to give us into the hand of the Amorites, to destroy us. Whither are we going up?" (Deut 1:27-28 RSV)

Almost all the questions look back longingly to life in Egyptian bondage as superior to life trekking through the wilderness. In Egypt, the menu offered some variety at least. A few questions even state an explicit desire to abandon the journey to the promised land and to return to Egypt (cf. Neh 9:17).

"Is it because there are no graves in Egypt that you have taken us away to die in the wilderness? What have you done to us, in bringing us out of Egypt? Is not this what we said to you in Egypt, 'Let us alone and let us serve the Egyptians'? For it would have been better for us to serve the Egyptians than to die in the wilderness." (Exod 14:11-12 RSV)

"O that we had meat to eat! We remember the fish we ate in Egypt for nothing, the cucumbers, the melons, the leeks, the onions, and the garlic; but now our strength is dried up, and there is nothing at all but this manna to look at." (Num 11:4-6 RSV)

"Who will give us meat to eat? For it was well with us in Egypt." (Num 11:18 RSV)

"Why did we come forth out of Egypt?" (Num 11:20 RSV)

"Would that we had died in the land of Egypt! Or would that we had died in this wilderness! Why does the LORD bring us into this land, to fall by the sword? Our wives and our little ones will become a prey; would it not be better for us to go back to Egypt?" (Num 14:2-3 RSV)

Underlying all these accusations is the fundamental suspicion that God is either unwilling or incapable of fulfilling God's promise to bring Israel into the land of promise. Two versions of the accusing question touch the heart of the matter. The first voices aloud the fear inherent in all the murmurings concerning provisions of food and water: "Can God spread a table in the wilderness. . . . Can he also give bread, or provide meat for his people?" (Ps 78:19-20). The second expresses the anxieties of promises delayed: "Is it too little that you have brought us up out of a land flowing with milk and honey to kill us in the wilderness, that you must also lord it over us? It is clear you have not brought us into a land flowing with milk and honey, or given us an inheritance of fields and vineyards" (Num 16:13-14). Once and once only, although in a story situated quite early in the narrative of the wilderness period, the people manifest the essential fear underlying all their murmuring and complaining, namely, whether "YHWH is among us or not" (Exod 17:7).

God Recognizes the Fundamental Problem: Lost Confidence. Although most of the accusations nominally address Moses, both he and God recognize that the people's mistrust of Moses as God's representative is tantamount to mistrust of God ("Your complaining is not against us but against the LORD"; Exod 16:8; cf. Exod 17:2; Num 16:11). Nowadays, the question of belief in God is usually understood intellectually and in relation to the alternative of atheism. Does one believe in, can one give intellectual assent to the notion of, the existence of God? For the Israelites in the wilderness, facing life and death questions threatening their very existence, the overarching issue shaping their relationship with YHWH was not whether YHWH existed, but whether YHWH could be trusted. Would YHWH remain with them throughout the hardships to come ("Is the LORD among us or not?" Exod 17:7)? Even if YHWH could be trusted not to abandon them along the way, the Israelites were not sure of YHWH's power to act for their benefit: "they had no faith [*'mn*] in God, and did not trust [*bth*] his saving power" (Ps 78:22; cf. YHWH's rhetorical "Is YHWH's power limited?" Num 11:23). Nor, looking from the vantage point of the harsh desert into a land populated by giants living behind walls, could they envision successfully taking possession of the promised land. What good is the presence of God in the face of armies of giants? In effect, "they despised the pleasant land, having no faith [*'mn*] in his promise" (Ps 106:24).[8]

A Failure of Memory and Interpretation. Perhaps the most startling aspect of the people's murmuring—or, to the contrary, seen as an example of the apparently universal human tendency toward anxiety, the most predictable—is their failure of confidence despite the evidence of God's benevolence and power. After God delivered them at the Reed Sea, their former fear of the Egyptians became reverence for YHWH whom they now trusted (*'mn*) to deliver (Exod 14:31; cf. Ps 106:7-12). Surprisingly, even this impressive demonstration of God's benevolent power did not ultimately convince them that God could and would protect them from danger and provide for their fundamental needs. At the climactic moment of the people's murmuring in the wilderness, their refusal to enter the promised land from Kadesh-barnea because of their fear of the inhabitants of the land, YHWH complained to Moses that the people refused to trust (*'mn*) him, "in spite of all the signs that I have done among them" (Num 14:11; cf. 14:22-23). In the parallel account in Deuteronomy, Moses likens YHWH's care for Israel to tenderness shown a small child, concluding that the people "have no trust [*'mn*] in the LORD your God" (Deut 1:30-32; cf. Pss 78:32; 106:24; Neh 9:17). A significant sub-motif in the murmuring materials characterizes the people's behavior as testing YHWH: challenging YHWH to prove his trustworthiness and power (Exod 17:2, 7; Num 14:22-23; Pss 78:18, 41, 56; 106:14).

God's Response: ". . . then you shall know. . . ." God responded to the Israelites' mistrust in three basic ways, corresponding roughly to periods in Israel's wilderness experience. At first, God reacted to the people's concerns, primarily dealing with water, by simply addressing the specific need (Exod 15:22-27 and 17:1-7). In passages dealing primarily with Israel's complaints concerning the quantity and quality of food available in the wilderness, however, God indicated that the provision to be made in response to the people's complaints should be interpreted specifically as responses to Israel's mistrust. God provided manna in the evening so that Israel "shall know that it was the LORD who brought [them] out of the land of Egypt," and in the morning so that they "shall see the glory of the LORD" (Exod 16:6-7). The purpose of the whole exercise is to demonstrate once more, in YHWH's words, "that I am the LORD your God" (Exod 16:12). When, weary of a steady diet of manna, the Israelites pled for variety, YHWH sent quails in abundance so that Israel, YHWH said, could "see whether my word will come true for you or not" (Num 11:23). Only after repeated expressions of Israel's mistrust did YHWH, in some frustration, turn to punishment. Even then, however, punishment demonstrated YHWH's presence and power ("'As I live,' says the LORD . . . " Num 14:28).

The Prophets on Israel's Mistrust

The prophet Jeremiah traced the sin of sixth-century Judah to its roots in Israel's wilderness mistrust of YHWH. Although YHWH had delivered Judah's ancestors from Egypt and led them safely in the wilderness, neither they (2:6) nor their religious leaders (2:8) learned from the experience to have confidence in YHWH. Instead, they behaved as though they had "found some wrong" in YHWH's care (2:5), and, like the wilderness generation, they "complained against [YHWH]" (2:29). In Jeremiah's view, Israel's transgenerational mistrust of YHWH manifested itself in two forms of misplaced trust: idolatry ("Has a nation ever changed gods—which really are not gods? Well, my people have exchanged their glory for something useless . . . my people have abandoned me, the fountain of living water, to hew themselves cisterns, broken cisterns that cannot hold water," 2:11-13) and politics ("You will be put to shame by Egypt as you were put to shame by Assyria. From it too you will come away with your hands on your head, for YHWH has rejected those in whom you trust," 2:36b-37). These two themes, along with a third concerning injustice against fellow human beings, constitute the core of the judgment message of Israel's prophets. In sum, the preaching of Amos, Hosea, Isaiah, Jeremiah and the others contends that the people of God have withdrawn their confidence in their deliverer to place it in gods "who are no gods" (Jer 2:11) and in foreign alliances. The moral decay of their society manifested their disconnection from the true source of their identity as God's people.

Idolatry. Interpreters of Israel's prophets typically and, for the most part, rightly describe prophetic anti-idolatry preaching as condemnation of Israel's willful rebellion against the most basic provision of YHWH's covenant with Israel: the first commandment. As a rule, the prophets made no effort to account for the motivation of Israel's apostasy. In their view, Israel's behavior was simply perverse and abominable. They were much less interested in explaining the causes and motivations for Israel's attraction to the worship of strange gods than in condemning and eradicating it. As a phenomenon in the context of Israel's exclusive relationship with YHWH, idolatry represents Israel's discomfort with the freedom and mystery of YHWH. Idol images can be seen and controlled. In contrast to a God who forgives freely, who provides and protects because of an undeserved and unearned commitment to a people, and whose presence with this people cannot be guaranteed or manipulated, idols can be placated, coerced by sacrifices made or withheld, and moved at the will of their worshipers. Relationship with YHWH depends on trust and mutuality; relationships with idols involve barter and management. Trust plays no role if one assumes that one can bribe one's god to forgive, that one can starve one's god into behaving as one wishes, or that one can guarantee the presence of one's god in the form of a physical representation. From the outset of the covenant relationship between YHWH and Israel, YHWH insisted that Israel acknowledge the impossibility of confining its Creator and Deliverer to any finite representation. The basis of Israel's relationship with YHWH would be trust, not control.

Jeremiah was not alone in tracing Israel's historic flirtation with other gods to an inexplicable failure of confidence. Hosea depicted YHWH's anguish over Israel's failure to recognize YHWH as the true source of Israel's prosperity (2:8), a failure that leads her to "go after [other] lovers" (2:5). Reconstructing the thoughts and attitudes of the exilic audience of the message recorded in Isaiah 40–55, one hears doubt that YHWH has the power or authority to deliver from exile. God contended that the nations are but "a drop from a bucket," indeed, "they are nothing . . . less than nothing, emptiness" (Isa 40:15, 17), presumably in anticipation or response to the exiles' concerns that the Babylonians will not permit them to leave. God did not need Babylonian permission. In the same passage, God challenged the audience to find a suitable comparison among the idols made of wood and cast metals for the creator of the universe, again, presumably in anticipation or response to the exiles' concerns that the Babylonian gods—who are no gods—would resist YHWH's plans. Again, the key issue, even in Isaiah's message of salvation, is trust in God's benevolence and power.

Although rare, a few prophets analyzed Israel's historic affinity for idol worship beyond the level of polemic. What would motivate a people whose ancestors YHWH had delivered from slavery, constituted as a nation, and sustained in a prosperous land to abandon that relationship? Hosea, Isaiah, and Jeremiah implied that disloyalty and disobedience result from a fundamental mistrust (cf. Deut 9:23, "neither trusting nor obeying"). Perhaps, by the time these prophets were active, the wonders of the exodus were so far in the past that many of the people could no longer draw confidence from them. (What have you done for me lately, God?) Perhaps, as is certainly true of moderns, they lacked the poetic vision, the eyes of faith, to see the everyday workings of the world—the rain, the sun, birth—as evidence of God's faithful provision. Perhaps the temptation to focus attention on penultimate concerns, because they are manageable, overwhelmed the discipline necessary to recognize that these concerns simply cannot sustain the confidence placed in them. Idols cannot save; they do not deserve devotion.

Politics. The prophets stated their case much more explicitly regarding Israel/Judah's geopolitical anxiety. The "founder" of the Israelite state, the prophet Samuel, chose its first king only reluctantly; YHWH did not initiate the monarchy, but only permitted it. In the view of God and God's prophet, the people's desire for a king was tantamount to a rejection of God's leadership. They had apparently grown weary of the instability and unpredictability of the charismatic leadership provided by the judges. They hoped that an institutional leadership could be more effective than God's deliverance (1 Sam 8 and 10).

This tension between confidence in the deliverer-God and reliance on the tools of statecraft paralleled Israel's flirtations with idolatry and dominated the relationship between the prophets and the throne throughout Israel's history. Like idolatry, statecraft involves penultimate concerns. Isaiah encouraged Ahaz, faced with the prospect of invasion by the allied kingdoms of Syria and Israel and tempted to appeal to Assyria for assistance, to "be quiet and unafraid" (7:4): God would see to the protection of Jerusalem. Ahaz needed only to "trust" (7:9). Of course, as any king might well, Ahaz found it impossible to be satisfied with passively trusting God. Faced with a geopolitical crisis, Ahaz resorted to geopolitical tactics and, in direct contradiction of Isaiah's instructions, called upon Assyrian assistance only to find himself forced into vassalage. The preaching of the prophets active during the crises of the eighth and sixth centuries contain many such warnings against trusting (*bth*) in military might (Isa 31:1; Jer 5:17; 48:7; Hos 10:13; cf. Deut 17:16; 28:52), in foreign alliances (Jer 2:26-37; 13:25; 46:25; Ezek 29:16), and, in one metaphorical reference to Jerusalem's geopolitical status, "beauty" (Ezek 16:15). Reliance on the methods of state embodied a lack of trust in God's intentions for Israel's good and in God's capabilities to effect God's intention. As Deuteronomy reminds its readers, God did not choose Israel because of its might (7:7); yet, despite Israel's weakness relative to other nations, God has protected. With YHWH on their side, Israel need not fear.

Isaiah's message for Ahaz was not a call to quiescence or to the abandonment of political structures, but to acknowledgement of politics as penultimate. God created the world in such a way that human beings have important work to do ("till the garden and keep it," Gen 2:15; "six days you shall labor," Exod 20:9; Deut 5:13) to sustain themselves and creation. Societies must be ordered, justice sought, children reared, and communities defended against their enemies. A long stream of biblical tradition, however, insists that all these worthy endeavors succeed only with God's sustenance and blessing. Early Israel fought against its enemies in so-called "holy wars" by sounding trumpets (Josh 6:1-21) and shining lights in the enemy camp (Judg 7:16-22) precisely so that the point could be made that their victories were "not by might, nor by power, but by the spirit [of YHWH]" (Zech 4:6). In the end, only God deserves ultimate trust; all else will disappoint.

Misplaced Trust and Wisdom Literature

Israel's wisdom applies prophetic logic concerning national behaviors to the level of individual lives. Just as the nation's reliance on the monarchy and the techniques of statecraft was driven by and manifested a lack of confidence in God's provision, an individual's false confidence in the tools and resources of personal power is tantamount to a lack of faith. The Wisdom literature, including the Psalter, is replete with warnings against placing trust in wealth (Job 31:24, a denial protesting innocence of this sin; Pss 49:6; 52:7; Prov 11:28), the bow and sword (Ps 44:6, likewise a denial), princes (Ps 146:3), one's own mental resources (Prov 3:5), and other human beings (Jer 17:5-8, a wisdom psalm). No less than idols or political stratagems, these objects of confidence are penultimate. They cannot justify the trust placed in them, trust that should properly be placed in God alone. Wisdom repeatedly admonishes and lauds trust (*bth*) in God as the sole key to authentic confidence (Pss 4:6 [5 Eng.]; 9:11 [10 Eng.]; 13:6 [5 Eng.]; 21:8 [7 Eng.]; 22:5-6 [4-5 Eng.]; passim; Prov 3:5; 14:26; 16:20; 22:19; 28:25; 29:25; cf. Jer 17:5-8). The wisdom teacher encourages his students:

> Trust in the LORD with all your heart,
>   and do not rely on your own insight.
> In all your ways acknowledge him,
>   and he will make straight your paths.
> Be not wise in your own eyes;
>   fear the LORD, and turn away from evil.
> It will be healing to your flesh
>   and refreshment to your bones.
> Honor the LORD with your substance
>   and with the first fruits of all your produce;
> then your barns will be filled with plenty,
>   and your vats will be bursting with wine. (Prov 3:5-10)

Jesus on Mistrust

Remarkably, according to the Gospels, Jesus had very little to say concerning the nature and structure of sin, once even refusing the opportunity to address the topic (John 9:3).[9] He encouraged extreme measures to avoid it (Mark 9:43-48 and par.; Matt 18:7 || Luke17:2; Luke 13:2; cf. John 5:14), and warned against being its occasion in others (Mark 9:42 and par.). In a few instances, he characterized people or groups as sinners or their actions as sin (Mark 8:38; Luke 6:32-34; 24:7; John 19:11). Once he spoke of the eradication of the causes of sin in the end time (Matt 13:41). Otherwise, Jesus focused not on defining the nature of sin and certainly not on moralistic preaching against it, but on forgiveness. His very purpose, he said, was to call sinners to forgiveness (Mark 2:17 and par.; cf. Luke 15:7, 10). At every opportunity, he forgave (Mark 2:5, 9-10 and par.; Matt

26:28; Luke 7:47-48; 24:47; John 8:7, 11), indeed with such freedom and authority that his opponents accused him of blasphemy and even debauchery. He called upon those forgiven and seeking forgiveness to forgive (Mark 11:25; Matt 6:12 par. Luke 11:4; Matt 18:15, 21 par. Luke 17:3-4), and entrusted the church with continuing his practice of forgiving sin (Matt 6:14-15; cf. John 20:23).

Fortunately, however, Jesus' discussions of anxiety, a symptom of mistrust in God's provision, and of the "unpardonable sin" in the synoptic tradition, along with his equation of sin with failure/refusal to believe in him as recorded in certain texts in the Gospel of John, provide sufficient insight into Jesus' understanding of the human condition as marred by unfaith. The good news is that God loves the world God created and cares for it enough to send Jesus even to die. God is present in and engaged with the world. God can be trusted. The proper response is faith; unfaith is mistrust.

Jesus on Anxiety. Trust God as a Child Trusts Its Father. Mark, followed by both Matthew and Luke, records Jesus' somewhat enigmatic sayings concerning children and the kingdom of God. Jesus reacts against the disciples' efforts to prevent children access to their master with the declaration that "to such belongs the kingdom of God" (Mark 10:14 and par.), which he then amplifies with the explanation that anyone who hopes to enter the kingdom must receive it "like a child." The enigma here involves this simile. Like a child in what respect? Innocence? Simplicity? Capacity for joy?

Fortunately, the Gospel writers provide several clues. First, Matthew treats the statements recorded in Mark 10:14 (|| Luke 18:16) and Mark 10:15 (|| Luke 18:17) separately (18:1-6 and 19:13-15), taking Mark's latter statement first, expanding it into a response to the disciples' question in 18:1-2 concerning who will be the greatest in the kingdom (answer: the least, the most childlike) and a further warning against misleading such innocence (vv. 5-6). Clearly, then, Matthew understands the simile as a reference to the humility of children, their awareness and acceptance of their relative powerlessness, which, in healthy circumstances, is a component of their capacity to trust their parents and other caregivers.

Second, while dividing Mark's one unit into two permits Matthew to insert, almost as a parenthesis, a series of units loosely structured around the themes of temptation to sin and forgiveness, Matt 19:13-15 returns to the basic outline of Mark and Luke. All three Synoptics, then, preserve Mark's association of the sayings concerning children and the kingdom with the account of the wealthy young man's question to Jesus concerning the requirements for inheriting eternal life. Not only does this account follow immediately after the children sayings, but its vocabulary establishes subtle ties between the two episodes: the young man's question concerning inheritance suggests a family context (i.e., children inherit); Matthew makes it explicit that the questioner is, himself, still a "youth" (νεανίσκος, *neaniskos*, 19:20, 22), while in Mark and Luke he responds to Jesus' citation of the Decalogue with an assurance that he has observed its requirements "from [my] youth" (ἐκ νεότητός [μου], ek neotētos [mou], Mark 10:20; Luke 18:21); in Mark (v. 24), Jesus addresses his disciples—who were astonished at the exchange between Jesus and the young man and, especially, at Jesus' declaration that wealthy people find entry into the kingdom difficult—as "children" (τέκνα, tekna). In sum, the Synoptics portray the rich young man (for Luke, a "ruler," 18:18) as the antithesis of the children entering the kingdom. The rich young man has worked hard to earn and to attain. He places his confidence in what he has done to deserve entry into the kingdom and in the material evidence of his prosperity. The possibility of returning to a childlike state of dependence and, therefore, *trusting* God to care for him regardless of his merits is too frightening.

Taken together, units in this complex on requirements for entry into the kingdom of God argue that the struggle to make one worthy for the kingdom misapprehends the nature of God's relationship with human beings. The kingdom is to be received, not earned. God is trustworthy; wealth and power are not. God saves; status cannot. As Craig A. Evans observes, "Paradoxically, the least powerful, least wealthy, least influential have a greater prospect of entering the kingdom than do those who are most powerful, wealthy, and influential."[10]

This interpretation of the sayings on children in Mark 10:13-16 and its parallels is consistent with Jesus' teachings in the Sermon on the Mount/Plain regarding God's parental provision and one's proper relation to the kingdom of God. Following in the wake of Jesus' teaching concerning prayer, in which he reminds his disciples that the purpose of prayer is not to gain God's good will—as "heavenly father" God both knows and desires what is truly needful and good for God's children—Jesus unfolds the implications of this fundamental truth in terms of the cares of daily life. If the "heavenly father" provides for the basic needs of the birds of the air and the lilies of the field, and if human beings are "much more valuable" (Matt 6:26 || Luke 12:24), and if the "heavenly father" knows what "his" children need (Matt 6:32 || Luke 12:30), will God not provide for humans? Therefore, Jesus admonishes, one must simply trust in God's provision, seek God's kingdom, and live in harmony with God's will.

Jesus must encourage these trusting attitudes and behaviors, however, because they are uncommon in human experience. Human beings find it difficult to trust God so thoroughly and fundamentally. Jesus labels the problem as having a "divided mind" (μεριμνάω, merimnaō, Matt 6:25, 27, 31, 34; Luke 12:22, 25, 26; μετεωρίζομαι, meteōrizomai, Luke 12:29), which is tantamount to being "of little faith" (ὀλιγόπιστος, oligopistos Matt 6:30 || Luke 12:28). As the father of the convulsive boy acknowledges, on everyone's behalf, it seems, no one trusts God wholly (Mark 9:24, "I trust, help my lack of trust"). Intellectually, the audience of Jesus' Sermon on the Mount would probably have found it quite simple to agree to orthodox statements of God's power, providence, and presence, but their everyday lives betrayed the sort of practical mistrust in God's goodness and care that drives individuals in modern Western society ever to acquire and horde as protection against coming shortages, ever to compete in efforts to assure their own survival, and ever to deny their lack of control over their own environments. This mistrust of God's good intention and constant provision drives frantic efforts to secure one's own existence despite the obvious limitations of being human. Jesus reminds his audience that, while they are much more important than birds and flowers, they are nonetheless dependent upon God to provide the essentials: none of them "by being anxious can add to the span of life" (Matt 6:27 || Luke 12:25). First, Jesus says, seek God's kingdom, God's will and way, and God will provide. God can be trusted.

God can be trusted because God does not deceive and trick. The serpent suggests to Eve that God is working some sort of cosmic deception, selfishly reserving for God's-self capacities from which the human pair could benefit. God's word conceals the full truth. Something more is going on than God reveals. Can God be fully trusted? Jesus also addressed these dynamics in the Sermon. Human fathers do not give their hungry children rocks instead of biscuits or scorpions rolled into balls instead of eggs. Human fathers want the best for their children. Why would "the heavenly Father" do otherwise (Matt 7:7-11)? God knows what human beings need; God can provide it; God wants to do for humanity, collectively and individually, what is good and needful. Eve's mistrust, however, is a universally human phenomenon.

The Synoptics on Mistrusting God's Presence: Blasphemy against the Holy Spirit. Mark (3:28-30), Matthew (12:31-32), and Luke (12:8-10) all preserve a saying of Jesus concerning the fact that one sin, and one sin only, lies beyond the possibility of forgiveness: blasphemy/slander against the Holy Spirit. As comparison of the relevant texts clearly demonstrates, the three Gospels preserve slightly different versions of the same saying.

| "Truly I say to you that all manner of sin will be forgiven the sons of man, even whatever blasphemy they may blaspheme; but whoever should blaspheme against the Holy Spirit will not have forgiveness in the coming age, but will be liable for his sin in the age to come." Because they had said, "He has an unclean spirit." (Mark 3:28-30) | "Because of this, I say to you, every sin and blasphemy will be forgiven to men, but blasphemy against the Spirit will not be forgiven. Whoever speaks a word against the Son of Man will be forgiven. But whoever speaks against the Holy Spirit will not be forgiven either in this age or in the one to come." (Matt 12:31-32) | "I say to you, everyone who confesses me before men, the Son of Man will confess before the angels of God. But the one who denies me before men, will be denied before the angels of God. Everyone who speaks a word against the Son of Man will be forgiven; but the one who blasphemes the Holy Spirit will not be forgiven." (Luke 12:8-10) |

Interpretation of the synoptic tradition concerning "the unforgivable sin" depends on three central observations: First, whereas Mark understands the reference to the sons of man generically, Q, the hypothetical Aramaic document thought to have served as a source for both Matthew and Luke, understands it as a reference to Jesus. Second, this distinction leads Matthew to declare that sins against "the Son of Man" are forgivable, a statement Luke apparently found objectionable. Thus, he corrects the saying by adding the statement concerning denying the Son of Man. Third, Mark and Matthew agree over against Luke (where the saying is somewhat unclear) as to the context to which this saying was addressed, a context that provides the interpretive key: observers of Jesus' healing and exorcising ministry have attributed his power to demons, not recognizing that, in Jesus, the kingdom of God is among them. As Vincent Taylor notes, "it is excusable to a point to fail to recognize the dignity of the One who hides himself under the humble appearance of a man, but not to disparage works manifestly salutary which reveal the action of the Divine Spirit."[11] In other words, this blasphemy expresses one's blindness to the real presence and ongoing work of God.

John on the Essence of the Matter: Trust Jesus. The Gospel of John, perhaps more clearly than any other biblical book, defines the fundamental question at stake in humanity's relationship with God in terms of essential trust/faith. According to John, God so loves God's creation that God became incarnate as Jesus of Nazareth in order to heal the breach of trust, to demonstrate the extent to which God will go to prove God's-self trustworthy. Other biblical texts touch on the idea, to be sure. Isaiah of the exile, for example, proclaims the good news that the return to Jerusalem depends not on the constancy of God's people—their faithfulness/trustworthiness is like grass that withers—but on God's steadfast commitment to God's people (Isa 40:6-7). In John, however, the notion of the incarnation makes it abundantly clear that the breach of trust/faith is a truly "personal" matter. Jesus repeatedly asserts that he and his Father are one. To see Jesus is to see God. So, in the person of Jesus, the incarnate *Logos* of God, humanity confronts the question of willingness to trust the Creator. John's Jesus puts the matter bluntly: "for you will die in your sins unless you believe that I am he" (John 8:24).

Indeed, for the Johannine Jesus, sin is not primarily the violation of covenant requirements, nor arrogant attempts to transcend the boundaries of humanity, nor a failure to realize the noble *imago dei* of authentic humanity.[12] Instead, sin is the failure to embrace God as revealed in Jesus, the failure to comprehend that Jesus' life and work demonstrate the love and provision, the trustworthiness, of God.

> "If I had not come and spoken to them, they would not have sin; but now they have no excuse for their sin. He who hates me hates my Father also. If I had not done among them the works which no one else did, they would not have sin; but now they have seen and hated both me and my Father." (John 15:22-24 RSV)

"And when he comes, he will convince the world concerning sin and righteousness and judgment: concerning sin, because they do not believe in me; concerning righteousness, because I go to the Father, and you will see me no more; concerning judgment, because the ruler of this world is judged." (John 16:8-11 RSV)

John 9 is a key text in the development of this Gospel's treatment of human (mis)perception of God's benevolent presence in Jesus Christ. Departing the Jerusalem temple after a dispute with his enemies, who accused him of being demon possessed (John 8:52), Jesus and his party pass by a man "blind from birth" (John 9:1). The disciples are interested in assigning blame (9:2-5). Jesus, like the priestly materials in the OT, is interested in restoration, not etiology. After the Pharisees learn that the man's sight has been restored, a division arises among them concerning the proper criterion by which to evaluate the significance of the event. Is Jesus a sinner because he "worked" on the Sabbath (i.e., strict observance of the law is the criterion) or does the beneficence of the act mark the actor as benevolent (9:13-17)? In an effort to avoid the controversy, the Pharisees seek a way out. Perhaps the man before them is an imposter (9:18-23).[13] Assured that, in fact, the man before them was born blind, the Pharisees choose Moses and the law over the evidence; in contrast, the blind man cannot escape the fact, no matter how mysterious its genesis (9:24-34). Jesus arrives on the scene, finally, to interpret events. Because Jesus has come into the world, the sighted are blind and the blind see (9:35-41). Blindness here is the "fundamental refusal on the part of human beings to expose themselves to God's revelation . . . [b]ecause they will not be shifted from their self-importance even by the great sign and the testimony of the man cured of blindness, their sin 'remains.'"[14] The Pharisees focus on individual acts of sin; "in contrast, John aims at a description of the *essence of sin*."[15]

In the end, while the vocabulary and conception are uniquely Johannine, the thrust of this material closely parallels the synoptic notion of the "unforgivable sin." All can be forgiven except the fundamental sin, the failure to recognize God at work in Jesus.

Paul on the Essence of the Matter: Salvation by Faith

Paul's theme of the righteousness of God asserts that the gospel is powerful good news because God can be trusted; the corollary theme of salvation by faith asserts that the fundamental human problem, lack of trust in God manifest in efforts to gain status with God or in the failure to embrace authenticity, can be resolved only by faith, fundamental trust. The relationship between God and humanity rests entirely on God's fidelity, God's trustworthiness (Rom 3:21-22 and passim). In other words, Paul's doctrine of salvation by faith implies a doctrine of sin. Simply put, if faith/trust is the solution to the human problem, unfaith/mistrust must be the problem itself. The fundamental injury to the relationship between God and humanity results from the human party's mistrust.

Psychologically Informed Theology on Mistrust

Modern depth psychology and, especially, developmental psychology have demonstrated that, as a rule, individuals confront the challenge of fundamental trust in the normal course of life, always only somewhat successfully. S. Kierkegaard described the basics of the human dilemma in his analysis of the condition of *angst*, "anxiety"—a fundamental sense of dis-ease. Anxiety arises in the conflict the individual feels between the possibility of transcendence (cf. Qoheleth's notion of the eternal in the human heart) and the reality of finitude—the familiar conflict of the duality of mortal creatures bearing God's image. This *angst*, which is not itself sin, but only its pre-condition, Kierkegaard argued, produces one of two courses of action: either one seeks to overcome the anxiety by assuring one's own existence or one abandons all hope of transcendence in fundamental despair.[16]

From a secular perspective, S. Freud, the founder of modern psychoanalysis, discovered the same dilemma, which he termed "the conflict of ambivalence," at the core of the human psyche. Opening a line of investigation that continues in the work of developmentalists today, Freud traced this anxious ambivalence to the conditions of infancy. Again, the familiar tension between autonomy and finitude felt already by the infant coming to consciousness produces a conflicted self. W. Lowe summarizes the process as follows:

> ... a period of protection is indispensable for the founding of those qualities of creativity, meaning and love which the humanistic psychologist so rightly celebrates. But now let us pause to note one point quite carefully, for the effect of this same period of nurturance is, by its very nature, to place the infant in a fundamental bind. Note first that protection gives gratification; there would be little point to it, did it not. And gratification which is protected and thus encouraged to luxuriate gives rise to desires and fantasies of a very specific sort: "... *the dream of narcissistic omnipotence*...." Note further that at the same time and just as inevitably, protection presupposes and fosters dependence; there would be little need for it, did it not. And sheltered dependence generates desires and fantasies which are of quite another sort: "... *a passive, dependent need to be loved.* ..."[17]

The influential developmental psychologist Erik Erikson documented the significant stages in human emotional development. According to his analysis, the infant's first developmental task involves the resolution of the conflict between what he termed "basic trust" versus "basic mistrust." Infants whose caregivers provide consistent, quality care—warmly, lovingly, competently, and regularly meeting the infant's needs for nourishment, affection, and comfort—develop confidence or trust in the benevolence of the world and, reciprocally, a healthy sense of their own value. Contrariwise, fickle, capricious care, neglect, or abuse engenders mistrust and a sense of worthlessness. If caregivers—the infant's primary point of interaction with the world—are unreliable, the infant experiences the world as impersonal, chaotic, and even malevolent. In this instance, the infant senses that his or her needs are not met because he or she is insignificant. The infant adopts a basic stance of mistrust toward the outside world.[18]

James Fowler pioneered the study of the development of the human individual's capacity for religious faith.[19] Fowler noted that Erikson's "basic trust" is nearly identical with the basis for religious faith, or better, it is identical with the *capacity* for religious faith. In more mature forms, of course, religious faith typically involves belief in some deity or divine power, incorporates some system of doctrine and morality, and is manifest in some overtly religious practice. That is, religious faith has a specific *object* (the deity) and some specific *content* (the worldview associated with worship of the deity). At the foundation of all religious faith, however, lies "undifferentiated faith," the ability and tendency to trust that someone cares and the confidence that this concern makes one worthy. In essence, believers trust that the world is not ultimately random, that it has purpose, and that their lives have value. Believers trust that God is engaged in the world, that God is fair and just, and that God cares about them. It is perhaps not too great an oversimplification to say that a core message of the Bible is that "God cares about God's creation."

Despite his emphasis on a slightly revised form of the "prideful rebellion" definition of sin, Reinhold Niebuhr, too, conceded that the fundamental sin is "lack of trust" in God,[20] which, in addition to false expressions of freedom, can take the form of immersion into finitude, the sin of "sensuality."[21] In the Niebuhrian tradition, L. Mercadante asserts that

> . . . sin is not first about behavior but about orientation. It is a religious category, not primarily a moral one, although these two overlap. Just as sin is not essentially about bad behavior or human willfulness, neither is it primarily about failing to realize our human potential, being alienated from self and others, lacking serenity. Although these things can be involved, sin is primarily separation from God.[22]

Ministry to Mistrust

Old Testament narratives recount several examples of sin as mistrust. The New Testament, especially John and Paul, define the most fundamental problem of human response to God not as disobedience to the commandments nor as failure to realize the potential of authentic humanity—these are effects, not causes—but as lack of trust in a trustworthy God. Not surprisingly, the Bible offers no etiology or psychological analysis of the roots and causes of humanity's mistrust in its Creator. Psychology, philosophy, and common experience, however, provide rather convincing descriptions of the phenomenon. Because human existence is precarious—balanced between finitude and mortality, on the one hand, and the godlike and God-given capacity and drive for transcendence, on the other—anxiety seems inevitable. The capacity for trust in the goodness and benevolence of the world is not innate, but must develop in the context of a safe, secure, and nurturing environment. From infancy onward, individuals interact with their environments, experiencing the world either as warm, accepting, and responsive or as cold, indifferent, and fickle. Individuals learn to trust or to fear.

Incarnate Trust

Now the point of connection between mistrust as unfaith in God and the psychological development of the capacity to trust as faith in God has not yet been established. A number of critiques of the faith development work done by Fowler and others based on Erickson's investigations into personality development have pointed out that the capacity for trust that they describe is only formally related to faith in God. That is, trust in the general benevolence of one's parents or of the world in general is not identical with trust in God. The object of trust, God, is an important component of religious faith.

C. Gestrich, for example, criticizes the tendency to equate Erickson's "basic trust"[23] with religious faith and flawed acquisition of basic trust with some basic component of sin expressed in the process of identity formation. At best, basic trust can be described (as Fowler does, but as Gestrich fails to note) as the capacity for faith, not as faith itself. Consequently, since sin is to be defined primarily in relation to God (not the parent responsible for assuring the infant of the trustworthiness of the world, for example), Gestrich recommends that "theology should turn its back on all of its attempts to verify sin on the basis of disruptions in the development of human identity."[24]

Gestrich's criticisms raise an important question for the ministry of the Christian gospel. While it is true that salvation comes by faith in God through Jesus Christ (and conversely, of course, salvation is made necessary by unfaith), not by trusting in some penultimate object of faith (parents, self, spouse, state, etc.), it is also true that, in the course of human development, God's presence and providence are mediated through the world God created. God's personhood is mediated through persons. The analogies and metaphors of the Bible and of Christian theology recognize and depend on this mediation. For someone with limited or no experience of loving parents or other primary caregivers, the biblical image of God as a loving parent has little or no power. In fact, the image may be an impediment to faith for such a person. For someone who has little or no experience of primary relationships in which the other party (or parties) has demonstrated consistent reliability and responsibility, the church's confession of a God who is steadfast and trustworthy may have little or no point of reference. Who, after all, has not learned the difficult lesson that even those whom one should be able most to trust prove at least sometimes to be unreliable? If one cannot totally trust one's mother, whom one has seen and touched, how can one fully trust God, whom one has not seen?

Preaching the gospel message is a key element of the church's mission. Teaching the gospel may be the most significant of the church's acts, however. In many cases, teaching people that God can be trusted first requires that they be taught the capacity for trust itself. Alternatively, to state it in a more theologically correct formulation, teaching people the gospel will require mediating God's trustworthiness in the church's role as the body of Christ exercising the ministry of reconciliation. This ministry of reconciliation, of teaching trust by incarnating God's faithfulness, cannot be conducted by publicity campaigns or annual fund-raising or gift baskets at Christmas. People need to *feel* God's committed love. The church is called to give it. Proclamation of God's love may be insufficient as the means of communicating to those whose life experiences have taught only mistrust. In such instances, *agape* love will mean long-term commitment to relationships that can model trustworthiness in order to incubate trust.

Suffer the Little Children

If the developmentalists are correct that individuals develop their capacities for trust in the context of the environments in which they are nurtured, the church can hardly give excess attention to the needs of children and families. Not only must the church support and shape the lives of the children of its members, but it must take interest in every aspect of the lives of children that can impact their growing senses of who they are in relation to the universe. In many cases this will mean attending to parents who were themselves poorly parented; in many cases it will mean political activism on behalf of children at risk; in many cases it will mean demanding work and long-term commitment on the part of the church. Proclaiming God's love is important, but it is not nearly enough. The church must be God's partner in the commitment to love those created in God's image.

I Believe, Help My Unbelief

Of course, no one in the church trusts God completely, either. Even believers trust while withholding trust at the same time. It is important to remember that trust, as used here, is not understood in terms of intellectual certainty. In other words, trust/faith and intellectual doubt are not antonyms. One need not fully understand the physiology and pathology of one's medical condition in order to entrust one's very life to one's surgeon. Within the church, many believe intellectually who are unable to entrust themselves to God's kingdom, seeking it first. These are the "practical atheists." Erikson commented on the puzzling inconsistency manifest by "many who profess faith, yet in practice mistrust both life and man [sic]."[25]

The church must help its members to identify this practical mistrust for what it is and resist the temptation to attempt its resolution in doomed self-security: possessions, reputation and status, the trappings of success, the cult of health, even membership on the right committees and boards of the church. All of these can be efforts to protect oneself from one's finitude, or more bluntly, one's mortality. Anxiety over death, the ultimate manifestation of human creatureliness, the ultimate affront to humanity's godlike aspirations, is apparently inevitable. Believers may as well confront it. Ultimately, human beings can and must trust that the seeds of eternity planted in the human heart are the evidence of things hoped for (Heb 11:1). Ultimately, persons can and must trust that God did not toy with humanity by creating it as persons somehow mirroring God's own personhood. Any other response to the question posed by humanity's compound nature is mistrust that produces pride or sloth. These inappropriate attempts to resolve existential anxiety are mistrust, sin.[26] To paraphrase Qoheleth, president and pauper alike ultimately face the same fate (Eccl 5:13-17). Ultimately, one must trust, with Abraham, that "the LORD will provide" (Gen 22:14).

CHAPTER FIVE

The Objective Nature of Sin: Intention Is (Relatively) Insignificant

> "... I am convinced that we should solve many things if we all went out into the streets and uncovered our griefs, which perhaps would prove to be but one sole common grief, and joined together in beweeping them and crying aloud to the heavens and calling upon God. And this, even though God should hear us not; but He would hear us. The chiefest sanctity of a temple is that it is a place to which men go to weep in common. A miserere sung in common by a multitude tormented by destiny has as much value as a philosophy. It is not enough to cure the plague: we must learn to weep for it. Yes, we must learn to weep! Perhaps that is the supreme wisdom."[1]

As has been shown, the conventional, juridical understanding of sin as willful rebellion against God oversimplifies the complexity of sin because it fails to account for the fundamental problem of mistrust that characterizes humanity's response to God and because it does not give sufficient attention to the dual inauthentic manifestations of human behavior that arise from this mistrust. The legal metaphor that controls the conventional view does not and cannot reflect the full scope of the biblical metaphor of humanity as *created*—and therefore finite—*in the divine image*—and therefore open to transcendence. In this sense, the juridical concept, or the "blame-justification model,"[2] of sin fails to provide the church a diagnostic framework for understanding and ministering to the full range of human sinfulness.

The conventional view, especially as it appears in typical Protestant thought and practice, accentuates the idea that forgiveness involves primarily, if not solely, God's willingness to declare the guilty party innocent. It fails as a diagnostic tool because it fails to acknowledge the real-world character of sin. That is, by restricting the idea of sin to guilt before the divine bar, the conventional view becomes limited to soteriological concerns, that is, to questions related to salvation. How can humanity, guilty of willfully violating God's commandments, hope to regain the innocence necessary for salvation? In these limited terms, the conventional view defines an important solution, of course: dependence on God's grace. By limiting its concern to the heavenly court, however, the conventional view tends also to limit its concern to assessing guilt and promising the gift of innocence. It does not address the real damage done by sin both to the sinner and to the sinner's environment. It offers no analysis of the nature of sin as real offense and, therefore, offers no suggestions for healing the injured. In effect, by wholly transferring sin to the juridical realm, the conventional view removes sin from the real, everyday world in which declarations of forgiveness for the sinner alone do at best only little to remedy the harm done by the sin.[3] As J. Gaffney has noted, in contrast to original sin, Christian theology has devoted little attention to "actual sin."[4]

Specifically, in practice, aspects of the conventional understanding of sin promote several dangerous attitudes. First, the Christian assurance that, in Christ, God redeems believers from the eternal consequences of their sin once and for all, while true and fundamental to Christian faith, tends to foster a quasi-gnostic attitude of libertinism.[5] For many, the assurance of forgiveness coupled with the conviction that human beings, even believers, are bound to sin in any case means that there is little reason actively and aggressively to seek to avoid sin. "Oh well, I am a mere human. I will inevitably make mistakes. I needn't trouble myself too much with holiness. Besides, God forgives everything anyway."

Similarly, this same assurance of forgiveness in the eternal realm draws the attention of many away from the dynamics of sin in the everyday world, especially from the mundane consequences of sin. For many, the problem of sin involves only the question of the sinner's salvation. Assured of forgiveness, these believers give no thought to the effects loosed on the world by their sin. In terms of the juridical metaphor, if the guilty party has been acquitted, the justice system can make no further claim. The conventional metaphor identifies the injured party solely with God, who has forgiven, overlooking the damage done to other people, to society, and to creation. In these instances, sin may be forgiven, but it may also continue to live on in the effects it has on the sinner's community. In contrast, the biblical notion of sin as a mishandling of the uniquely human calling to bear the image of God in creation implies responsibility not only to God—first and foremost, of course—but also, in fulfillment of the call, to other people and to the created order. Forgiveness must, therefore, include remedy and healing. Korean theologian Andrew Sung Park has addressed this failure of the conventional theology of sin through an analysis of the Korean concept of *han*, the real injury that outlives the act of wrongdoing. He observes that:

The Objective Nature of Sin: Intention Is (Relatively) Insignificant

> In pulpits we have preached the one-sided theology of the sin-repentance model for everyone, including the sinned-against and the wounded: "Repent of your sin and be saved." Toward victims, we have done wrong. The God of Job is angry at this simplistic sin-repentance formula the church has applied to the victims of sin, overlooking their *han*. It is overdue for us to provide a sensible theology of healing for the victims of sin and tragedy. Our present one-dimensional theology is under God's wrath. Theologians owe burnt offerings to God and our apology to the victims.[6]

Finally, at least since Peter Abelard,[7] Western Christianity has considered intention a definitive element of sin. In order to meet all the criteria necessary for categorization as sin, an act must be willfully wrong. For modern Westerners, the moral quality of an action cannot be judged primarily either by the nature of the act itself or by the nature of the consequences of the act. A bad act that produces bad results is not sin if the agent had no intention to do evil. Modern Western theology typically categorizes such acts as error or (morally neutral) wrongdoing, tragic accidents. In this, of course, theology mirrors "the most fundamental affirmations of modernity's turn to the subject: [namely] that the individual is autonomous, and that autonomy is the sole basis for establishing responsibility and guilt."[8] This turn to the subject, however, leaves the matter, the act, outside the bounds of theological qualification. In other words, when theology defines an act that is clearly evil in character and consequence not as sin, but merely as tragic error, it places that act beyond the realm of redemption and salvation. Such acts are problems for the philosophy of religion; they do not fall within the purview of the gospel. As Paul Ricoeur has commented:

> My problem was to distinguish between finitude and guilt. I had the impression, or even the conviction, that these two terms tended to be identified in classical existentialism at the cost of both experiences, guilt becoming a particular case of finitude and for that reason beyond cure and forgiveness, and finitude, on the other hand, being affected by a kind of diffused sense of sadness and despair through guilt.[9]

The conventional emphasis on the intentionality of sin hopes, of course, to avert the conclusion that human beings sin because God created them as sinners. If the errors human beings commit as the result of their creaturely limitations are sin in the full sense, then creatureliness itself is sinful.[10] "Tygers, to use Blake's image, were created carnivorous—and humans were created fallible."[11] As Mercadante observes, "Either we equate our sinfulness . . . with will deliberately and wrongly used (Pelagianism) or with our inherent finitude and weakness (Manicheanism)."[12]

Yet common experience teaches that a significant proportion of the injury and harm felt in human existence stems not from intentional evil but from mistake and inadvertence. Further, the criterion of intention too often supplies the wrongdoer with a ready excuse for avoiding responsibility for the consequences of the wrong done—"I didn't mean to"—however inadvertently. Is it possible to extend the gospel to such mishaps without accepting the implications of the serpent's temptation to regard human finitude as itself a crippling limitation? Is it possible to distinguish between the guilt of willful wrongdoing and responsibility for wrong done even unintentionally?

Much of the Bible operates, in fact, on the assumption that the quality of evil is inherent in a sinful act regardless of the agent's intention.[13] In this way, the Bible takes seriously the harmful, dangerous nature of the act itself and continues to hold the agent responsible in the everyday world.

Sin and the Priestly Function in the Hebrew Bible

Ancient Israel's priests devoted significant attention to the "objective" quality of wrongs done as a pastoral problem. An entire section of the priests' handbook, Lev 4:1–5:26 (4:1–6:7 Eng.) outlines the steps to be undertaken in the event that an Israelite commits an "unintentional" or "unwitting" sin (Lev 4:2, 13, 22, 27; 5:15, 18; cf. Num 15:27-28; 22:34; Ezek 45:20). In such cases, the true nature of the act is "hidden" from the wrongdoer (Lev 5:2-4), who, therefore, does not "know it" (Lev 5:17). The priests take for granted that an act or condition can, in and of itself, be wrong; the actor's intentions and even the actor's awareness (cf. the situation that Pharaoh and Abimelech confront in the episode of the so-called "Endangered Ancestress," Gen 12:17-20; 20:1-18)[14] have no bearing on the quality or potential consequences of the act.[15] Wrong has been done, and as soon as the wrongdoer recognizes that fact, steps must be taken to atone for the wrong and, as far as possible, restore proper conditions. Indeed, the priests so consistently held the notion that wrong inheres in a situation, regardless of the intention of the actor, that they could use the language of sin to discuss skin diseases (Lev 14:1-32) and mold in houses (Lev 14:33-53), cases in which it is meaningless to consider the intention of an actor.[16] The priests saw wrong, however it came about and in whatever realm, primarily as a matter to be atoned, remedied, and healed (Ezek 45:18).

As texts elsewhere in the priestly body of literature in the Hebrew Bible demonstrate, the priestly concern for the inherent wrongness of an act or situation extends to incidents of manslaughter, or unintentional homicide (Num 35:9-34; Deut 19:1-13; Josh 20:1-6), and to cases in which the perpetrator cannot be identified (Deut 21:1-9). Those who commit manslaughter may escape the legitimate retribution of the slain person's kinsman, the "avenger-redeemer" (Hebrew גֹּאֵל, go'el), by fleeing to certain levitical cities, the so-called "cities of refuge," located throughout Israel. Tests of motive (hatred [Num 35:20-21; Deut 19:11]), premeditation (evidenced by a history of animosity [Deut 19:4, 11] or by the fact that the killer was "lying in wait" for his victim [Num 35:20;

Deut 19:11]), and method (use of a lethal weapon, designed to kill, suggests intent [Num 35:16-18]) established whether the killer had truly acted "unintentionally and unwittingly" (בִּשְׁגָגָה בִּבְלִי־דָעַת, *bishgagah bibliy da'at*; Josh 20:3; "unintentionally" alone in Num 35:11, 15; Deut 19:4; and Josh 20:5). Failing these tests, the killer was a murderer, for whom there could be no mercy (Num 35:21, 30-34; Deut 19:11-13). Meeting the tests, however, did not relieve the killer of responsibility entirely. While the killer was to be permitted refuge in the levitical city from the kinsman avenger, the killer was restricted to this city for the duration of the current high priest's lifetime. Should the killer venture outside the city walls, the avenger could exact retribution (Num 35:25-28; Josh 20:6). For the priests, the key issue motivating this provision involved dealing with the reality of the victim's death—hence the restrictions on the manslayer's freedoms—and, at the same time, avoiding the possibility that further innocent blood, which pollutes even the land, might be shed (Num 35:28).[17]

This concern for the wrong inherent in the taking of innocent life accounts for the priestly ritual designed to deal with possible homicides committed by unknown actors. If the accidental nature of the manslayer's acts does not render him entirely free of restrictions, and the danger posed by the possibility that the community may mishandle innocent blood motivates such careful regulation, then the fact that in other instances the perpetrator may be unknown to the community does not relieve the community of responsibility for dealing with the known reality, innocent blood shed in their midst. The Deuteronomic code specifies measures to be taken upon the discovery of a corpse lying in the open field. Although perpetrator, means, and motive are unknown, the elders of the city nearest the discovery must sacrifice near a flowing stream a heifer that has never been worked by breaking its neck, not by shedding its blood. Then,

> all the elders of that city nearest to the slain man shall wash their hands over the heifer whose neck was broken in the valley; and they shall testify, "Our hands did not shed this blood, neither did our eyes see it shed. Forgive, O LORD, thy people Israel, whom thou hast redeemed, and set not the guilt of innocent blood in the midst of thy people Israel; but let the guilt of blood be forgiven them." (Deut 21:6-8 RSV)

In this manner, Israel would be able to " purge the guilt of innocent blood from [their] midst, when [they] do what is right in the sight of the LORD" (Deut 21:9 RSV).

The priests' concern for the inherently wrong nature of certain acts, regardless of the actor's intention or awareness and even of whether the actor can be identified, seems odd to the sensibilities of modern Western Christians. After all, is it not true that God looks upon the heart? Will God hold one accountable for error in the same way God holds one accountable for willful evil? Did God not know that the elders of ancient Israelite cities were innocent of the blood shed in a nearby field? Had God not witnessed the event? Such questions view the problem of unintended wrong in relation to the justice of God and to matters of eternal judgment and salvation. Ancient Israel's priests seem to have taken a more practical, even mundane, view of wrongdoing. Undeniably harmful or proscribed acts are inherently wrong. Manslaughter kills as truly as does murder. Wrongdoing affects the well-being of individuals and of the community regardless of the purposes of the actor. From a pastoral perspective, therefore, ancient Israel's priests found it necessary to address the wrong done in a way that could, as far as possible, restore harmony and balance to the system. Failure to do so risked permitting the wrongful act to continue in effect, polluting and profaning the system.

In this regard, incidentally, modern objections that one cannot be considered guilty for mistakes, since, after all, one did not mean to do harm are somewhat disingenuous. Ancient Israel's priests viewed the world from a practical standpoint not unlike that of good parents seeking to instill in their children a sense of the fragility of life and the need to take appropriate responsibility even for accidental harms done. At some point in a child's development, parents meet the excuse "I didn't mean to" with reminders that carelessness often causes harm, with admonitions to apologize, with encouragement to sympathize in the pain or loss of the injured party, and with the requirement to make restitution, if possible. Even the Western legal system recognizes that, although the intention to violate the law heightens responsibility for the wrong done, people must be held accountable for ignorance, malfeasance, negligence, and incompetence that results in injury or damage (cf. the requirement stated in the Deuteronomic code that Israelites construct parapets on the roofs of their houses to avoid the possibility of incurring liability in the event of an accidental fall, Deut 22:8). Ancient Israel's priests did not hold a cartoonish view of the world in which the laws of physics and the principles of social life apply only when an actor invokes them through an act of will. Intended or not, wrongful acts produce real harm and the harm done must be addressed.

In other words, the priests treated wrong not primarily as a topic for systematic theology but as a problem for pastoral care. One notes, for example, in the section on "unintentional sin" in the priestly manual, that the writer assumes that his readers do not need definitions for the kinds of acts covered by the term "sin" (חטא, *ht'*).[18] He refers only to instances in which someone has "done what YHWH commanded not be done" (see Lev 4:2, 13, 22, 27, etc.). Since YHWH's commandments were well known, the priestly author can omit the specifics in order to concentrate on the proper treatment of situations in which someone who has transgressed a divine commandment unintentionally and unknowingly subsequently becomes aware of the transgression. If the commandments were well known, how could one possibly violate one and fail to recognize the fact? The structure of this section in the priestly manual offers some guidance on this issue. It first classifies the situations a priest may confront in terms of the status

The Objective Nature of Sin: Intention Is (Relatively) Insignificant

of the offender in descending order of gravity: the anointed priest (Lev 4:3-12), the whole congregation (Lev 4:13-21), a ruler (Lev 4:22-26), and, finally, a commoner (Lev 4:27-35). The remainder of the section suggests, apparently as illustrative examples, a variety of situations involving degrees of unintentional wrongdoing (Lev 5:1-26 [5:1–6:7 Eng.]). Grouped into three subsections (vv. 1-13, 14-19, 20-26 [6:1-7 Eng.]) marked by the introductory formulae at 5:14 and 5:20 [6:1 Eng.], these examples provide insight into the priestly mindset.

The third of these subsections (5:20-26 [6:1-7 Eng.]) presents a particular problem for interpreters and should, therefore, be treated first before being set somewhat to the side. It deals with instances in which an individual sins against YHWH by deceiving, robbing, oppressing, or defrauding another Israelite. Surely such actions must necessarily involve the actor's intention ("[if] he has found what was lost and lied about it, swearing falsely" [5:22 (6:3 Eng.)]). The editor of this section apparently includes it in the category of unintentional sins for two reasons. First, like the second subsection immediately preceding (5:14-19), it deals with trespass[19] against the sacred, in this case through the false oath common to all the cases listed. That is, the guilty party in these cases has involved the name of YHWH in a lie. In other words, in the view of this section of the priestly manual, the obvious property crimes under discussion mask an even more critical trespass against God. Such trespasses have been the subject of the preceding section and may have suggested the association. Second, although the crimes discussed must surely have been conscious acts, the text envisions the lapse of some time between the commission of the act and the moment when the actor acknowledges guilt (5:23 [6:4 Eng.]). In this sense, these cases resemble those involving unwitting sin of which the sinner becomes aware only subsequently. How the priests viewed the fact that a robber can only subsequently acknowledge/feel guilt involves the connotations of the key term אשם ('shm) discussed below.

Chiastic structure (an ABCCBA or "concentric" pattern) governs the first subsection, which deals with sins of speech (5:1, 4) and of improper contact with uncleanness (vv. 2-3). At first glance, failure to volunteer testimony in a case about which one has actual knowledge does not seem to represent a lack of intention. The reluctant witness knows quite well what he or she is doing. Nonetheless, verse 5 of the summary statement utilizes the same verb (אשם, 'shm) used in Lev 4 (vv. 13, 22, 27) to describe the process of dawning awareness of sin. Consequently, the precise connotation of this term, which is thematic in Lev 4–5, deserves attention. It is often translated simply "to be guilty" or "to incur guilt," although throughout Lev 4–5 it refers to a moment subsequent to the commission of the act in which the actor perceives its true nature. In the absolute sense, the actor becomes responsible for the act in the moment of commission even though the actor will only later become aware. Thus, the verb must mean either "to recognize guilt/responsibility"[20] or, more subjectively, "to feel guilty."[21] In the context of unintentional and unwitting sins, the former seems well suited. Those who have done wrong without knowing it become fully responsible for their acts at the moment when they "come to know" what they have done. In that moment, they "recognize [their] guilt." But, as Jacob Milgrom, the chief proponent of the second understanding of the term, has argued, the notion of "recognizing guilt" does not conform well to the situation described in Lev 5:1 and suits even more awkwardly the situation described in 5:20-26 [6:1-7 Eng.]. The reluctant witness (5:1) and "the defrauder, embezzler, robber, and the like are quite aware of their guilt. It is their consciences that subsequently disturb them."[22] Reserving the problem presented by 5:20-26 [6:1-7 Eng.] for below, it is safe to assert for now that the verb אשם (*'shm*) denotes the perception of guilt, either as an act of recognition or of the conscience.

How is the case of the reluctant witness an instance of unwitting sin? Rolf Rendtorff has noted that the expression "it is hidden from him" replaces the former "unintentionally" and argued that intention is not at issue for the cases cited in 5:1-6 because these misdeeds are not violations of express commandments (cf. 4:2, 13, 22, 27). Instead, they are "sins of omission."[23] The distinction between absent intention and lack of information seems too fine, however. As in Lev 4, the actors described in 5:1-6 become responsible for their actions when they "come to know." Indeed, the summary statement in verses 5-6 classes all four "sins" in a common category and assumes that, at some point, the actors have become aware of their wrongdoing—the same process envisioned in Lev 4. Rendtorff's observation concerning the nature of the misdeeds in relation to express commandments, on the other hand, is on point. The Torah contains several prohibitions against "bearing false witness" (Exod 20:16; 23:1-2; Deut 5:20; 19:16-18), but offers no injunction requiring the giving of testimony. Nor does the Torah prohibit making vows (Lev 5:4). In contrast, however, contact with unclean things is very closely regulated (see Lev 11:8, 26, 27, etc.).

To summarize: by juxtaposing the case of a reluctant witness (who, although in violation of no express commandment, has nonetheless failed to do the right thing) and the case of the individual who vows rashly (again an act technically in keeping with the requirements of Torah) with cases of unwitting contact with uncleanness, the priestly manual establishes that "unintentional sin" covers the whole gamut of behaviors short of willful sin that can result in terrible injury and harm. The silent witness may avoid entanglement in public controversy, but this silence may result in a miscarriage of justice. He has broken no law, but he has nonetheless caused, or risked causing, real harm. According to priestly logic, silence, an act of omission, brings responsibility for the outcome of the legal proceeding, just as Jephthah's rashly spoken vow would result in his daughter's death (Judg 11:29-40)[24] or Saul's rash oath would endanger the life of his son, Jonathan (1 Sam 14:24-46). Admittedly, Jephthah could not have known that his daughter would come to meet him nor could Saul that his son, ignorant of his father's oath, would violate it. Nevertheless, prudent fathers very likely

The Objective Nature of Sin: Intention Is (Relatively) Insignificant

would have anticipated the possibilities. The hasty, rash, ill-advised statements of Jephthah and Saul became unintended, unwitting sentences of death for their children.

The second subsection of the discussion of "unintended sin" (5:14-19) deals with unwitting trespass against the sancta—sacred objects, areas, times, and abstractions. In contrast to modern sensibilities, ancient Israel understood the concept of holiness as a quality, something like a force, that inheres in places, things, and persons, rendering them objectively off-limits, even dangerous, for those not qualified for contact. Such trespasses in ancient Israel could include mistaken consumption of food set apart as the tithe, inadvertent contact with holy objects such as priestly clothing or implements belonging to the sanctuary, misuse of the divine name, etc. As a crude comparison, radioactivity offers a certain analogy. An object may seem ordinary to the casual observer and yet emit dangerous levels of radiation. Even casual, unwitting contact with such an object may be dangerous. This view of the quality of holiness inherent in certain places (Moses on "holy ground," for example; Exod 3:5), objects, and persons explains a series of events involving the ark of the covenant narrated in 1 Sam 5-6 (concerning the sojourn of the ark among the Philistines) and in 2 Sam 6:1-7 (concerning the death of Uzzah). As the symbol and locus of God's presence with Israel, the ark was the most sacred object in the ancient cult. Only a select few Israelite priests were qualified to have contact with the ark of the covenant; that is, only they were considered to possess a similar degree of holiness. After its capture by the Philistines, 1 Sam 5-6 records that the ark of the covenant toppled the statue of the Philistine god, Dagon, and caused the outbreak of a plague among the Philistine populace. Much later, when Uzzah, who was not one of the properly qualified priests, touched the ark to prevent it from falling during its journey to a new home in David's Jerusalem, the inherent holiness in the ark killed him.[25]

Obviously, modern Western Christians, especially Protestants, have no comparable sense of the sacred as an inherent, sometimes dangerous, force. Nonetheless, appreciation for the priestly viewpoint holds potential as a corrective for aspects of the modern worldview. Perhaps it does not border too closely on allegory to suggest parallels between the priestly view of the inherent quality of an act or an entity and the real, everyday world experience of the inherent harmfulness—to persons including the "unintentional sinner" him- or herself, to relationships, to the environment—of certain actions, entirely without regard for the intentions of the actor. The first pair did not intend to introduce shame and mistrust into their relationship with one another, with God, and with the rest of creation. However, shame and mistrust were inherent in their sin. God did not impose it as a penalty.

Most importantly, the priestly view stresses the need for restitution and restoration in the aftermath of wrongdoing. In every case, the wrongdoer shall offer a "sin" offering to atone, "and [the wrongdoer] shall be forgiven." Furthermore, in the event that the wrong done involves trespass against the sacred, and thus against God directly, or against another Israelite, so that there has been some real injury, the wrongdoer is to make restitution, more than fully restoring (120 percent) that which had been lost to the injured party. In short, ancient Israel's priests saw the world, as God had created it, as a harmony of order and well-being. Wrong—intention has no bearing—disrupts the balance. Wrong has its own reality. The death of the innocent victim is a wrong, regardless of the killer's motives and intentions. Motive and intention simply do not alter the objective reality. The killer's "error" resulted in the death of an innocent. Whether intentional or not, the Bible takes for granted that such states of "wrongfulness" must and can be remediated. They cannot be safely left unresolved. So far as possible, the wrongdoer must take steps to set wrong right. Failing that possibility, the community must act.

Israel's priests did not speculate as to the precise point along the spectrum of willfulness and inadvertence at which one becomes morally culpable in the legal sense, the point at which the modern distinction between error and "sin" can be invoked. Instead, their approach was much more pastoral: whatever the psychological and ethical dynamics preceding and underlying a wrong, the priests saw their role primarily in terms of healing, restoration, and restitution.

Sin and the Priestly Function in the New Testament

Some will no doubt protest that not only does this objectification of sin—divorcing it from the will of the sinner—seem foreign to modern Western sensibilities, it also represents a more primitive ethic than that found in the New Testament. Jesus, for example, offered a rather extensive analysis of the requirements of obedience to the Decalogue in which he emphasized that truly *fulfilling* the intent and spirit of the law requires much more than merely avoiding certain overt acts—killing, adultery, etc. (Matt 5:17-48). Matthew preserves Jesus' discussion of the commandment against killing most extensively, detailing the logic of Jesus' interpretation, probably to provide a model for reading the much more succinct continuation of Jesus' argument. Perhaps not coincidentally, Jesus seems to have based his thinking regarding the commandment against killing on the priestly texts regarding unintentional homicide discussed above and especially, further, on the version found in Deut 19 along with its context.

Jesus agrees (Matt 5:22) with these texts that intent defines murder in contradistinction to manslaughter (Num 35:11, 22-23; Deut 19:4; Josh 20:3), and, further, that anger and hatred give birth to intent (Num 35:20-21; Deut 19:11; Josh 20:5). Since the sequence of attitude, decision, and action is seamless, Jesus argues—extending the argument of the unintentional homicide texts a step further—that the attitude itself already renders one "liable to judgment." The desire to kill makes one a killer. The act only manifests the killer's decision.

Jesus also agrees with the broader context of Deut 19, in which the Deuteronomic code explicates the case law pertinent to the commandment against killing based on the principle of the supreme value of human life (extending even to the executed criminal; see Deut 21:22-23).[26] In Jesus' view, any diminishment of another human being is a form of killing. Insults, deprecation, and murder arise from the same source (Matt 5:22). The danger posed by anger is so great, in fact, that Jesus encourages his disciples not only to avoid it themselves, but also to seek actively to protect both friend (Matt 5:23-24) and enemy (Matt 5:25-26) from its effects. Because anger makes murderers, one should avoid becoming the irritant. One should quickly be reconciled with any who are in danger of becoming haters. In Jesus' view of the kingdom of God, in which all are their siblings' keepers, the potential victim loves the potential murderer enough to snuff out the chain of events leading to transgression.

The book of James resonates with Jesus' discussion of obedience to the law in its discussion of the source of temptation. Perhaps in order to counter a misunderstanding of the "lead us not into temptation" clause of the Lord's Prayer,[27] the book of James rejects the notion that God can be such a source. Significantly, it does not appeal to Satan or the "evil inclination" often cited in the Jewish texts of the day, "but to a psychological analysis."[28] At issue is the moment when "desire," itself morally neutral, becomes "sin," that is, when it seeks "to convert its relativity into an absolute and its finitude into infinity."[29] Similarly, Jas 2:9 and 4:17 assert the unity of the law. James 2:9 maintains that there are no degrees of transgression; but the Holiness Code has distinguished between "intentional" and "unintentional" sins, and the "unforgivable sin" traditions in the New Testament have maintained that a certain category of sin surpasses all others in severity. James can be harmonized with these traditions if it is understood to be speaking objectively of the *hata'* nature of sin; that is, wrong is wrong without reference to intent or degree. In a fashion similar to the position taken in Lev 5:1, Jas 4:17 argues that the failure to act according to one's knowledge of righteousness is to sin. That is, the absence of the intention to do right has the same consequences as the will to do wrong.

In this analysis, Jesus expanded the priestly notion of sin as an objective reality to include intention as a category in the discussion of sin, but did not, as Abelard would later, make it definitive of sin. Jesus, and in his wake, James, offered a psychological analysis of the process that *can* result in overt acts of sin. That is, Jesus maintained that the attitudes at the root of sinful behavior are also sinful, or perhaps better, become sinful when they become decisions.

Neither Jesus nor James, however, forwarded the argument that all sin results from such a process, as becomes apparent in Jesus' discussion of hypocrisy. Nor did they assert that an otherwise sinful behavior could be rendered innocent by virtue of the lack of intention to do harm. In fact, whereas the ancient priestly view saw an act as "sin" regardless of intention based on its inherent quality alone, Jesus argued that even apparently good deeds such as almsgiving

(Matt 6:1-4), prayer (Matt 6:5), and fasting (Matt 6:16-18) could be tainted with sin if marred by evil or misdirected intention (cf. also Matt 7:21-23). Like the prophet Jeremiah, Jesus recognized that one's intentions, rarely pure, are often opaque even to oneself: "The heart is devious above all else; it is perverse—who can understand it?" (Jer 17:9).[30]

In the Sermon on the Mount, Jesus contended, then, that evil intention can be consonant with evil action, or that evil intention can be masked by an apparently good deed. Nevertheless, Jesus' overarching concern in the Sermon on the Mount seems to have been a call for integrity of attitude and behavior: "Have integrity [31] as your heavenly Father has integrity" (Matt 5:48). Those with pure intentions will see God (Matt 5:8; cf. purity of vision, Matt 6:22-23, and of purpose, Matt 6:33). Because God loves wholly, God sends the blessing of life-giving rain to the righteous and the unrighteous alike; God's children should likewise love with integrity, not differentiating between persons (Matt 5:45-46). Citizens of God's kingdom do not have two distinct sets of behaviors because they do not have two masters (Matt 6:24). Finally, since they have only one master, they will ideally marry a single intention with a style of behavior. Intention and action will be integrated. Good trees bear good fruits, therefore "by their fruits, you will know them" (Matt 7:20). In effect, although by way of a quite different course of logic, Jesus comes very close in the Sermon on the Mount to affirming the priestly notion that, at least in many cases, a bad act is inherently bad. He adds that these acts can, in fact, even evidence evil intent.

The objection does hold that Jesus' teaching supercedes and transcends the ancient priestly view of wrong as a quality inherent in certain acts by shifting the center of gravity away from the external act to the human heart. Jesus examines the relationship between intention and action, to be sure, in ways Israel's priests did not. Nonetheless, the complex picture of the role of the human will that emerges in the end seems to argue that, since human motives are most often mixed, the observer must still evaluate the "fruits" in terms of their inherent qualities. Bad fruit is inherently bad. One can conclude from this evidence that it came from a bad tree. This, however, is a deduction.[32]

Although the Gospels preserve no other discourse of Jesus even impinging on the subject of the concrete reality of sin, Jesus' behaviors manifest his priestly concern for the inherently wrong quality of sin. As a rule, Jesus forgave sin and healed its consequences in tandem. That is, Jesus recognized that sin has reality in the world and, therefore, cannot be relegated solely to the spiritual realm. Modern theologians (rightly) warn against the erroneous thinking of Job's friends that misfortune—sickness, disease, loss—always represents God's punishment on sinners. Innocent suffering is an all too familiar phenomenon. Indeed, in one of his very few statements on the subject, Jesus explicitly rejected the automatic equation of sin and suffering, too (John 9:3).[33] Nonetheless, Jesus did not, as the church so frequently does, view sin as a purely psycho-spiritual problem: Jesus not only *forgave* sinners their sin, but he *healed* them from sin's effects, as well.

Surpassing ancient Israel's priests in the capacity to set wrong right, Jesus did not simply pronounce forgiveness, he addressed the concrete, real-world footprint of sin—he restored, he replaced wrong with right. The instructive account of Jesus healing the man born blind recorded in John 9 exemplifies Jesus' approach toward concrete wrong manifest in illness and disease. The disciples are interested in assigning blame: "Who sinned, this man or his parents?" (John 9:2). Jesus' response rejects their reasoning and asserts that he sees such wrongs as matters to be set right. The man's condition presents an opportunity for "God's works [to be] revealed" (9:3). He will no longer live in darkness, because Jesus, "the light of world," dispels inherently chaotic darkness. In sum, like the priestly materials in the OT, Jesus' first and foremost concern was to restore the order and goodness of God's creation.

One additional passage in the New Testament, Heb 5:1-4, expresses the priestly view of error and inadvertence. As examined in chapter 2, the book of Hebrews attempts to encourage Christians facing persecution for their faith to stand firm, or, from another perspective, to admonish them against abandoning their confidence in the hope offered through Jesus Christ. In the author's view, such apostasy would be tantamount to renouncing salvation, closely akin to the Synoptic Gospels' concept of the unpardonable sin. Clearly, however, the author of Hebrews does not intend to advocate perfectionism. The disobedience discussed in 3:12-19 does not encompass all "sins." Instead, Heb 5:1-4 places the reader back in the context of Lev 4–5 and the category of "unintentional sins." Because Israel's priests were themselves "subject to weakness," the limitations of being human, they could sympathize with "ignorant and errant" individuals whose wrongdoings were unintentional, although no less harmful. The priest's responsibility is to guide the errant to restored relationship.

The Priestly View of Sin and a Tragic Vision

Consideration of the Bible's discussion of unintentional sin requires one to entertain the possibility of bearing responsibility for an act committed "innocently" and raises all manner of questions concerning what might be termed "fairness"—innocent suffering, well-intentioned wrongdoing. The arena of concerns parallels in many ways those explored in classical tragedy. In everyday usage, "tragedy" has come to refer to virtually any *catastrophe*—an airplane crash, a famine, a killer tornado, a terrorist attack. In its classical usage, however, it refers to a particular kind of dilemma that closely parallels the "unintentional sin" notion of ancient Israel's priests.[34] It may be helpful to delineate the similarities between the worldview espoused by the priests who envisioned the possibility of unintentional sin and the tragic worldview of classical literature and philosophy.

Neither the priests nor the tragedians focused attention on purely innocent suffering resulting from natural disasters or the overtly evil acts of other persons.

Deaths resulting from violent weather are lamentable, but the victims of these catastrophes are just that, passive victims. Their choices and behaviors cannot usually be identified as the precipitating cause of their fate. Nature has behaved according to its rules, indifferent to its impact on human lives. Tornadoes and earthquakes make no choices and bear no moral responsibility; victims—usually[35]—suffer for merely being present at an inopportune moment. In cases of violent crimes, on the other hand, perpetrators do make choices and bear moral responsibility, but the victims are similarly passive (for the most part).[36] Such instances of victimization are horrendous, but they are not tragic in the sense that they present the moral dilemma of an agent, acting in good faith and with good intention, acting erroneously nonetheless and bringing upon him- or herself tragic consequences.

The biblical book of Job illustrates the limited applicability of the tragic conception quite well. It does not fit the category of "tragedy" in the limited sense. Job suffered loss as the result of natural catastrophes (the fire from heaven and the wind that took his servants, livestock, and children, and the illness that befell him personally) and at the hands of human agents (the Sabean and Chaldean raiders). Significantly, *his suffering was entirely passive*. As he asserted, and God confirmed, Job did nothing to entangle himself in the matrix of events that brought his suffering. In fact, he undertook extraordinary measures to avoid such difficulties, offering sacrifices on his children's behalf, for example. To the contrary, tragic protagonists suffer as the direct result of their own actions.[37] The tragic component involves the fact that they act in good faith and with good intentions, ignorant of the true character of their deeds.

Job raises other questions concerning God's moral responsibility, not Job's, questions that receive at least two types of response in the book. On one level, as readers of the book of Job know, but Job himself did not, God permitted, or even directed, the disasters that befell Job. The book portrays a complicated conception of agency at this level. The satan persuades God to permit measures against Job. The measures taken, however, involve the immediate agency of human beings (Sabeans and Chaldeans) and of nature (fire, wind, illness). The book never satisfactorily addresses how responsibility for Job's suffering is to be meted out among human, angelic, and divine agents. Every expression of human evil ultimately raises the question of God's responsibility for permitting human beings freedom of will and action. More fundamentally, the book offers no convincing response to Job's charge that God, the permissive authority behind Job's suffering, has acted arbitrarily.

On another level, God did respond to Job in the end, but in enigmatic portrayals of the "universe [as] an amoral arena of powerful forces clashing,"[38] suggesting that even the forces and creatures of the natural world exercise a degree of free agency. Contemporary process theology recognizes as a corollary to the notion that God is other than God's creation the notion of the independence of the created order. With a view to God's portrayal to Job of the wildness of God's creation, the independence of creation helps to situate the category of "catastrophe" theologically. God creates and preserves the universe as "other," giving even the created order the freedom manifest in "the indeterminate natural occurrences that recent physics has uncovered at the most elementary levels of physical reality, the random events that biology finds at the level of life's evolution," as well as "the freedom that emerges with human existence...."[39] Still, in the context of the book of Job, at least, the fire, the wind, and the illness came specifically at God's behest, or at least with God's permission, not as an expression of nature's freedom.

At any rate, Job correctly asserted that the moral questions raised by his suffering are not questions to be put to him. He has not acted, either intentionally or unintentionally, in such a way as to have set the moral machinery of the universe justly into motion against him. Instead, the moral questions raised by Job's suffering are for God to answer. Job is not a tragic figure in the pure sense.

"Tragedy" does not describe the circumstances of those who suffer as pure innocents; that is, conversely, it includes only those who have somehow, without intending to commit wrong, set into motion events that will exact the price of responsibility. Nevertheless, just as tragedy does not apply to those who suffer without cause, it also does not apply to those who do wrong with some degree of awareness and intention. It is a commonplace, following Aristotle's analysis of the "tragic flaw" of tragic protagonists, to define tragedy in terms of the overreaching (*hubris*) of tragic characters. Oedipus' defiant efforts to escape the destiny predicted by the gods, so the argument goes, led him down the path to the fulfillment of the prediction. The problem posed by tragedy in this reading hinges not around the protagonist's innocent suffering, but around the scale of the suffering, incommensurate with the degree of the crime.[40] In fact, however, it was Laius, Oedipus' father, who sought to avoid the fulfillment of the prophecy by exposing his infant son, so that a chain of circumstances, unforeseen and unrecognized by the actors, especially Oedipus, could culminate in the very fulfillment of the prediction.[41] While it is true that Oedipus abandoned his parents—unknown to him, his adoptive parents—also in an effort to avert the prophecy repeated to him when he came of age, one surely cannot charge a dutiful son with arrogant defiance of the gods for taking steps to avoid fratricide. In fact, he fled to protect them from the prophecy when they refused to answer his questions concerning his paternity. Filial loyalty, like that of Oedipus and Shakespeare's Cordelia, is surely not *hubris*.

Oedipus faces tragic outcomes because he acted based on tragically limited information. He left home in a noble effort to avoid any possibility that he could kill his father, not knowing that he was, in fact, adopted. He killed Laius in a contest and for reasons that the culture would have judged honorable, except that, unknown to either of them, Oedipus was Laius' true son. He unknowingly married his mother as a result of saving Thebes from a monster. When the gods plagued Thebes because Laius' murder had not been resolved (cf. Deut 21),

Oedipus vigorously searched for the truth despite warnings from the oracle, Teiresias, to leave well enough alone. Oedipus is not guilty of *hubris*; he is guilty of determination to live according to the standards of decency and honor required by his culture. Indeed, after trying to avoid answering Oedipus' pointed requests to reveal the identity of Laius' killer so that the plague could be lifted, Teiresias responded with a statement very much in the tenor of ancient Israel's priests: "You are the slayer whom you seek . . . you do not see where you are in sin" (I:362, 367).[42]

Sophocles' Oedipus and the Bible's Jephthah became entangled in circumstances that can be qualified as "tragic" precisely because they were acting in good faith and with pure intention, but without full knowledge of the context of their actions. Factors unknown to them affected the quality of their deeds, transforming innocent intentions into harmful outcomes. Or, as with Sophocles' Antigone and the Bible's Jephthah, the tragic protagonist finds it impossible to satisfy competing claims: the law demands one thing, fidelity to a brother demands its opposite; keeping a vow requires the sacrifice of a child. The paradox involves the contrast between the tragic protagonist's understanding and the full scope of reality revealed in the course of events resulting from the protagonist's actions. The situation is tragic because the protagonist cannot have avoided suffering:[43] either ignorance of the true nature of the situation precludes wise decision-making, or competing and mutually exclusive claims mean that, in acting to satisfy one claim, the protagonist *must* violate the other. In any case, although they are not intentional wrongdoers, "tragic heroes . . . always have a hand in their own destruction."[44]

The Rush to the Comic

Christians typically experience discomfort with the notions of unintentional sin and tragedy. Indeed, critics point out Christianity's tendency to rush past tragedy toward a comic vision of reality, thus denying tragedy its full reality. Christianity wants an orderly, meaningful world that fully acquits God of responsibility for the world's messiness. J. Morreall has argued, indeed, that monotheism is fundamentally anti-tragic because of its belief in God's providence, omniscience, and omnipotence. "*Whatever* happens, including all instances of evil, is the will of God, and is ultimately for the best."[45] Similarly, A. MacIntyre (following Nietzsche) has contended that, since Christianity is a divine comedy (i.e., everything ends well regardless of the circumstances), "it cannot account for moral tragedy."[46] These analyses of Christianity presume the identity of Christian theology and a particular, Calvinistic-deterministic version of it. What becomes of the monotheistic rush to the comic in a version of Christianity that takes seriously the notion that God created human beings so that they might exercise an appropriate degree and kind of autonomy? What if God truly enters into relationship with God's creation, genuinely reacting and responding to decisions and actions rather than controlling outcomes?

The Objective Nature of Sin: Intention Is (Relatively) Insignificant

Often, especially in the everyday settings of hospital emergency rooms and pastors' offices, Christianity offers alternative, but flawed, explanations of tragic suffering meant to salvage meaningfulness and orderliness. Three such explanations predominate: (1) suffering is redemptive; (2) suffering is edifying; (3) suffering is penultimate. In an examination of the Christian understanding of tragedy and its role in interpretations of the Holocaust—indeed, its function as an enabling factor—Michael Steele urges that, "In the matter of unearned and unredeemed suffering, Christianity must eventually grapple directly with the implications of its position on suffering and transcendence." Christianity's theory of tragedy permits it facilely to assert the meaningfulness of suffering. Yet, in efforts to comprehend the Holocaust, Christianity can make appeal neither to the Jews' "tragic flaw" revealed in the moral order's meaningful exaction of consequences nor to the possibility of transcendence opened by the Jews' suffering. Often, entirely undeserved suffering does no apparent good whatsoever.[47] Similarly, Christian eschatology and hope threaten to make it impossible "to take the tragic tragically."[48]

If Christianity too often effectively denies the reality of tragic suffering, it does not do so because the Christian gospel requires it. As L. Ruprecht has pointed out, Christianity is, at root, a tragic faith. In contrast to modernity's pessimism, its "tragic posture," with its Humpty-Dumpty vision of a broken world beyond repair, Christianity sees a broken world that may be restored. That is, Christianity need not, ought not, deny the brokenness. Instead, Christianity must embrace the paradox of pointless suffering. After all, Christianity's savior redeems by dying on a cross.[49] In other words, the categories of "unintentional sin" and tragedy attest to the uncomfortable but no less basic reality of the conflict between human finitude and human autonomy.

Human beings are finite; finitude produces tragedy. One acts on incomplete knowledge and chooses wrongly, sometimes disastrously. One undertakes to do good, but is incompetent and in the end only does harm. Christian theology and ministry must take into account the reality of human limits and must, further, clarify the relationship between limitation and "sin" as the problem. Human beings are limited and will make mistakes. Apparently, this is inherent in human nature—God created humanity to be thus—and is not, therefore, the human problem. Nonetheless, the church cannot ignore the harm resulting from human limitations. At the same time, limited human beings have a degree of autonomy; that is, there are at least two wills operative in any moment.[50]

Theodicy, the justification of God's ways in the world, especially in regard to the problem of evil and innocent suffering, is not the subject of this study. Nonetheless, unintentional tragedy, to combine the priestly and the Greek terminology, raises the question quite forcefully, both with respect to human finitude and to human autonomy. On the one hand, God created human beings as finite creatures. By nature, then, humans will, from time to time, lack the full knowledge and competency required to choose a wise course of action. Had

111

Oedipus only known the identity of his parents, or even that he was adopted, he could and surely would have made appropriate decisions; had Jephthah only foreseen the possibility that his daughter would greet him on his return from battle, he could and would have modified his vow. This finitude is not humanity's *fault*, it is humanity's God-given *nature*. On the other hand, though limited, human beings also enjoy autonomy, again as God-given. L. Ruprecht summarizes Hegel's view of this dialectic: "God creates free beings whom God remains free to love, but is no longer free to control. God has created, in effect, the rock too large to lift. This, then, is a setting ripe for tragedy—our world, a stage, the theater for tragic collisions."[51] Human beings exercise their autonomy in a context in which the limitations of being human bind total freedom. In a real sense, God must take responsibility for creating such a world.[52] The church, however, must also face the facts that only in such a world would creatures be privileged to bear the image of God, that only in such a world would God share fully in the tragedy in Gethsemane and on Golgotha, and that denial of this tragic reality fails to comprehend the full scope of God's work to reconcile the world to God's-self.[53]

The gospel, after all, reminds us that there is no Sunday without Friday and that the resurrected Jesus bears Friday's scars.[54] Emphasizing too quickly the victory of Easter is ministering "as if the agony and delusion, the sheer monstrous reality of physical and spiritual suffering which he bore were a mere charade."[55] Christian theology must revision tragedy within the gospel so that Christian ministry and practice will have a basis on which to address serious (no less so for being accidental) wrong.

A Tragic Vision and the Priestly Function of the Church

The juxtaposition of the ancient Israelite priestly concept of "unintentional sin" with the classical understanding of tragedy suggests that the church typically fails to include tragic error and its consequent suffering among those human phenomena addressed by the gospel. Defining "sin" primarily as the voluntary violation of the divine will in keeping with modern Western emphases on individual autonomy and responsibility, the church has no theological framework for dealing with tragedy and error. The ministry of the church to the full range of human wrongdoing and pain can benefit from the recovery of several aspects of the priestly understanding of, and pastoral approach to, unintentional sin.

First, the church must be willing to acknowledge the meaninglessness of some suffering and resist the urge to pacify the threat posed by an unpredictable world. "Language that makes us feel better does not insure that we see better."[56] A motorist, driving at night in the rain, punctures a tire on a broken bottle discarded earlier by another motorist. The puncture causes the SUV to swerve, topple, and roll into oncoming traffic. Several people suffer serious injury and the young mother of two driving one of the vehicles caught up in the crash dies on the scene. She had not secured her seat belt. Who sinned? If the question means, who intended to do wrong and cause injury, the answer, of course, is no one. What does the gospel have to say to these people? That their suffering makes sense somehow as redemptive, or that it is ultimately insignificant?

Jesus' approach to the man born blind, and indeed, to everyone he healed of infirmity, is instructive. The first task is to acknowledge the reality of the tragic circumstance and to deal with it. Attempts to redefine catastrophe as redemption in disguise gain nothing. As L. Ruprecht has poignantly observed,

> The Christian goes "beyond tragedy" *not* when he or she believes in resurrection, *but only* when he or she claims that this faith will take your pain away. Tragedies *can* end well—and still be "tragic." But if genuine suffering is ignored, or simply painted away in colors that distract the eye, if the agony of the struggle to believe and to understand is not faced in all earnestness, *then* it is no tragedy. *Salvation is **through** suffering, not **from** it.* Suffering is not necessarily tragedy's last word, but it is decidedly the first. . . . [57]

Second, the church must consciously embrace a priestly role with respect to the tragic conditions created by "unintentional sin." That is to say, as far as possible, the church should imitate the priestly concern with restoration and restitution. Harm, injury, pain, suffering—these are all experienced in the real world as the result even of simple error. Modern Christianity tends to see the gospel as pertinent *only* to eternity. Israel's priests knew that, even though accidental, certain actions upset the equilibrium God intended. Imbalance, regardless of its source, will damage the community or members of it (whether one purposefully sets fire to one's house or *only* fails to properly extinguish the candles on the dining table before bed makes no difference), so the priests saw it as their responsibility to help restore equilibrium to the extent possible. Jesus forgave *and healed*. Repentance is not the only proper Christian response to injury and harm. In some cases, Christians can and should assume responsibility for actions for which they have no guilt.

Third, dealing with persons caught up in situations of tragic wrongdoing, the church, while emphasizing the need for restoration and healing, can imitate Jesus and ancient Israel's priests (Heb 5:1-2) by avoiding the blame game. People find themselves in these situations because they are limited human beings, unable to anticipate every circumstance and control every condition. Inevitably, however, people will place blame. It would be common for people like the driver of the overturned SUV in the example cited immediately above to blame themselves. The chief insight of ancient Israel's priests into the nature of the tragic maintains that, while real wrong may result from a person's error, responsibility and guilt are distinct in such cases. Good people can, even with the best of intentions, do bad things entirely by accident. They do not thereby become evil themselves. They bear no guilt—responsibility yes, guilt no. Healing involves addressing not only the reality of the harm done, but also the innocence of the wrongdoer. The "innocent wrongdoer" deserves priestly protection.

Fourth, the church must offer a critique of Western civilization's concepts of hyper-individualism and absolute autonomy in relation to the privatization and interiorization of sin. By definition, "unintended sin" in a tragic setting defies analysis as a private experience rooted in the depths of an individual psyche. Tragedy occurs in the marketplace, where people interact, where unintended consequences can be as devastating as the more carefully planned atrocity. Relatedly, the church, through its teaching, preaching, and public advocacy, in relation both to individual and public decision-making, must take a cautious stance with respect to the value of good intentions. Human intentions cannot be trusted. Human beings, by virtue of human limitations, must beware the unforeseen. The church should continually remind people of the precarious quality of human wisdom.

CHAPTER SIX

Guilt as a Condition and a Consequence: Sin and Systems

> "Of all that was done in the past, you eat the fruit, either rotten or ripe....
> For every ill deed in the past we suffer the consequence:
> For sloth, for avarice, gluttony, neglect of the Word of GOD,
> For pride, for lechery, treachery, for every act of sin.
> And of all that was done that was good, you have the inheritance.
> For good and ill deeds belong to a man alone, when he stands alone on the other side of death,
> But here upon earth you have the reward of the good and ill that was done by those who have gone before you."[1]

As has been shown, Western individualism and the prevalent juridical theological metaphor encourage a conception of sin that focuses on the sinner's intention to commit a wrong. Biblical tradition and common experience, in contrast, suggest that such a sin concept fails to account for vast proportions of human wrongdoing and suffering. Individualism and legalism also influence thinking on sin toward a somewhat atomistic concept that overlooks the systemic nature of sin. Western justice deals with crime by assessing guilt and exacting a penalty. The objectives are to identify the individual or group of individuals primarily and intentionally responsible for the wrong done, and to prescribe a jail sentence commensurate with the severity of the crime. Western justice systems take scant notice of the fact that in many cases a familial or cultural system has created the conditions in and out of which an individual acts: that is, others than the individual before the bar have contributed to the crime. Increasingly, even the mental state, native intelligence, and psychological condition of the wrongdoer have no bearing on guilt or innocence:[2] that is, society is unwilling to give account for its inability or unwillingness to care for the mentally and emotionally ill and for the disadvantaged. Nor do Western justice systems have at their disposal tools for addressing guilt that is organically related to the nature of the crime and suited to redressing and repairing, as far as possible, the injury. Only one penalty exists: jail time, varied in duration according to society's assessment of the severity of the crime.

The recent trend of trying juveniles as adults points to the weaknesses of this system.[3] Parental neglect, benign or otherwise, communities that fail to provide opportunities for constructive activity, educational systems that fail to respond to bullying and societies that pamper and privilege athletes and entertainers, and business and corporate environments willing to profit from violence and sexuality in advertising and entertainment all contribute to the acts of the twelve-year-old boy who kills his six-year-old neighbor while playing at professional wrestling.[4] Surely he bears appropriate responsibility for his actions; but the adult world that nurtured his fascination with violence and permitted him to act it out, unsupervised, bears a greater degree. Just as surely, true justice would make available some redress other than confinement behind bars. Medical practitioners diagnose a problem and prescribe a course of treatment designed to address the specifics. Bloodletting is no longer a panacea.

Juridical individualism is not the only distorting factor operative in popular Christian thought. Modern Christianity has difficulty reconciling faith in a God who remains involved in God's creation and in the course of human history with the messy manifestations of right and wrong. Many Christians, for example, were rightly horrified and embarrassed by Jerry Falwell's assertion on Pat Robertson's *700 Club* just a few days after the events of September 11, 2001 that these events were God's punishment on America because of the secularization of its society: "[T]he pagans and the abortionists and the feminists and the gays and the lesbians who are actively trying to make that an alternative lifestyle, the ACLU, People for the American Way—all of them who have tried to secularize America, I point the finger in their face and say 'you helped this happen.'"[5] Some were embarrassed because Falwell had issued a blanket condemnation of persons based solely on their sexual orientation, others because Falwell's statement reveals a degree of disregard for the separation of church and state fundamental to American life, and still others because of Falwell's underlying assumption that American culture has fallen into secularity from a previous state of sacredness or chosenness. Many more, however, are embarrassed by any discussion of God's anger or justice. Modern popular Christianity wants to avoid all images of the "angry" God of the Old Testament, thinking that in the affirmation that "God is love" Christianity has matured beyond Jonathan Edwards's "Sinners in the Hands of an Angry God," beyond moralism and legalism. Falwell certainly went too far in claiming to know the mind of God and he certainly condemned people for actions whose sinfulness is open for debate. Nevertheless, in defense of his assertion that actions have consequences and that God has a stake in the relationship between the two, common sense and experience teach that sin creates conditions that perpetuate wrongdoing and that often rebound against the sinner. While this is not the place to enter into a lengthy and detailed theological analysis of the situation, it may be in order to observe that the September 11 terrorists hated America for some reason. Their actions were vile and reprehensible. Yet one can only wonder, if American interests in the Arab world were directed less toward sustaining non-democratic regimes and more toward economic development to benefit the people, if they were concerned equally with justice, freedom, and security for Palestinian mothers and for Israeli fathers, and if they were motivated less by energy policy and corporate interests and more by the American values of equal opportunity and self-determination, whether Arab youths would hate America so violently as to be willing to die in the commission of mass murder.

As it happens, the Bible speaks neither of a God whose love amounts to toleration of wrongdoing, nor of a God who sits above watching and waiting for someone to break a rule and merit punishment, nor of a God who keeps a balance sheet to determine how one's account will be settled in eternity, nor of a God who punishes innocents for the wrongdoing of their fellow citizens. In the popular Christian mind, then, juridical individualism, coupled with a substrate layer of gnostic discomfort with the everyday world, translates into a view of sin and judgment that ruptures the organic connection between wrongdoing and consequences. In the popular Christian mind, God sits in God's heaven, tallying up individual sins, issuing pardons in response to repentance, and waiting to exact the penalty of eternal damnation on the unforgiven. The nexus of sin and its consequences—its afterlife in the everyday world—has no place in the popular Christian mind. The situation created by sin and everyone's "situatedness" in a sinful system, both noted with open eyes by tragic viewpoints, are overlooked.

The Biblical View: An Organic System of Sin

The biblical view, evidenced most clearly in the Hebrew Bible in the broad semantic range of the noun עָוֹן ('*awon*, "sin, iniquity, guilt, consequence")[6] and in New Testament texts that presume the Hebrew viewpoint, envisions the sinful deed, the sinful condition it produces, and the resulting sinful consequences together as one organic continuum. In analogy to the ripples produced by dropping a pebble in water, the biblical perspective on the relationship between deed and consequence does not distinguish discrete aspects of the system created by the impact of sin on reality. As a rule, the Bible does not separate the act from the effects that follow fluidly and organically. As a result, usages of the Hebrew noun can be roughly classified into three categories along the deed-consequence continuum:[7] (1) to refer to the wrongful act itself; (2) to denote the state of guilt into which the agent enters; (3) to indicate the consequences suffered by the agent and the environment as guilt "matures" into results. Not surprisingly, since the Hebrew worldview used the same word for all three phases, reflecting the fact that this worldview regarded the continuum as a whole, several instances of the term are difficult clearly to assign to one category. Instead, they convey elements of both the act and the guilt borne by the agent or of that guilt and the negative consequences that stem from it. These "bridge" usages serve as the most obvious reminders to the modern Western reader that the categorization of usages is an artificial harmonization to Western thought. For the ancient Israelite, *'awon* encompassed deed, guilt, and consequence together. The common modern limitation of the term "sin" to the act alone is foreign to biblical thought, as are the notions that sin will have no natural consequences in the life of the sinner and on the social and physical environment or that "punishment" for sin will take the form of some unrelated penalty.

Significantly, the Hebrew Bible nowhere specifies the criteria by which an action can be judged *'awon*. Similarly, as is true for *ht'*, the criterion of intentionality is not a key element of the semantics of *'awon*. R. Knierim has forcefully refuted the common assumption that *'awon* always presumes conscious intention: (1) Several instances clearly presuppose an act to have been unconscious and unintended: Gen 15:16; 19:15; Lev 22:16; Num 18:1, 23; 1 Sam 14:41 LXX; 20:1; 2 Sam 14:32; 1 Kgs 17:18; Isa 6:7. (2) Many cases are not concerned with the issue of conscious or unconscious intentions but with the relationship between deed and consequence: Gen 4:13; Deut 19:15; 2 Kgs 7:9; Isa 5:18; Ps 25:11; 31:11, etc. (3) Passages like Deut 9:15; Amos 3:2; Ps 103:3, etc., emphasize the totality of all transgressions, regardless of the type. (4) The term *'awon* can occasionally interchange with the term חַטָּאת *hatta't*. (5) Since the term refers not only to deeds but also to their consequences, the conscious-volitional factor is nonessential, because the consequence often occurs unknowingly, or at any rate unintentionally.[8] The term centers, then, not on what constitutes and defines an improper act, but on the natural and, if left alone, inevitable maturation of such an action into guilt and ultimately into consequence.[9]

Beyond the semantics of the Hebrew term, the Bible in both Testaments offers a rather consistent and coherent concept of the dynamics of sin as an organic continuum. The essential features of this sin nexus idea can be summarized in only a few statements: Sin creates a real circumstance that lingers in the world until it comes to fruition—sometimes with the assistance of accusers and sometimes with God's "permission" or even encouragement—or until it is deactivated. Unfortunately, the nature of sin's impact on the sinner's environment—its almost independent afterlife—means, however, that even forgiveness is sometimes unable to terminate sin's continued effects.

Sin Twists Reality

Most often, the term designates the condition created in the life of the wrongdoer, including the wrongdoer's social and physical environment. The psalmist (Ps 32:5) can thank God that when, instead of enduring the conditions resulting from his wrongdoing, he confessed his sin to God, God "took away" (Hebrew נשא, ns', "to bear, carry, take") the *'awon* resulting from the supplicant's *ht'*. English translations regularly render this verb in the context of sin as "to forgive." The notion of forgiveness suits the juridical metaphor that calls for God to acquit the sinner. In contrast, the Hebrew concept calls for the condition resulting from acts of wrongdoing to be remedied. The psalmist's unspecified wrongdoing produced an *'awon* state that only God could render inert (see also Jer 33:8). "Guilt," as understood from modern legal (culpability) or psychological (a feeling) perspectives, simply does not adequately convey the organic nature of this relationship between the deed and the conditions it produces.[10] Acts of *'awon* twist and pervert reality.[11]

The book of Isaiah, especially the masterful treatise on the twistedness that is *'awon* found in Isa 59, marvels at the power of perversion. *'Awon* so contorts reality that people living in its environment are simply unable to see clearly or walk straightforwardly: "The way of peace they do not know, and there is no justice in their paths. Their roads they have made crooked [עקש, *'qsh*]; no one who walks in them knows peace" (Isa 59:8). *'Awon* constitutes a barrier between God and people (59:2). It confuses the distinction between light and darkness (59:10), between justice and transgression, and between truth and "lying words" (59:13-15). Elsewhere, the book of Isaiah describes people who "drag their *'awon* along behind them on cords," who, in the throes of this twisted reality, cannot distinguish evil from good, darkness from light, bitter from sweet, folly from wisdom, and oppression from justice (Isa 5:18-23). Indeed, Isa 1:4 contends that conditions are so twisted that children (the Judeans) do not even know their father (God).[12]

Sin Lingers in the World in Its Aftereffects

The perverse conditions that are the afterlife of sin linger in the world well after the original action. Hosea (13:12) speaks of the way in which "Ephraim's *'awon* is bound up; his *ht'* is kept in store."[13] Phinehas and representatives of the ten Cis-jordanian tribes rebuke the Reubenites, the Gadites, and the Manassites living in the Transjordan for constructing an unauthorized altar near the Jordan. Their rebuke, based on the historical examples of the sin at Peor ("from which even yet we have not cleansed ourselves," Josh 22:17) and of the sin of Achan (who "did not perish alone for his *'awon*," Josh 22:20), warns that sin's afterlife extends beyond the sinner and even beyond the sinner's generation in the life of Israel. Once loosed in the world, *'awon* can take only two courses. Unaddressed, it will mature; only atonement and forgiveness *may* interrupt its life cycle.

Significantly, as will be discussed in detail shortly, the ancient Israelite worldview understands this idea of the maturation of sin into its consequences as a central principle of the divinely ordained and sustained moral order. In a very natural manner, sin produces genetically related consequences. Psalmists confess that their sins continue to reverberate throughout their environments and threaten their lives. "My *'awonot* [Hebrew plural of *'awon*] have gone over my head, they weigh like a burden too heavy for me" (Ps 38:5 [4 Eng.]). "My *'awonot* have overtaken me until I cannot see" (Ps 40:13 [12]).[14] God explains to Abraham that the promised gift of the land of Canaan must await the day when the sins of the current inhabitants have matured to the point that expulsion from the land at the hands of Abraham's descendants will be the appropriate consequence ("for the *'awon* of the Amorites is not yet mature," Gen 15:16).

The Hebrew Bible's attitude toward ancestral guilt borne by subsequent generations, an attitude that moderns often regard as primitive by current standards of fairness, can best be understood as an expression of the underlying notion of *'awon* as embracing sin and its consequences as a continuum. In brief, ancient Israel was convinced that sin creates a perverted condition that, left alone, can only twist the perceptions and decisions of subsequent generations so that, by their own choice, they too perpetuate their ancestors' sin. That is, ancestral guilt is not a debt left for later generations to pay, but a heritage in which subsequent generations participate, a tradition that they continue.

Now, modern readers of the Bible commonly balk at any notion of corporate guilt or responsibility. Post-Enlightenment ideals highlight the individual. Individuals act independently and bear sole responsibility for their actions. Western ideas of fairness require that a mother cannot be held responsible for her daughter's actions. In fact, post-Enlightenment interpreters of Scripture often think that they have found evidence of an evolution away from corporate thought to individualism within Scripture itself. The parade example of this supposed evolution, Jer 31:31-34, notwithstanding (see below), it is simplistic to think of the evolution of Israelite thought from primitive collectivism to enlightened individualism for at least three reasons: First, the idea of the afterlife of sin in subsequent generations occurs in texts not only from Israel's early period but also in the very latest documents (i.e., Ezra 9:6-7; Neh 9:2). Second, as will be shown immediately below, the idea resounds also in the New Testament—indeed, on the lips of Jesus himself. Third, and most important, the idea is much more sophisticated than the contention that God (unfairly) exacts from *innocent* children the penalties owed by their ancestors. Furthermore, it is simplistic to think that modern romanticism regarding the absolute autonomy of the individual accurately describes conditions in the real world. In truth, no one is an island. The sins of the father do, indeed, impact the lives of the children, creating conditions that negatively affect the possibilities open to them, that predispose them to certain choices, and that contribute destructively to their identities. In short, rather than reflecting the primitive tribalism of an ancient society, now debunked by enlightened views of human society, the biblical view, in many ways, represents a more accurate analysis of the workings of human families and communities.

A key to the Israelite conception of the intergenerational transmission of *'awon* is the credo, often repeated in the Hebrew Bible and often troubling to modern readers convinced of the strict individualism of responsibility, that God holds children accountable for their parents' *'awon* "for three and four generations of those who [continue to] hate me" (Exod 20:5; 34:7; Num 14:18; Deut 5:9-10; Jer 32:18, etc.). Grammatically, the participle "those who hate me" refers to the third and fourth generation of "haters." In other words, the credo assumes that the behaviors of the ancestors will be perpetuated in subsequent generations and implies that God will hold these generations accountable, not arbitrarily or unfairly for their ancestors' sins, but for their solidarity with their ancestors. *'Awon* can be inherited, not in the form of legal guilt, but in the tendency to perpetuate parental behaviors. Jeremiah 36:31 makes this solidarity clear by referring to the cumulative *'awon* of King Jehoiakim, his offspring, and his servants, as does God's warning in Isa 65:6-7: "I will repay your *'awonot* and your ancestors' *'awonot* together."[15]

Interpreters often appeal to texts such as Jer 31:29-30 ("In those days it will no longer be said, 'The parents have eaten sour grapes, and the children's teeth are set on edge.' But all shall die for their own sins", cf. Ezek 18 and contrast Jer 32:18) to support the notion that an advanced state of Israelite religion recognized the inequity involved in primitive collectivism and rejected it. Such an approach, however, overlooks the rhetorical function of statements such as Jer 31:29-30 in the context of the discussion surrounding, in this case, the Babylonian crisis. Jeremiah 31 seems to respond to excuses such as Lam 5:7 ("Our fathers sinned and are no more, and we bear their iniquities"), in which the generation that experienced the exile attempts to displace responsibility for its fate onto its ancestors. Such statements imply a qualitative difference in the behaviors of parents and children: "We have not continued in our parents' footsteps." Yet the argument of the book of Jeremiah depends on precisely the opposite contention, namely, that the children have, indeed, perpetuated their parents' error: "They have returned to the *'awonot* of their ancestors" (Jer 11:10; cf. 7:26; 9:13; 16:11-12; 17:2; 19:4; 23:7; 34:13-18; 44:9-10, 21-23).[16] The objection that they are being unfairly punished is specious.

The subtleties and nuances of the problem of the afterlife of *'awon* as it affects subsequent generations undergoes exquisite analysis in Jesus' statement to the Pharisees regarding the transgenerational quality of systemic sin recorded in the Gospels of Matthew (23:29-36) and Luke (11:47-51). Probably one of a series of "woes" contained in the hypothetical Q source thought to be common to Matthew and Luke, Jesus' statement seizes on the ironic contrast between the Pharisees' participation in memorializing Israel's prophets, slain by previous generations of the religious leadership, and the Pharisees' own culpability in the treatment of God's spokespersons in their midst.[17] The Gospel writers develop the core of Q's version[18] of the woe in unique ways in keeping with their individual theological interests,[19] although they agree substantially with regard to the conclusion of Jesus' warning.

Luke's version, the shortest, depends on a very simple ironic juxtaposition to drive its logic. The Pharisees build memorials to prophets although their ances-

121

tors rejected and murdered them (11:47). Luke understands this behavior to be tantamount to agreement with the acts of the ancestral killers (11:48, literally, "you think well along with [συνευδοκεῖτε, *suneudokeite*] the works of your fathers"). Surely, however, one can memorialize heroes such as the prophets without thereby agreeing with the criminals. Those who maintain Holocaust memorials and observe Martin Luther King holidays do not thereby celebrate the deeds of murderers and assassins. How did Luke view the nature of the children's culpability in the parents' sins? Luke's conclusion, very closely paralleled in the Matthean version, describes this culpability as a reiteration. The flaw involved in the Pharisees' apparent respect for prophets of old, wrongly slain by Israel's disbelieving and disobedient leaders, involves the children's propensity to perpetuate parental behaviors. Regardless of the symbols of respect constructed for dead prophets, when the children face a new generation of God's living spokespersons, the children will reject God's representatives as surely as did their parents.

Matthew analyzes the phenomenon much more extensively. The Pharisees memorialize the prophets as they delude themselves with claims that they are nothing like their ancestors: "We would not have shared in the blood of the prophets" (23:30). This confession of theoretical innocence becomes self-condemnation (23:31-32) when exposed by the sending of new "prophets and wise ones and scribes" (23:34) whom the Pharisees will kill and persecute. In this way, the cycle of sin's afterlife will reach fruition. Children replicate their parents' behaviors, even after hypocritically and arrogantly denying the possibility of such systemic sin. Because, however, the children do so despite the warning of historical precedent and in relation, now, not only to prophets but also to *the* Prophet, the cycle will reach its climax. The entire history of guilt for "all the blood of the righteous [Matt 23:35]/the prophets [Luke 11:50]"—from Abel, the victim of the first murder, to Zechariah, the last such victim in the Old Testament canon[20]—will mature into consequences for "this generation" (Matt 23:36; Luke 11:51).[21]

Sin's Aftereffects and "Punishment"

The point at which the biblical view of the continued viability of sin through its aftereffects diverges most sharply from modern popular concepts of sin involves the idea of "punishment" for sin. Operating within the framework of the juridical understanding, popular Christian thought envisions punishment for sin as an event, discrete from sin itself, imposed on the sinner. The biblical viewpoint, on the other hand, views sin and its consequences in holistic, organic terms. In short, sin matures into "punishment" quite naturally.

Indeed, in the biblical view, agents, including God, who stand outside—or perhaps better, alongside—this deed/consequence nexus intervene in only three ways. On occasion, a human agent can function as a catalyst to speed the process of sin's maturation into consequences by bringing the sinner's '*awon* to light. Numbers 5:15, for example, employs the standard formulaic expression to describe the offering designed to "bring '*awon* to remembrance" in the case of the trial by ordeal of the wife accused by a jealous husband. In 1 Kgs 17:18, the widow of Zarephath attributes the role fulfilled by the sacrifice in Num 5 to the prophet Elijah when she expresses her fear that the prophet "[has] come to bring my '*awon* to remembrance." The operative expression, זכר עָוֺן (*zkr 'awon*, "to remember guilt"), points to the fact that, for the ancient Israelite, remembering was much more than a mental exercise. To remember something is to actualize it (cf. the German "vergegenwärtigen"). To remember '*awon* is to revitalize its force.[22] Remembering '*awon* is tantamount to activating the final stage in the process of its maturation (Isa 64:9; Jer 14:10; Ezek 21:28, 29 [23, 24 Eng.]; 29:16; Hos 8:13; 9:9; Pss 79:8; 109:14; cf. 2 Sam 19:19).[23]

God's role, as the Bible understands it, is not to impose punishment, but to sustain and enforce the moral order.[24] In a pregnant parallel expression, Hosea (8:13; 9:7, 9) announces that God will remember Israel's '*awon* and visit Israel's *ht'* on the people, equating actualization of guilt with the maturation of sin. Personified Lady Jerusalem speaks of the horrors she faces at the hands of the Babylonians as the organic consequence of her perverse political dalliances with foreign "lovers" (Lam 1:2-13). Indeed, she describes the situation she created for herself as though God has gathered her actions together, bound them into a yoke, and placed them on her neck (Lam 2:14). Isaiah 65:6-7 announces the intention to bring '*awon* to maturity in an expression that is difficult to render adequately in English. The RSV renders it " . . . I will repay into their bosom their iniquities and their fathers' iniquities." The verb שׁלם (*shlm*), translated "to repay," conveys the basic idea of "completion" and can take on the sense of "repayment" in the context of debts completed by being brought to an end. The usage in Isa 65:6-7 connotes the "completion" of the Judeans' sins by means of their return, now matured, to their authors. God does not intend to exact revenge, as the English term "repay" can suggest; instead, God intends to enforce the normal process by seeing Judah's '*awon* to maturity. An enigmatic expression repeated as a refrain in Amos's denunciations of the crimes of Israel, Judah, and their neighbors (Amos 1:3, 6, 9, 11, 13; 2:1, 4, 6) offers another example of the way in which English translations sometimes obscure the subtleties of the biblical concept of God's involvement in the course of sin's maturation. The RSV translates, "For three transgressions of Damascus [or Gaza, Tyre, etc.] and for four, I will not revoke the punishment." The Hebrew reads "I will not turn it back," with no clear antecedent to the pronoun. Against the background of ancient Israel's understanding of sin as a continuum, a plausible, even probable, understanding of the expression would relate it to the maturation process. Having set events into motion by three, and now four, egregious violations of the standards of common human decency, the nations to whom Amos addresses these denunciations must be prepared for God to allow matters to take their full course.

In the Old Testament, the notion that God punishes is not as common as the popular imagination has it. Most often, passages that English versions render with the verb "to punish" employ the formula פקד עָוֹן עַל, *pqd 'awon 'al* ("to visit guilt/consequences on [someone]"; see Exod 20:5; 34:7; Lev 18:25; Num 14:18; Deut 5:9; 2 Sam 3:8; Isa 13:11; 26:21; Jer 25:12; 36:3; Amos 3:2; Ps 89:32; Lam 4:22). Although translators persist in translating this phrase "to punish," it quite forcefully reflects ancient Israel's deed-consequence worldview. God does not "punish," God gathers the consequences of the guilty party's actions, the *'awon* loosed in the world, and brings it home. That is, God actively enforces the moral order God created. Sooner or later misdeeds bear fruit—sometimes God hastens the harvest, but God does not arbitrarily impose penalties.[25]

Josef Scharbert has pointed out, in fact, that in the Old Testament this understanding of sin's maturation is the predominant view expressed in the prophets and the deuteronomistic literature. Israel's historical sins (especially the golden calf and the long history of idolatry) represent an accumulating burden of guilt, to which every generation of Israel adds and which every generation must bear—until it reaches critical mass.[26] The New Testament, especially Paul, shares this understanding of sin as its own penalty. In Rom 1:18-32, Paul outlines the manner in which the wrath of God is being revealed in the course of human history.[27] Because human beings consistently "exchange the glory of the immortal God" for mere replicas of created beings, worshiping images only resembling the creation rather than the Creator, Paul says *three times* (vv. 24, 26, 28) that God "gives them up" or "hands them over" (παραδίδωμι, *paradidōmi*) to what they have chosen. In other words, in the course of the argument in this section Paul agrees with Amos in defining the "wrath of God" as God's decision to allow *'awon* to take its course. God's wrath is not arbitrary. To the contrary, it is supremely consistent with God's righteousness. "Guilt and punishment remain materially the same."[28] Elsewhere, Paul warns against deceiving oneself concerning the vitality of *'awon*: "Be not deceived . . . whatever you sow, you will also reap" (Gal 6:7). Jesus, too, affirms the material consonance of deed and consequence: "Those who live by the sword, die by the sword" (Matt 26:52).

Sin's Aftereffects Must Be Neutralized

The Bible's conviction that the afterlife of sin presents a real danger to individuals and to the community manifests itself in language describing the remedy and in cultic practices designed to deactivate it, such as the scapegoat that bears away the community's *'awon* (Lev 16:21; cf. the ritual to be enacted in cases of unsolvable homicides, Deut 21:1-9;[29] and the manner in which Aaron is to assume the *'awon* of the people, Exod 28:38). In common Christian parlance, the usual remedy for sin is God's forgiveness, understood as God's gracious disregard. Remarkably, in contrast, the Bible employs verbs denoting the act of forgiving in a definite minority of instances,[30] preferring instead verbs that describe methods for the removal of sin and the truncation of its afterlife. Even the semantics of the expression denoting the forgiveness of *'awon* (סלח לְעָוֹן, *slh la'awon*, "to forgive guilt," Exod 34:9; Num 14:19-20; Jer 31:34; 33:8 [parallels the expression "cleanse their guilt"]; 36:3;[31] Pss 25:11; 103:3[32]), which seems to contradict the precedent established by the other phrases describing means for dealing with *'awon*, remains unclear.[33] Originally, the verb seems to have denoted the act of sprinkling or pouring. Scholars hypothesize a cultic setting in which some "poured" or "sprinkled" offering was associated with atonement for sin such that the verb came to denote not the act of pouring but the intended result, "forgiveness." If this is indeed the case, the translation "to forgive" misses the background implication that *'awon* must be "washed" away in some fashion. To simply forgive it does nothing to remove it from the world.

Other expressions refer to "bearing [away]," "covering," "removing," and "washing away/cleansing from" *'awon*. Perhaps the most common image of the way in which *'awon* may be deactivated involves the expression נשׂא עָוֹן (*ns' 'awon*, "to bear guilt/consequences"). The imagery is important for an appreciation of the Hebrew Bible's viewpoint. R. Knierim [34] argues against the common practice of translating this expression contextually and thereby obscuring the imagery. Most egregiously, many translations render the expression "to forgive sin" in some contexts involving God's intervention, entirely obliterating the fact that the Bible uses but one phrase to describe bearing responsibility for one's sins and having that responsibility borne by another. In fact, someone *must* bear *'awon* once it has been unleashed!

In terms of the identity of the guilt-bearer, usages of this phrase fall into three categories: (1) one can bear one's own guilt/consequences, that is, one can allow them to go unremedied until they mature (Gen 4:13; Exod 28:43; Lev 5:1, 17; 7:11; 17:16; 19:8; 20:17, 19; 22:16 [|| *'shmh*]; Num 5:31; 14:34; 18:1, 23; Ezek 14:10; 44:10, 12[35]); (2) guilt/consequences can be shifted onto another person, animal, or even object (Exod 28:38; Lev 10:15; 16:22; 18:25; Num 18:1; Ezek 4:4, 5, 6; 18:19, 20); or (3) God can bear the consequences (Exod 34:7 [*'awon* parallels *psh'* and *ht'h*];[36] Num 14:18 [|| *psh'*], 19; Isa 33:24; Hos 14:3 [2 Eng.]; Mic 7:18-19; Pss 32:5; 85:3 [2 Eng.]; Job 7:21). The notion that God can and does "bear the guilt/consequences" of the guilty is much more powerful theologically than the notion that God "forgives (= disregards) sin." The latter focuses on the commission of sin, the former on the afterlife of the act. The former acknowledges that the results of a misdeed must be addressed; the latter implies that a change in attitude on God's part suffices.

Old Testament priestly and cultic contexts frequently portray the "covering" of sin (כפר עָוֹן, *kpr 'awon*, "to cover guilt/consequences"—1 Sam 3:14; Isa 22:14; 27:9 [|| חטאה hitph, נו, נשׂא hiph. *ht't*, "to remove sin"]; Jer 18:23 [|| *ht'h*]; Ps 78:38; Prov 16:6; Dan 9:24; cf. Job 14:17, טפל, *tfl*, "to smear or cover over [as with plaster]"; כסה, *ksh*, "to cover"—Neh 3:37 [4:5 Eng.]; כפר חטאה, *kpr ht'h*— Exod 32:30; Lev 4:26, 35; 5:6, 10, 13; 16:16 [|| *psh'*], 30, 34; 19.22 [|| *'shm*]; Ps 79:9; 2 Chr 29:24; כפר אשם, *kpr 'shm*— Lev 5:16; 19:22; cf. Ps 32:1). Similarly, sin can be "removed" (עָוֺן עבר hiph. *'br* hiph. *'awon*, "to remove guilt/consequences"—2 Sam 24:10 ‖ 1 Chr 21:8; Zech 3:4; Job 7:21; חטאת hiph. עבר *'br* hiph. *ht't*—2 Sam 12:13; עָוֺן hiph. מוּשׁ, *mush* hiph. *'awon*, "to remove"—Zech 3:9). The image of washing away appears commonly in association with *'awon*: כבס עָוֺן, *kbs 'awon*, "washing away guilt/consequences" (Ps 51:4 [2 Eng.]; cf. Jer 2:22; 4:14; Ps 51:9 [7 Eng.]);[37] חמעון piel נקה *nqh* piel *me'awon*, "to make clean from guilt/consequences" (Job 10:14; cf. Ps 19:13 [12 Eng.]);[38] טהר עֲוֺנוֹת, *thr 'awonot*, "cleansing away guilt/consequences" (Lev 16:30; Ezek 33:8; 36:33; Prov 20:9; cf. Num 8:7). Clearly, in the Old Testament view, once loosed in the world, *'awon* must either come to fruition or be disabled in some fashion.

Obviously, the Old Testament employs this language somewhat metaphorically, and the New Testament does so to an even greater degree, as attested by the restricted range of the vocabulary and the distancing of the language from its figurative roots. The ancient Israelites certainly did not think that one could literally wash sin away as though it were physical matter, dirt. Nonetheless, the authors of neither Testament viewed sin and its consequences in purely accounting terms either, as evidenced, for example, by the close association between forgiveness and healing in Jesus' ministry. Like the Old Testament, the New Testament views sin as more than a mark against one's name in the heavenly ledger. It is not enough merely to erase the mark in the ledger. The reality of sin requires that it be deactivated. In fact, the New Testament contends that, in order to neutralize sin and its effects, it was necessary for Jesus to die.

The New Testament commonly employs a verb, often translated "to forgive," that connotes the idea of the removal of sin, although New Testament usage seems somewhat static. That is, New Testament usage of this verb does not evoke any clear image, as do its Old Testament equivalents. Employed in the LXX as an equivalent for *ns'* ("to take away, bear"), *slh* ("to forgive"), and *kpr* ("to cover/atone") with God as the subject and sin as the object, the Greek verb ἀφίημι (*aphiēmi*), "to send away, send forth, put away," acquired a legal use in *koine* Greek.[39] The New Testament employs the verb twenty-eight times with sin, transgression, lawlessness, and so forth as the object and roughly an additional sixteen times without an object. The related nouns ἄφεσις, *aphesis* (fifteen times) and πάρεσις, *paresis* (once), both meaning "forgiveness," usually take the genitive object "sin." Imagery and language used in parallel with the New Testament idea of forgiveness, on the other hand, enrich the metaphor. Sin can be forgiven because Jesus' blood covers it (Matt 26:28; Heb 9:22; cf. Rom 4:7). Forgiveness follows repentance (Acts 5:31; Luke 24:47) and is closely associated with the washing of baptism (Mark 1:4 and parallels; Acts 2:38); consequently, it takes the forms of cleansing (1 John 1:9; 2:12) and redemption (Col 1:14; Eph 1:7).

Moreover, the New Testament also speaks of "covering" sin (καλύπτειν πλῆθος ἁμαρτιῶν, *kaluptein plēthos hamartiōn*—Jas 5:20;

1 Pet 4:8, proverbially;[40] ἐπικαλύπτειν—Rom 4:7) or of "redeeming" from sin by using a verbal root associated in the LXX with the Hebrew root כפר (*kpr*) "to cover/atone" (λυτρόειν, *lutroein*, "to redeem"—Titus 2:14). That is, the redemption idea in the New Testament involves more than merely canceling a debt.[41] Against the background of baptism,[42] the New Testament speaks of "washing away" sins (ἀπολούειν, *apolouein*, "to wash away"—Acts 22:16; 1 Cor 6:11; λουτρόν, *loutron*, "washing"—Eph 5:26; Titus 3:5; καθαρίζειν, *katharizein*, "to cleanse"—Acts 15:9; 1 John 1:7, 9; Heb 9:14, 22, 23; καθαρισμός, *katharismos*, "cleansing"—2 Pet 1:9; Heb 1:3; ἐκκαθαίρειν, *ekkathairein*, "to clean out," in reference to the corrupting influence of the sin/sinner tolerated in the Corinthian church—1 Cor 5:7). The key observation to be made regarding the remedy for sin as understood in both Testaments concerns the fact that the Bible views sin and its aftereffects as a matter that requires a remedy more effectual than God's willingness to overlook it: sin must somehow be removed, neutralized.

To the Extent Possible

The Bible is also clear, however, that sometimes no measure can completely terminate the afterlife of sin. Here the Bible reflects a stubborn truth discernible in everyday experience. Sometimes the consequences of an act of wrongdoing are irreversible. This assertion—that some sin cannot be prevented from continuing to shape reality—may seem trivial. Still, contemporary Christians may need to be reminded that God did not create an Alice-in-Wonderland world. While it is true, as preachers love to preach, that God is eager to forgive and to heal, it is also true that God does not regularly alter the physical and moral principles that give the world its structure. Sincerely to repent of one's decision seconds after jumping from a bridge does not prompt God to reverse the effects of gravity. Sincerely to repent of one's actions after drunkenly driving into an oncoming van occupied by a family of four does not prompt God to annul the laws of inertia. Sincerely to repent of years of neglecting and abusing one's children does not automatically heal the emotional scars that diminish the quality of the children's lives.

In individual terms, this means that one must sometimes live with the real-world consequences of sin even after repentance and forgiveness. The author of Hebrews encourages readers of the book to beware the defiling consequences of bitterness and contention for the community (Heb 12:12-17), appealing to the fate of Esau as an illustration of the irreversible consequences of some actions. Esau was both perpetrator and victim. He so undervalued his birthright as to exchange it for a single meal. Esau's brother Jacob, being the "supplanter" that he was, and having made the very profitable exchange, would not rescind the agreement; in fact, the Bible records no overture on Esau's part. "Bitterly as Esau regretted his hasty action, he was denied any chance of having its consequences reversed by a subsequent μετάνοια [*metanoia*, lit. 'change of mind' and thence 'repentance']."[43] Subsequently, Esau's folly was only compounded by Jacob's greed and Isaac's naiveté in the theft of Esau's blessing. Now clearly a victim, Esau could not reverse the chain of events that he had helped to set into motion by his disdain for his birthright or prevail on his father to invalidate the blessing already given Jacob. What was done, was done: " . . . though he wept loudly and bitterly there was no way of retrieving the situation. His father could not and would not call back the blessing pronounced on Jacob."[44]

Modernity's hyper-individualism and artificial discrimination between an act and its aftereffects misses the real power of sin to twist persons and situations. As A. McFadyen observes:

> . . . the autonomous core of the individual subject is assumed to remain untouched and unaffected by the concrete history of its own action, just as the person is supposedly unaffected by external influences in any significant way. Freedom as a formal capacity for unconstrained choice has no preconditions but itself. . . . Neither anything in the social, nor in one's own personal, inheritance effects a distortion of one's inner, personal core of freedom. That inner, personal core always stands in an external relationship to both one's own history of action and to social and other realities external to the self. So, one's acts have no significant after-life in relation to one's freedom. There is no accretion of the consequences of action which might diminish the freedom constitutive of one's status as an autonomous subject. One returns to neutral, so to speak, after each action. Each and every act is consequently the free act of the autonomous subject, isolated from and purified of any personal, social or material influence.
>
> [In contrast,] the history of sinning may be described as a kind of decision about the self; or, better, as a life in which the self is decided and through which freedom not to sin is progressively lost. Here freely chosen acts gradually bind the self in an orientation on sin which can no longer adequately be spoken of in purely axiological terms. For sin pertains now not just to the bad acts performed by the free self, but to the enduring structure of decision-making, of selfhood. . . . This is an internal, *self*-binding in sin, not the impersonal inheritance and transmission of an external distortion, bondage and guilt. It is decisive, self-involving life-in-act.[45]

In terms of families, communities, even humanity as a whole, the inevitable maturation of some sin means that sin is endemic to the system because no one, other than the first pair, has been or will be born into a pristine situation free from the distortions of sin's aftereffects. Sin, as a continuum, twists reality and passes on this contorted system as an antecedent reality to those who come after, limiting their freedom to perceive reality properly and, thus, also their freedom to choose rightly. Sin as aftereffect both precedes one and proceeds from one. Understood in this way, the notion of sin's maturation holds rich implications for the Pauline doctrine of "original sin" and the Old Testament notion of "inherited sin," which turn out to be different ways of speaking about the same phenomenon. If, once loosed, *'awon* lives on and is not neutralized, one's sin can ripple throughout society far beyond one's own life and long after one has gone.

From this perspective, a major component of society's ills can be characterized as the accumulated *'awon* of the generations. Until this *'awon* is addressed, society will continue to suffer from "original sin." It may be most fruitful to speak of sin, in this regard, as a system preceding any individual and compounded by individual actions.

Furthermore, the tension inherent in the traditional version of the doctrine of original sin between the notion that all human beings subsequent to Adam are born into sin and the requirement of modern Western thought that responsibility and guilt can only apply to free agents[46] can be resolved by revisioning the doctrine in relation to the concept of sin's perverting effect on reality. After the first human beings sinned, twisting their relationships with God, one another, and the rest of creation, no subsequent human being found the existential possibility of complete freedom to act in accordance with God's will. The first sin had already perverted the options.[47]

Beginning with the observation that often Judaism is thought not to share with Christianity a doctrine of original sin, Kepnes points to Exod 34:7 ("visiting the *'awon* of the parents on the children"), Gen 4:7 ("sin crouches at the door"), and Gen 8:21 ("the plans of the human heart are evil from youth") and argues that "Judaism also has a Hebrew term [*galut*, "exile"] that, like 'original sin,' is suggestive of a state or condition that limits the human ability to be in free contact with God." In Kepnes's view, "the concept of exile," understood comprehensively in reference to expulsion from Eden, alienation from the land, Babylonian captivity, or any other such condition of separation from home, "has affinities with original sin because both are states or conditions that affect the whole person, the human community, and the world, and because both require divine help to be rectified."[48]

M. Volf helpfully extends Kepnes's exile metaphor, noting "that sin is not simply a condition that human beings suffer passively. Affected by it, they act, and by acting they make their own small or large contributions to keeping themselves and others in exile. Sin is a corporate condition we inherit ('original sin'), and sin is an act we personally commit ('actual sin'); the one makes the other worse, and both shape human identities."[49]

Paul chooses yet another metaphor, but one that is still consistent with the Hebrew worldview. Paul describes existence in this contorted system that twists perception and limits choice as bondage to sin. Once introduced into the world, sin ruled in death (Rom 5:12-21). Ubiquitous and antecedent to every human existence save that of the first pair, sin distorts the system so as, in effect, to enslave every individual human being (Rom 6:20-23) save one, Jesus Christ. Indeed, one's perceptions and judgment are so distorted and twisted by this prevenient sin, one's choices so limited by the constraints of a perverse system, that one cannot choose freely. As Paul put it, "I do not understand my own actions. For I do not do what I want, but I do the very thing I hate" (Rom 7:15). There can be little wonder that the whole of creation groans under the weight of the system of sin, longing for the redemption of humanity that will set the world free (Rom 8:19-23). Furthermore, for Paul, "the Christian stands in the tension of a double reality."[50] That is, the Christian, although forgiven, continues to live in a world twisted and contorted by sin ("Let not sin reign in your mortal bodies," Rom 6:12). Sin's afterlife vibrates throughout the system such that, so long as the world awaits the coming of the kingdom of God, sin will continue to twist existence and limit freedom.[51]

Two Biblical Case Studies of the Dynamics of Sin and Systems

Nowhere does the Bible spell out in doctrinal fashion the dynamics of sin as an organic system of wrongdoing and its afterlife. The Bible does offer, however, several accounts portraying the dynamics of the sin continuum in narrative fashion. These accounts offer views of family and society that appear remarkably contemporary in terms of social science's analysis of dysfunctional systems twisted by sin and its continued effects. In these biblical accounts, one sees sinners whose actions reverberate beyond their own lives to twist the reality in which others must act. One sees how sin closes doors on choices that could have been made, diminishing the freedom to choose wisely and well. One sees sin lingering in the world, distorting perceptions, offering inauthentic possibilities, skewing the system, perpetuating itself. One sees the material identity of sin and "punishment." One sees that forgiveness granted the first sinner in the chain of causation is sometimes, sadly, unable to interrupt the sequence if the seeds sown in the environment have already taken root in the lives of others.

David and Bathsheba: David's Sons Follow in His Footsteps

Perhaps the clearest of these narratives, the story of the aftermath of David's adultery with Bathsheba, illustrates every aspect of the continuum model of sin outlined above. The key passage in the account records the confrontation between the prophet Nathan and David (2 Sam 12:7-15) after David has concealed, at first blush successfully, his adultery with Bathsheba by murdering her husband, Uriah (2 Sam 11:14-15), and after the son produced by David's illicit union with Bathsheba has been born (2 Sam 11:26-27). Nathan indicts David and outlines the consequences—initially two, later to be joined by a third—that will result from David's actions. Very significantly, these consequences relate organically to David's sin (i.e., sin is its own punishment): David's violence will give birth to violence ("the sword shall never depart from your house," 2 Sam 12:9-10), David's sexual predation will be replicated "from within [his] own house" (2 Sam 12:11), and the child born to David and Bathsheba will die (2 Sam 12:14).

Notably, although Nathan, speaking on God's behalf, attributes to God a degree of agency in the second consequence ("I will raise up trouble against you," 2 Sam 12:11), the unfolding of this consequence in the subsequent account of the rest of David's life and career takes a seemingly very natural course.[52] In fact, Nathan's predictions of the continuation of violence in David's household and of the death of Bathsheba's son are couched in passive verbs attributing no direct agency: these events will simply happen in and of themselves. Except for the death of Bathsheba's son,[53] the account does not relate that God intervenes actively to bring about any of the consequences of David's sin; that is, God's role seems to be to maintain and reinforce the organic maturation of David's behavior. David's sin—sown and matured into fruit—is David's punishment.

Remarkably, although Nathan responds to David's confession of sin and his implied repentance with an assurance of forgiveness, he does not rescind the predictions concerning violence and sexual predation. In fact, Nathan announces the impending death of Bathsheba's son only *after* David confesses and receives assurance of forgiveness. In the context of this discussion of sin as a continuum embracing sin's afterlife, the wording of Nathan's statement offers a tantalizing clue: Nathan assures David that his wrongdoing, *ht'*, has been "taken away" (*'br* hiph.) so that David himself will not die, but he says nothing of the consequences, the *'awon*, of David's sin (cf. Ps 32:5; Jer 33:8). David has loosed something in the world that God will not or cannot call back.[54] Sin has taken on its own life, and forgiveness cannot reverse its course in the world.

And how are these consequences realized? In the lives, actions, and deaths of David's sons. The infant son dies. David's eldest son, Amnon, follows his father's example, replicating David's sexual predation in the rape of Tamar (2 Sam 13:1-19). David's sin has become the antecedent condition of Amnon's actions, twisting his perceptions of reality, distorting his interpersonal relationships, and robbing David of moral legitimacy as example and guide for his children. David, morally bankrupt (Could he hold his beloved first-born to a standard higher than he followed himself? Would he expect Amnon not to do as his father had done? Could the father who murdered and escaped direct accountability hold the rapist son accountable?), takes no action against Amnon. Absalom, Tamar's full-brother, bitter at the injustice, bides his time, exacts vengeance, and flees David's kingdom (now two sons are dead, the second at the hands of his brother). Confronted with his complicity in Amnon's death,[55] David agrees to permit Absalom to return home, only to discover that Absalom's bitterness at David's compromised position on matters of justice has not subsided (2 Sam 15:3-6). Absalom rebels, seizes Jerusalem, takes possession of David's harem, and dies at Joab's hands (the third son dead, the second by violence). Adonijah's rebellion—again involving desire for a woman—and ultimate execution brings the cycle to its end (the fourth son dead, the third by violence, and the second by his own brother's hand).

Manasseh, Jeremiah, and the Babylonians

On the societal level, portions of the Hebrew Bible grapple with the ramifications of the afterlife of sin in a context that parallels in some ways the international terrorism crisis facing the contemporary West. The book of Jeremiah, for example, contains materials dating to the final period leading up to Babylon's conquest of Judah and the series of deportations of Jews and represents, in its final form, a document composed and edited in the period following the crisis. Thus, it offers a highly reflective consideration of events from a theological perspective. On its face, Jeremiah forwards a very straightforward argument such as one would expect from a Hebrew prophet: Roughly the first half of the book announces that the Judeans, especially their leadership, are apostate and, unless they truly repent, God will send the Babylonians to execute just punishment. The latter half recounts the consequences of the Judeans' failure to heed Jeremiah's message, up to and including the destruction of Jerusalem and the so-called "great deportation" of thousands of the Judean upper crust into Babylonian exile.

This straight-line surface reading of Jeremiah obscures, however, the complexity and intricacy of the dynamics of sin and repentance *experienced* by the editors of the book and reflected in the many strands of discussion incorporated into the book.[56] Any brief treatment of this complexity runs the danger of oversimplifying, of course. Nonetheless, the discussion can be serviceably characterized in terms of three driving themes/issues associated in the book with key figures: (1) Despite the prophet Jeremiah's call to repentance, Judah's sin had accumulated to such critical mass that even repentance may have been unable to dampen the momentum of unfolding events (King Manasseh of Judah). (2) In the face of national sin and its international consequences, the repentance and righteousness of individuals is ineffective in sparing righteous individuals the common fate (Jeremiah himself and his friend and collaborator, Baruch). (3) God may and does commission human agents—both individuals and nations—to act in history on God's behalf, but God does not control these agents; in other words, God's human agents retain free will—witness the Babylonians.

Manasseh and Critical Mass.[57] As the book records it, at least early in his public preaching prior to the destruction of Jerusalem, Jeremiah offered Judeans the clear-cut alternative between continued apostasy and its consequences or repentance and forgiveness (see esp. Jer 18:1-11; cf. 4:1-2; 7:1-15; 26:1-6; etc.). In "private" discourse with God (Jer 7:16–8:3; 11:14-17; 16:1-9)[58] and in a few public sermons (Jer 11:1-13, for example) and explications of symbolic acts (Jer 19:1-15), however, Jeremiah hears from God, and sometimes passes the message along, that the die has already been cast. Jeremiah was to preach a message of repentance, but God already knew that the people would not listen (Jer 7:27); Jeremiah should not bother to pray for the people (Jer 7:16-20; 11:14-17; 14:11-12) or mourn them (Jer 16:1-4). It is too late. Judah's history of sin had accumulated to such a degree, as manifest especially by the atrocities of King Manasseh in the generation just before Jeremiah (Jer 15:1-4; cf. 2 Kgs 21:1-18; 24:2-4), that the course of events was set.[59] Judah's massive *'awon* had reached maturity.

Righteous Innocents: Jeremiah and Baruch. One of the more puzzling features of the book of Jeremiah for interpreters involves a series of texts in the book in which the people or some subset thereof seem, in fact, to respond positively to Jeremiah's call for repentance (Jer 3:22b-25; 14:1-9, 19-22)—albeit to no avail. Interpreters typically explain the discrepancy between God's offer of the possibility of repentance and the people's fruitless response by suggesting that the people's repentance is insincere or that Jeremiah (or the editors of the book) put these (in this view only hypothetical) confessions on the lips of the people. Surely God would not fail to respond to sincere, actual confessions of sin! Jeremiah's own so-called "confessions" (Jer 11:18-20; 12:1-6; etc.) and an isolated complaint voiced by Jeremiah's scribe, Baruch (Jer 45), point to another possibility. The complaints of both Jeremiah and Baruch focus on the injustice of their individual fates. Although they have been God's faithful servants, they have been misunderstood, persecuted, and, in the end, they will suffer along with the sinners in Judah's downfall. As Baruch puts it, "Woe is me! YHWH has compounded my pain with sorrow; I am weary from groaning; I find no rest" (45:3). God's response to Baruch is telling: "I am about to break down what I have built, and pluck up what I have planted—namely, the whole land. But you, you seek great things for yourself? Do not seek them; for I am about to bring ruin on all flesh . . . but I will give you your life as plunder of war. . . . " (45:4-5). Such is the nature of societal *'awon*: societal in scale, it transcends individual justice. The Babylonian invaders will not distinguish between the apostate and the righteous. Surely Jeremiah and Baruch were not the only righteous individuals in Judah, but events were too far progressed. In an ironic inversion of the circumstances associated with the destruction of Sodom and Gomorrah, national sin has reached such proportions that the righteousness or repentance of a few can have no impact (contrast Gen 18:17-33).

The Babylonians: Out of God's Control? Does this mean that God *would not* forgive or that God *could not* counteract the power of Judah's *'awon*, so massive had it become? This question revolves around the role of the Babylonians as God's agents. While God commissioned, as it were, the Babylonians and their king, Nebuchadnezzar, whom God even famously called "my servant" (Jer 25:9), the Babylonians were unaware of, or unwilling to acknowledge, that role *per se*. From their perspective, they were acting freely, of their own choosing. Moreover, as texts clearly dating from immediately after the crisis indicate, God accused them of exceeding their mandate: "I will repay Babylon . . . for all the wrong done in Zion."[60] The conclusion to be drawn from this simple observation with respect to the question of God's ability to cut off the afterlife of Judah's sin focuses on the contingency inherent in a system involving multiple agents, each with some degree of freedom. The prophets, including Jeremiah, argued that Judah's apostasy from God had an international component. Judah had become entangled in international power politics. Their actions impinged upon the Babylonians. God, so said the prophet, allowed the relationship between Judah and Babylon to take its course. Neither Judah, a free agent, nor Babylon, a free agent, acted fully in accordance with God's preferences. Because *'awon* loose in the world twists entire systems, clean and clear-cut or fair and balanced outcomes may be beyond possibility.

Sin and Systems: Implications for Ministry

According to the biblical view (and common experience), sin is nondiscrete. An act of sin sends shock waves throughout the sinner's environment. Sin's afterlife continues to impact the sinner and others in the sinner's proximity, sometimes well after the original act. In this sense, sin twists and perverts the system in which it exists, causing injury both to the sinner and to the innocent and setting preconditions that limit the capacity to see clearly and to act rightly, preconditions that prejudice choices toward the perpetuation of sin, contaminating family systems, communities, and whole societies. The gospel message cannot fail to offer hope for counteracting—for taking away—"the sin of the world." In particular and practical ways, this understanding of sin as systemic suggests that the church's ministry to individuals and groups caught up in structures of reverberating sin must be prepared to address at least three typical circumstances: the residual impact of sin in the life of the forgiven sinner, the suffering of innocent parties victimized by systemic sin, and the perverting effect of antecedent sin.

Sin and Forgiveness in a World of Consequences

The story is told of a teenage boy who despised the neighboring farmer. As a youthful prank, he sowed the neighboring fields with johnsongrass—a particularly hardy and virulent weed common in the southeastern U.S. As fate would have it, he grew up to fall in love with and marry the despised neighbor's daughter, *and* to spend the rest of his adult life battling the johnsongrass in what were first his father-in-law's and, later, his own fields. It is a harsh reality of life that one reaps what one sows. Furthermore, changes of heart, repentance, and forgiveness are often simply incapable of altering the realities established by one's sin. God surely forgives, but God does not *yet* restore the original conditions unmarred by sin. Sin changes things that cannot be changed back—at least not on this earth.

Ministers confront ignorance and denial of this almost self-evident truth in many situations. Counselees despair of God's grace and power because their acts of repentance and contrition do not cancel the consequences of their sin. "I have sincerely asked God to forgive me for my substance abuse and to heal me, but I still suffer from cirrhosis, my son has started to drink heavily, and I cannot get a good job. Why is God punishing me?" In these situations, the gospel offers assurance that God has forgiven along with the promise of strength and courage to deal with sin's continued effects. Parishioners of all ages and walks of life, but especially the young, come to presume upon the promise of God's willingness to forgive and risk behaviors that can drastically alter the courses of their lives. "It's only sex. God will forgive me." Here, the gospel warns that even forgiven sin damages lives and calls believers to holiness.

Systemic Sin and Innocent Suffering

Collective sin manifests itself in perverted systems. Hierarchies that differentiate between groups of people according to some presumed degree of value (slavery, subjugation of women, devaluation of children, racism, classism) are perverted systems that have incorporated oppression and injury into the very structures of society. Western capitalism, based on self-interest (greed) that opposes the gospel's call for self-sacrifice and the assumption of scarcity that denies the gospel's promise of blessing, and so well established that Western Christians often find it difficult to imagine any other economic structure, depends on exploitation for profit to fuel its machinery. Cheap sneakers from Wal-mart require sweatshops in Indonesia; the global economy is so inextricably and intricately intermeshed that one hardly knows whether pulling a particular string will remedy a flaw or unravel the whole fabric. Nonetheless, Jesus' clarion call to "seek first the kingdom of God" resounds.

Antecedent Sin and Original Sin

Individuals learn to sin before they know what sin is. No one is born into a pristine, sinless setting. A white baby boy born in the South in the late 1950s learned racial prejudice before he was mature enough to competently assess its morality. Antecedent sin twisted his vision. To be sure, he reached a point at which his background and upbringing could not be an excuse for holding on to racial prejudice. Environment is not destiny; but environment can be a handicap, a predisposing factor. A firstborn girl in an alcoholic family learned that her worth depended on keeping others, if not happy, at least free from annoyance. Hers was the responsibility to see that daddy had no reason to be upset. She accepted his abuse to protect her little brothers. Later, she even protected her mother from her father's drunken temper. Later still, she married an abusive husband and began to drink herself.

C. Gestrich has observed that contemporary society suffers from its failure to recognize the continuum between sin and consequences evidenced in the competition between theological and psychoanalytical interpretations of the human condition.

> *Therefore, the churches are not doing everything that should be done about sin and guilt by struggling against "structural sins," against "evil that has become objectified in society."*

> Of course, the *one thing* that should certainly be expected in this regard is the solidarity of Christian churches with the oppressed. But the *other thing* that should certainly be expected from Christian churches is that they view and address *all* people, even the oppressed, as subjects and perpetrators of their sins . . . If they abandon the latter task they have ceased being Christian churches.[61]

The idea of "the bondage of sin" must mean, among other things, that the sin of the world is already standing there to greet each and every human being who comes to full moral consciousness. By that moment, each and every human being has already been shaped and predisposed by systemic sin. To perpetuate this sin is easy, and almost normal, but it is not necessary. To leave it uncontested is to reject Christ's commission to the ministry of reconciliation.

In Conclusion: Three Case Studies Revisited

In the final analysis, then, this investigation maintains that sin cannot be reduced to a single, simple concept. Instead, the term "sin" refers to a system of organically related phenomena, a nexus of cause-effect-cause. Fundamental lack of trust manifests itself as compensatory arrogance or despondent passivity—or, paradoxically, as both at once. Nor can sin be reduced to a discrete event; instead, a perverted environment precedes any individual's act, limiting the individual's absolute freedom, distorting the individual's view of reality, replicating itself in the limited, distorted choices individuals make. Once committed, the act changes reality itself, perverting conditions, harming relationships, injuring victims, and twisting and distorting options for future action. Unaddressed, these injuries and perversions fester, creating the conditions that further limit and poison the environment in which subsequent decisions must be made and actions taken. Analysis can isolate no single element of this nexus as *the* moment of sin. All are present in any sinful act. Salvation must address the whole; the church's ministry of healing and reconciliation must address the spectrum of sin.

The irreducibility of the sin system accounts for the inadequacy of traditional definitions of sin as a diagnostic tool for ministry in real-life situations. As the case studies discussed in the introductory chapter indicate,[62] an appreciation of sin as a system opens a broad vista on the human condition. A moralist considering the case of the unwed teenage mother will likely focus on her violation of sexual mores, although, viewed organically, her sexual behavior represents only the fruition of the system of sin comprising the environment that has failed to nurture her and her resulting immature ego. Her mother's choices have created a situation that has damaged her. She has grown to adolescence in a home that has taught her that father figures come and go, that the adults in her life cannot be trusted to make her appropriate needs a priority, that women must devote significant energies to keeping or attracting a man, and that all love is conditional and must be earned. In short, she has enjoyed precious little opportunity to learn the basic trust fundamental to maturation as a fully human person. Similarly, the factory owner reacts primarily out of fear and the drive for self-preservation. Whatever his background, he seems unable to exercise the trust—in God, in himself, in other human beings—that enables one to act on the decision to do what is right and good; instead, he thinks and acts out of fear of shortage, on the conviction that he must protect himself even at the cost of others' well-being, with no confidence in the trustworthiness of God and God's moral order.

In the teenage mother's life, this stunted capacity for trust has manifested itself primarily not in rebellion against God's law or God's authority—although her behavior results effectively in such rebellion—but in acceptance of the lie of her unworthiness, in believing that she must earn affirmation, "love," from any available source. She is an incompetent truster. She trusts the untrustworthy and fails to trust in God and in the power of the image of God stamped on her own life. Not surprisingly, she has sought affirmation in unwise sexual relations with a dangerous, unreliable young man, replicating her mother's behavior. What other model does she have? She has no deep sense of her own value as a young woman created in the image of God, gifted with the capacity to *become* fully human, to find purpose, to realize her innate skills and talents, to relate to others out of a sense of potential instead of a desperate hunger. She acted out, then, not to rebel against a rule, but in a desperate attempt to be valued. The lie of unworthiness affected the mother of the son with the birth defect in a very similar fashion. At one point in her life, she had acted out against a fundamentalist religious upbringing that must have been repressive with its core negative message of her innate sinfulness and unworthiness. If one accepts the notion that, from the outset of one's life, one is essentially unworthy, incapable of authenticity and goodness, one has taken the first step toward living a life that demonstrates the shameful truth of the notion.

In any case, for both mothers, the act has been committed. Now the weight of the matter lies on the immediate and long-term futures of their children—indisputably, the absolutely innocent victims of their mothers' choices. The situation of the mother of the son damaged *in utero* by her substance abuse clearly attests to the objective reality of sin's effect, to the tragic component of sin. Her son will likely never overcome the severe disadvantage he faces as the result of his mother's unwise behavior. Regardless of the fact that his mother had no such intention, he is permanently damaged. Sin does that to people sometimes. Her only responsible course of action, her only possibility for redressing the wrong she has created, albeit unwittingly, will be to care faithfully for her son as best she can or to provide for his care in the event his needs surpass her abilities and resources. In either case, the boy deserves to be treated as one created in God's image. Even though the potential for the full realization of this image is severely restricted in his case, it merits mention that this potential is stunted to some degree and in some manner in every human life. Sin has done that to people.

The situations of the teenage mother-to-be and of the businessman constitute circumstances in which the sins of the principal actors threaten to assume tragic proportions if left unaddressed; that is, their sins threaten to replicate themselves in the lives of a succeeding generation. Unless the teenage mother can mature into the trusting, self-aware, competent young woman inherent potentially in her nature as a person created in the image of God, she will likely perpetuate the choices and behaviors her mother modeled for her. The cycle will continue for yet another generation, and likely for generations to come. Until the factory operator can come to see the conditions in which his employees work and live— and rear their children—as the environment that dictates to a great degree his employees' choices and behaviors, he will likely continue to support a system that deprives children of opportunities for education, stability, good nutrition, and safety. Ironically, his actions will teach the children of his workers to fear that the system is stacked against those who do not fight to protect themselves, that they cannot trust, that they are unworthy. The cycle will continue.

If this analysis of sin in these cases accurately outlines its full scope and true nature, the tasks of the church's ministry of reconciliation and healing take on specific features that can be clustered around two themes: (1) the proclamation and cultivation of trust—generally and particularly in God and God's order—as an essential for human maturation, and (2) the redress of the afterlife of sin manifest in the perversion of the environment of the sinner. The church must be concerned with the circumstances of any child and all children, for example, who are growing to maturity in conditions that hinder and frustrate the human need to trust one's family unit, the world, and the world's Creator. The church must find every responsible opportunity to incarnate trustworthiness. It must raise its voice on behalf of any who face an environment of neglect and hostility not of their own making. It must model God's reliable and aggressive concern.

The traditional form of the gospel message stressing human rebellion and unworthiness not only fails to correspond to the dynamics of sin in these situations, but it also risks increasing the danger that its hearer will slip into despondency, passivity, and sloth. The gospel message is less about the fact that human beings *cannot* earn worth in God's eyes because they are inherently unworthy and more about the fact that human beings *need not* earn God's regard because God has already given it as a gift. Human beings need not grasp after a godlikeness beyond their reach because God has created humanity with a potential for a godlikeness that is humanity's destiny. The ministry of reconciliation must involve, among other things, the reassurance that God has created all humanity in God's image and the offer of assistance in growing into the mature image of God modeled and enabled by Jesus Christ.

Furthermore, the ministry of healing inherent in the Good News of Jesus

Christ calls the church to confront the reality of sin's afterlife in the lives of individuals and in the world. The church must not overlook restitution, healing, and remediation—in short, the priestly tasks—in its efforts to fulfill its purpose. Otherwise, real injuries continue to fester, real distortions of family and communal life continue to pervert relationships, real economic and social injustices continue to restrict and constrain the opportunities of those trapped in the system. Victims become sinners because they facilely accept the system as the only reality. The church cannot allow itself to become complicit in the sin of the world by passively permitting its self-replication.

Notes

Introduction

1. Kevin O'Shea ("The Reality of Sin: A Theological and Pastoral Critique," *Theological Studies* 29 [1968]: 241-43) objects that the common view of sin is "insufficiently realistic, insufficiently historical, and insufficiently communitarian to convey the insights of the biblical revelation on sin." O'Shea refers to the biblical emphasis, not on the individual act, but on the covenant context of human existence, humanity's relationship with God. From this perspective, the common view is too atomistic. The common view is also reductionist and isolationist in terms of its individualism. Sin is a historical or transgenerational phenomenon in that its effects become the environment for later generations. Sin is a social or corporate phenomenon in that no one is an island, a perspective expressed in the biblical concept often termed "corporate responsibility."

2. Compare Patrick McCormick, *Sin as Addiction* (New York: Paulist, 1989).

3. Nor, it may be added, does it have a valid claim to catholicity. Orthodox theologians typically charge Western Christianity with distortion of the biblical perspectives through its overemphasis on a juridical schema. As Daniel Clendenin (*Eastern Orthodox Christianity: A Western Perspective* [Grand Rapids: Baker, 1994], 124) observes, however, "the real issue here seems to be a difference of emphasis—the East emphasizing mystical union through theosis, the West emphasizing juridical categories. No necessity forces us to choose between the two or to see them as mutually exclusive categories that are contradictory. Rather, they, and a host of other New Testament salvation motifs besides (adoption, reconciliation, redemption, ransom, sacrifice, forgiveness, *Christus victor*, propitiation, deliverance), are complementary."

4. The comments of Christof Gestrich (*The Return of Splendor in the World: The Christian Doctrine of Sin and Forgiveness* [trans. D. Bloesch; Grand Rapids: Eerdmans, 1997], 257) regarding the Old Testament's understanding of the corporate dimension of sin are typical: " . . . in our present situation, the task that faces a Christian theology called upon to develop an improved, renewed understanding of sin is *not* to attempt a return to Old Testament hamartiology! . . . Here it must be expressly stated that it will prove to be wrong, even impossible, to return to a time prior to the Western developments of a highly individualistic, highly subjective, and highly personal approach to sin and guilt, to return to more archaic, collective, perhaps even 'national' forms." Gestrich recommends that the church safeguard Enlightenment gains regarding interiority and subjectivity in any attempt to advance a view of sin more appropriate to the current context.

5. James Barr, *Biblical Faith and Natural Theology: The Gifford Lectures for 1991 Delivered in the University of Edinburgh* (Oxford: Clarendon, 1993), 49.

6. J. Barr (*Biblical Faith and Natural Theology*, 220-21) laments "the violent separation between biblical studies as they are actually carried on and the ideas of theologians about the place and authority of the Bible."

7. Ibid., 118.

8. See, for example, Harvey Cox, *On Not Leaving It to the Snake* (New York: Macmillan, 1964); Susan Dunfee, "The Sin of Hiding: A Feminist Critique of Reinhold Niebuhr's Account of the Sin of Pride," *Soundings* 65 (1982): 316-27; Justo L. González, *Mañana: Christian Theology from a Hispanic Perspective* (Nashville: Abingdon, 1990); June O'Connor, "Sin and Salvation from a Feminist Perspective," in *Problems in the Philosophy of Religion: Critical Studies in the Work of John Hick* (ed. Harold Hewitt, Jr.; New York: St. Martin's Press, 1991), 72-81; Juan Luis Segundo, et al., *Evolution and Guilt* (trans. J. Drury; A Theology for Artisans of a New Humanity 5; Maryknoll, N.Y.: Orbis, 1974).

9. See, for example, Henri Rondet, *Le péche original dans la tradition patristique et théologique* (Paris: Fayard, 1967); Alfred Vanneste, "De Theologie van de erfzonde," *Collationes Brugenses et Gandavenses* 12 (1966): 289-312; Erich Gutwenger, "Die Erbsünde und das Konzil von Trient," *ZKTh* 89 (1967): 433-46; Karl Schmitz-Moormann, *Die Erbsünde: Überholte Vorstellung—Bleibende Glaube* (Freiburg: Walter, 1965); Jerome Murphy-O'Connor, *Becoming Human Together: The Pastoral Anthropology of St. Paul* (Good News Studies 2; Collegeville, Minn.: Liturgical Press, 1982); Joseph W. Ciarrocchi, "Spirituality for High and Low Rollers: The Paradox of Self-esteem in Gambling Recovery," in *Addiction and Spirituality: A Multidisciplinary Approach* (eds. Oliver Morgan and Merle Jordan; St. Louis, Mo.: Chalice Press, 1999), 173-91; compare also B. McDermott, "The Theology of Original Sin: Recent Developments," *Theological Studies* 38 (1977): 478-512.

10. See, for example, P. McCormick, *Sin as Addiction*, Linda Mercadante, *Victims and Sinners: Spiritual Roots of Addiction and Recovery* (Louisville: Westminster John Knox, 1996); Harold Doweiko, "Substance Use Disorders as a Symptom of a Spiritual Disease," in *Addiction and Spirituality*, 33-53; Lee Jampolsky, "Healing the Addictive Mind," in *op. cit.*, 55-74.

11. See, for example, Søren Kierkegaard, *The Concept of Anxiety: A Simple Psychologically Orienting Deliberation on the Dogmatic Issue of Hereditary Sin* (trans. and ed. R. Thomte and A. Anderson; Princeton: Princeton, 1980); Jean-Paul Sartre, *Being and Nothingness: An Essay on Phenomenological Ontology* (trans. Hazel E. Barnes, New York: Philosophical Library, 1956), Piet Schoonenberg, *Man and Sin: A Theological View* (Notre Dame, Ind.: Notre Dame, 1965).

12. See, for example, Alistair McFadyen, *Bound to Sin: Abuse, Holocaust and the Christian Doctrine of Sin* (Cambridge: Cambridge University Press, 2000); Stephen G. Ray, Jr., *Do No Harm: Social Sin and Christian Responsibility* (Minneapolis: Fortress, 2003); Miroslav Volf, "The Lamb of God and the Sin of the World: Paul's Conversion and the Christian Doctrine of Salvation," in *Christianity in Jewish Terms* (eds. Tikva Frymer-Kensky, et al.; Theology in a Postcritical Key 1; Boulder, Colo.: Westview Press, 2000), 314-15.

1. Clearing the Deck

1. S. Kierkegaard, *The Concept of Anxiety: A Simple Psychologically Orienting Deliberation on the Dogmatic Issue of Hereditary Sin* (trans. and ed. R. Thomte and A. Anderson; Princeton: Princeton, 1980), 49-50.

2. See Reinhold Niebuhr, *The Nature and Destiny of Man: A Christian Interpretation* (Library of Theological Ethics; Louisville: Westminster John Knox, 1996), and the discussion by Tatha Wiley, *Original Sin: Origins, Developments, Contemporary Meanings* (New York: Paulist Press, 2002), 137-48.

3. See the more complete discussion in T. Wiley, *Original Sin*, 5.

4. See the useful summaries of the doctrine by T. Wiley, *Original Sin* (especially p. 72), and Henri Blocher, *Original Sin: Illuminating the Riddle* (New Studies in Biblical Theology; Grand Rapids: Eerdmans, 1997), 18.

5. At the Council of Trent, the Catholic Church reaffirmed the Augustinian view. See Jerry D. Korsmeyer, *Evolution and Eden: Balancing Original Sin and Contemporary Science* (New York: Paulist, 1998), 23-24, 43-44.

6. Marjori Hewitt Suchocki, *The Fall to Violence: Original Sin in Relational Theology* (New York: Continuum, 1994), 17-19. Suchocki argues that "neither the traditional definition of sin as rebellion against God nor its corollary concept of original sin as rooted solely in human freedom is adequate to account for the enormity and variety of ways by which we manage to inflict ill-being upon ourselves, one another, and our environing earth" (17). She prefers a "relational" concept of original sin: "Sin as the unnecessary violation of the well-being of any aspect of creation is my primary definition of sin. The language of sin as a 'rebellion against creation' indicates not a primacy of one being against another, but a primacy of the well-being of all, against which one rebels in sin. In this sense, sin can be called a 'rebellion against creation.' While the focus is on the violation of creation, in a relational universe the violation of creation is *also* a violation of God. If God feels the effects of every

Notes

sin, then every sin is not only against creation, it is against God as well. Therefore, sin as rebellion against creation necessarily entails sin against God" (48).

7. James Connor, "Original Sin: Contemporary Approaches," *Theological Studies* 29 (1968): 215 (215-240).

8. T. Wiley, *Original Sin*, 103-26. L. Mercadante observes, "Our focus on biological predisposition [for addictions] today may be an experiment with a contemporary and secularized version of original sin divorced from original guilt" (*Victims and Sinners: Spiritual Roots of Addiction and Recovery* [Louisville: Westminster John Knox, 1996], 126).

9. J. Connor, "Original Sin," 215; T. Wiley, *Original Sin*, 103-26; H. Blocher, *Original Sin*, 37-38.

10. T. Wiley, *Original Sin*, 103-26; H. Blocher, *Original Sin*, 37-38; J. Connor, "Original Sin," 215.

11. For a thorough yet concise summary and assessment of options for translating and interpreting this key Greek phrase, see Stanley E. Porter, "The Pauline Concept of Original Sin, in Light of Rabbinic Background," *Tyndale Bulletin* 41 (1990): 22-25.

12. Compare H. Blocher, *Original Sin*, 37-38.

13. James Gaffney, *Sin Reconsidered* (New York: Paulist Press, 1983), 50-51; see also Justo González, *Christian Thought Revisited: Three Types of Theology* (Nashville: Abingdon, 1989), 29-31; Constantine Tsirpanlis, *Introduction to Eastern Patristic Thought and Orthodox Theology* (Theology and Life 30; Collegeville, Minn.: Liturgical Press, 1991), 47-49. The pertinent texts in Irenaeus are: *Adv haer.* 2.25.3; 4.11.1; *ad Autol.* 2.25; *Strom.* 2.22. Others shared his views (i.e., Procopius of Gaza [d. 529 CE]: see *In Gen.* 2.8).

14. See C. Tsirpanlis, *Introduction to Eastern Patristic Thought*, 50.

15. Panayiotis Nellas, *Deification in Christ: Orthodox Perspectives on the Nature of the Human Person* (trans. N. Russell; Contemporary Greek Theologians 5; Crestwood, N.Y.: St. Vladimir's Seminary Press, 1987), 33. The Greek Church extends this line of reasoning in its doctrine of theosis/deification/Christification. Nellas comments, for example, that "the fact that Adam was created in the image of Christ implies that it was his vocation to be raised up to the Archetype or, more precisely, to be purified and to love God so much that God would come to dwell within him, that the Logos would enter into a hypostatic union with man, and thus appear in history as the Christ, be manifested as the God-man" (35). This (over-)extension of the Alpha-Omega principle can seem to border on adoptionism or even pantheism. Orthodox theologians reject this appearance, however: "Orthodoxy consistently rejects the idea that humans participate in the essence or nature of God. Rather, we remain distinctly human by nature but participate in God by the divine energies or grace" (D. Clendenin, ed., *Eastern Orthodox Theology: A Contemporary Reader* [Grand Rapids: Baker, 1995], 130).

16. P. Nellas, *Deification in Christ*, 38.

17. *Enchiridion* viii, 27-ix, 29.

18. P. Nellas, *Deification in Christ*, 94-95.

19. A. Hulsbosch, *God in Creation and Evolution* (trans. M. Versfeld; New York: Sheed and Ward, 1965; as cited by J. Connor, "Original Sin," 233); others holding similar "Christic" views include H. Rondet, *Le péche original*; A. Vanneste, "De Theologie van de erfzonde"; and E. Gutwenger, "Die Erbsünde," who speaks of Auf-Christus-hin-sein. The work of Teilhard de Chardin with respect to Christ as the Omega point is summarized and extended by K. Schmitz-Moormann, *Die Erbsünde*; compare also B. McDermott, "The Theology of Original Sin: Recent Developments," *Theological Studies* 38 (1977): 478-512.

20. J. D. Korsmeyer, *Evolution and Eden*, 122-23, citation p. 122, summarizing Charles L. Birch and John B. Cobb, Jr., *The Liberation of Life: From the Cell to the Community* (Denton, Tex.: Environmental Ethics Books, 1990), 120.

21. J. Gaffney, *Sin Reconsidered*, 48-49.

22. Post–Vatican II Catholic theologians, struggling to reinterpret the doctrine of original sin, have appealed to existentialist categories. They fall roughly into two categories: "situationalists" (Karl Rahner, for example), who use existentialism to describe the state of human beings "thrown"

into existence with freedom limited by two factors, God's prevenient grace and a historically accrued absence of holiness. "One is born into the world and into a historical sinful situation. . . . Original sin is not a static situation that occurs at birth, it grows in time as we participate in sinful humanity" (according to Karl-Heinz Weger). Similarly, P. Schoonenberg speaks of the human race's solidarity in sin. Among Catholics, "personalists" (Urs Baumann) "reduce original sin to the factual universality of actual sin in the world. . . . As soon as a child becomes a moral person . . . that child will freely, but inevitably, sin in the first act of the will" (A. Vanneste). Situationalists stress the already-there quality of sin in the lack of personal freedom. Personalists stress that very freedom, but with a tinge of fatalism. See J. D. Korsmeyer, *Evolution and Eden*, 62-65; B. McDermott, "The Theology of Original Sin," 478-512.

23. L. Mercadante, *Victims and Sinners*, 32.

24. Paul Tillich, "On the Transitoriness of Life" and "The Destruction of Death," in *The Shaking of the Foundations* (New York: Charles Scribner's Sons, 1948), pp. 64-75, 169-72, respectively. See the helpful discussion by Bonnie J. Miller-McLemore, *Death, Sin and the Moral Life: Contemporary Cultural Interpretations of Death* (American Academy of Religion Academy Series 59; Atlanta: Scholars Press, 1988), 129-35.

25. J. D. Korsmeyer, *Evolution and Eden*, 57.

26. P. Schoonenberg, *Man and Sin*, discussed in T. Wiley, *Original Sin*, 132-37.

27. "Insights from the social sciences have been helpful in consideration of the transmission of original sin, said by Trent to occur by generation, not imitation. But Trent did not discuss the meaning of 'generation.' For modern theologians it is considered to apply to the whole process of socialization that occurs when humans enter the world and are assimilated into the family, the local community, and the wider social sphere. The principal idea is that humans find themselves thrust into a world where sinful people, activities and structures are already in place, and influencing and training the mind long before it is capable of making fully free moral decisions. We are contaminated by evil just by being born, by our generation into the human race, and not just by imitating our ancestors." J. D. Korsmeyer, *Evolution and Eden*, 57. Compare H. Blocher, *Original Sin*, 123. Blocher holds to the essence of the traditional doctrine of original sin, but with accommodations. He typically rejects dichotomies. For example, he regards as simplistic the Augustinian/Pelagian debate over whether sin is transmitted by "generation" or "imitation." Why not both? Sociological and psychological factors can surely transmit "the radical deformity of sin."

28. Advocates of this reading of Gen 3 find support in Paul's discussion in Rom 5–7, in which he describes a time (perhaps in his own life; the issue of the possible autobiographical nature of the passage is hotly debated) before the "age of accountability" when, in innocence, there is no knowledge of or guilt from sin. Attaining a mature knowledge of the law, however, brings sin to life.

29. See C. Gestrich, *The Return of Splendor*, 84-85.

30. Robert Gordis ("The Knowledge of Good and Evil in the Old Testament and in the Qumran Scrolls," *Journal of Biblical Literature* 76 [1957]: 123-38) argued on the basis of a passage in the *Community Rule* from Qumran (1QSa 1:9-11), which recommends that male members of the community refrain from sexual intercourse until the age of twenty, "when he knows good and evil," that the Hebrew phrase "the knowledge of good and evil" consistently refers to sexual awareness. Gordis argued that the phrase in Gen 3 could not mean "moral judgment," since Adam and Eve could not be held accountable for their actions if, prior to consuming the fruit, they were morally incompetent. Nor can Gordis imagine that God would have created the first pair without moral sensibility. Similarly, Gordis rejects the idea that the fruit of the Tree imparted knowledge in a general sense. Adam was able to name the animals before he ate. In fact, biblical and rabbinic traditions celebrate Adam as a paragon of wisdom (Ezek 28:12ff.; Ps 82:6ff.). Finally, in Gordis's view, objections to the "moral judgment" interpretation apply equally to the notion that Adam and Eve experienced an "enlargement of capacity" for knowledge comparable to the maturation of a child into adulthood. God would have created them in a state of perfection. Gordis's argument is seriously flawed. First, he assumes that God created Adam and Eve in a state of "perfection," that they would not have

"matured" in any way by eating of the fruit. Yet, in his argument, they would have been ignorant of sex. Second, the appeal to biblical and rabbinic tradition overlooks alternate traditions, such as Qoheleth's analysis concerning Adam's wisdom. The biblical perspective seems to be, not that Adam was a "paragon" of wisdom, but that Adam's wisdom was precarious. Like the Mesopotamian Adapa, Adam was wise enough for discourse with deity, but not wise enough to attain deity. Finally, Gordis's interpretation is tantamount to identifying sex and sin, whereas the divinely intended goodness of sexuality is inherent in the creation of two genders in God's image and in the injunction to multiply.

31. *Mañana: Christian Theology from a Hispanic Perspective* (Nashville: Abingdon, 1990), 137-38.

32. Medieval theology focused a great deal of attention on "sloth," although it did not rank it alongside "pride" as a component of primal sin. As early as the mid-1960s, H. Cox anticipated the revival of the term by contemporary liberation and feminist theologians (*On Not Leaving It to the Snake* [New York: Macmillan, 1964], ix).

33. Indeed, taking her cue from the actions of the first pair, feminist theologian S. Dunfee ("The Sin of Hiding: A Feminist Critique of Reinhold Niebuhr's Account of the Sin of Pride," *Soundings* 65 [1982]: 316-27) terms this variety of primal sin "hiding."

34. " . . . And she also gave some to her husband [who was with her, and presumably had been all along], and he ate" (Gen 3:6).

2. Sin: To Be More Than Human

1. Blaise Pascal, *Pensées* (New York: Penguin, 1966), 90; cited in Patrick Kerans, *Sinful Social Structures* (New York: Paulist, 1974), 41; Kerans goes on to talk about the human experience of "disproportion."

2. Seminal figures in this field include Jean Piaget (*Judgment and Reasoning in the Child* [London: Routledge and Kegan Paul, 1928]; *Origins of Intelligence in the Child* [London: Routledge and Kegan Paul, 1953]; etc.) on cognitive development, Lawrence Kohlberg (*Essays on Moral Development* [2 vols.; San Francisco: Harper & Row, 1981, 1984]) on moral development, Eric Erikson (*Childhood and Society*, etc.) on emotional development, and James Fowler (*Stages of Faith: The Psychology of Human Development and the Quest for Meaning* [San Francisco: Harper & Row, 1981]) on faith development. Fowler's *Faith Development and Pastoral Care* (Theology and Pastoral Care Series; Philadelphia: Fortress, 1987) is a particularly helpful summary of the basic insights of personality development theory, a summary with the added value of a pastoral orientation.

3. S. Ray, Jr., *Do No Harm: Social Sin and Christian Responsibility* (Minneapolis: Fortress, 2003), 42.

4. *Childhood and Society* (2nd ed.; New York: Norton, 1963), 247-51; J. Fowler, *Stages of Faith*, 119-21.

5. J. Fowler, *Faith Development and Pastoral Care*, 62.

6. *The Eternal Now* (New York: Charles Scribner's Sons, 1956), 52, 56.

7. Walter Lowe, *Evil and the Unconscious* (AAR Studies in Religion 30; Chico, Calif.: Scholars Press, 1983), 3.

8. The root appears outside the Bible, post-biblical Hebrew, and Jewish Aramaic only in Syriac in the divergent meaning "to be numb, terrified; to act foolishly." A substantive in the meaning "crime, sin" appears occasionally in Ugaritic. In the Bible, the verb occurs 41 times (except for one niphal, always in the qal) and the noun 93 times.

9. For example, by inclusion in lists with חטא (*ḥṭ'*) and/or עָוֹן (*'awon*): Lev 16:16, 21; Num 14:18; Josh 24:19; 1 Kgs 8:50; Isa 43:25, 27; 44:22; 50:1; 53:5, 12; 58:1; 59:12; Jer 5:6; Ezek 21:29; 37:23; 39:24; Mic 1:5, 13; 6:7; 7:18; Pss 25:7; 32:1, 5; 51:5; 59:4[3]; 65:4[3]; 89:33[32]; 103:12; 107:17; Job 7:21; 8:4; 13:23; 14:17; 31:33; 33:9; 35:6.

10. Connotations of the term seem to divide neatly into two not easily reconciled categories: (1) uses, especially of the verb, in political contexts to designate acts of rebellion (verb: 1 Kgs 12:19 ‖ 2 Chr 10:19; 2 Kgs 1:1; 3:5, 7; 8:20, 22 ‖ 2 Chr 21:8, 10; noun: 1 Sam 24:12[11]; 25:28; Prov 28:2, regarding which compare Crawford Howell Toy, *A Critical and Exegetical Commentary on*

Notes

The Book of Proverbs [ICC 18; Edinburgh: T. & T. Clark, 1948 (=1899)], 495; and Richard J. Clifford, *Proverbs: A Commentary* [OTL; Louisville: Westminster John Knox, 1999], 169); and (2) instances, "especially where a legal life situation is perceptible," involving "criminal offenses to be adjudicated" (so Rolf Knierim, *Die Hauptbegriffe für Sünde im Alten Testament* [Gütersloh: Gerd Mohn, 1965], 176; see especially Exod 22:8; cf. Gen 31:36; 50:17; Prov 28:24; Amos 1, 2; Mic 3:8). Based on the "political" use of the verb, Ludwig Köhler suggested "to rebel" as the basic meaning of the verbal root ("Zu Ex 22:3—Ein Beitrag zur Kenntnis des hebräischen Rechts," ZAW 46 [1928]: 213-18). In addition to texts involving a clearly political component, a number of passages in which both verb and noun parallel various terms for rebellion seem to support Köhler's suggestion (|| מרד, *mrd*, "to rebel [unsuccessfully]," a term appropriated from the realm of international law—Ezek 2:3; 20:38; || נדד, *ndd*, "to depart, stray, wander"—Hos 7:13; || מרה, *mrh*, "to be obstinate, rebellious"—Exod 23:21; Ps 5:11[10]; Lam 3:42; || בגד, *bgd*, "to deceive"—Isa 48:8; שקר, *shqr*, "to lie"—Isa 57:4). In contrast, R. Knierim (*Hauptbegriffe*, 151; see also Hans Wilhelm Hertzberg, "Die 'Abtrünnigen' und die 'Vielen': Ein Beitrag zu Jesaja 53," in *Verbannung und Heimkehr: Beiträge zur Geschichte und Theologie Israels im 6. und 5. Jahrhundert v. Chr.* [FS W. Rudolph; ed. Arnulf Kuschke; Tübingen: Mohr, 1961], 97-108) has argued that Köhler's suggestion fails to explain the use of the noun in certain legal contexts, especially Exod 22:8[9], and that the idea of "rebellion" alone does not address a key component of the situations addressed in the political contexts, namely, whether the rebellion is described as successful. Exodus 22:8[9] is the crux. Knierim (*Hauptbegriffe*, 162) catalogued sixteen possible translations of this quite ambiguous text before concluding that, in this and similar texts, פשע, *psh'* denotes property and personal crimes, as indicated not only by the subject matter of Exod 22:8[9], for example, but also by vocabulary found in association with פשע, *psh'* in several literary contexts (Gen 31:36, גנב *gnb*, "to steal"; 1 Sam 24:10-14, שלח יד ב, *shlh yad be...*, "to raise one's hand against" הרג, *hrg*, "to slay"; Prov 28:24, גזל, *gzl*, "to rob"; Gen 50:17, kidnapping). With a view to the connotations of "property crime" manifest in such texts, Knierim turned to 2 Kgs 8:20, 22—the parade example for the "rebellion" understanding of פשע, *psh'* and called attention to the idiom מתחת יד, *mtht yd*, "from the control of." He argued that this phrase "demonstrate[s] clearly . . . the fact of completed separation, self-extrication from foreign dominion, and thus a type of property removal" (R. Knierim, "פֶּשַׁע *pesha'* crime," *TLOT* 2, 1033-34. See also Ina Plein, "Erwägungen zur Überlieferung von 1 Reg 11:26-14:20," ZAW 78 [1966]: 10).

11. R. Knierim, *Hauptbegriffe*, 177-78; idem, *TLOT* 2, 1036.

12. Amos probably regarded the cultic objects established at various sanctuaries in the northern kingdom to be idols. Therefore, worship at the sanctuary in Bethel, for example, would be tantamount to idolatry, rejection of the basic covenant with YHWH, *psh'*. Micah equates the sanctuary in Jerusalem with a "high place," the technical term for the hilltop sanctuaries of Canaanite religion. Judah's "rebellion" is its syncretistic worship.

13. See Mark E. Biddle, *A Redaction History of Jeremiah 2:1-4:2* (AThANT 77; Zurich: TVZ, 1990), 52-55.

14. Cf. Mark E. Biddle, *Deuteronomy* (Smyth & Helwys Bible Commentary 4; Macon, Ga.: Smyth & Helwys, 2003), 442-52.

15. "Thus 'to have sin' is distinguished from 'to sin' as the sinful principle from the sinful act itself" (Brooke Foss Westcott, *The Epistles of St. John: The Greek Text with Notes* [Abingdon: Marcham Manor, 1966], 22).

16. *1, 2, 3 John* (WBC 51; London: Paternoster, 1984), 159-63.

17. See Frederich Hauck, "μένω, κτλ," in *Theological Dictionary of the New Testament* IV (ed. G. Kittel; trans. G. Bromiley; Grand Rapids: Eerdmans, 1967), 575-76; Jürgen Heise, *Bleiben: Menein in den johannischen Schriften* (HUTh 8; Tübingen: J.C.B. Mohr [Paul Siebeck], 1967); James Rosscup, *Abiding in Christ: Studies in John 15* (Grand Rapids: Zondervan, 1973); Dorothy Lee, "Abiding in the Fourth Gospel: A Case Study in Feminist Biblical Theology," in *A Feminist Companion to John*, II (eds. A.-J. Levine and M. Blickenstaff; New York: Sheffield Academic Press, 2003), 64-78.

Notes

18. *The Johannine Letters: A Commentary on 1, 2, and 3 John* (Philadelphia: Fortress, 1996), 104.

19. First John may document one of the church's earliest encounters with a theology, heavily influenced by Greek idealism, that maintained a sharp line of demarcation between the spiritual and the material worlds. Those who held this view believed that spirit is pure and flesh is evil. This being so, they concluded, God could not become incarnate. Therefore, Jesus only "seemed" (Greek δοκέω, *dokeō*, "to seem," hence "docetism") to have been a physical human being; in truth, Jesus the Christ, as the Redeemer sent from God, was a spiritual being unable to suffer and die.

20. The New Testament attests two other "unforgivable sin" traditions: the synoptic (Mark 3:28ff.; Matt 12:31ff.; Luke 12:10; cf. *Did.* 11:7) and that of the book of Hebrews (6:4-6; 10:26-31; 12:16ff.). That the three perspectives may be harmonized is evident in the Synoptics' identification of "blasphemy against the Spirit" as a failure to recognize the significance of Jesus' healing ministry. Thus, all three traditions regard failure fully to recognize Jesus as the ultimate sin (cf. the Gospel of John's definition of sin as unbelief; see below).

21. Paul Ellingsworth (*The Epistle to the Hebrews: A Commentary on the Greek Text* [New International Greek Testament Commentary; Grand Rapids: Eerdmans, 1993], 532) observes that Judaism had expanded definitions of sins of ignorance to include sins of folly (*T. Jud.* 19:3) and those committed under duress (*T. Zeb.* 1:5).

22. Note, for example, Michael Fox's *Qoheleth and his Contradictions* (JSOTSup 71; Sheffield, England: Almond, 1989).

23. The expression יצא את־כלם, *yetse' 'et-kullam* is difficult to translate. Some take the verb to mean "escape" (LXX, Sym, Syr; cf. NIV). Michael Fox (*A Time to Tear Down and a Time to Build Up: A Rereading of Ecclesiastes* [Grand Rapids: Eerdmans, 1999], 262) objects that, in the context, the alternatives referred to by the 3mp pronominal suffix are "counsels of *desirable* behavior" and, thus, not something to be escaped. He suggests, admitting the problem of retrojection, "to do one's duty" on the basis of rabbinic usage. The translation above, which agrees substantially with NIV, is based on the idea that the Teacher does not consider the alternatives to be "desirable" behaviors, but the boundaries marking the arena of desirable behavior. The common translation of the verb with the direct object marker in other occurrences (e.g., Gen 10:14; 27:30; 44:4, 28; Exod 5:20, etc.) expresses motion away from. One who fears God will certainly "proceed away from" folly and evil; in the Teacher's view, the fear of God should also motivate one from arrogantly moving toward the other extreme, as well—too much wisdom. Fear of God points toward the middle path.

24. Commentators recognize the clear parallels between Eccl 3:20 and 12:7 and Gen 3:19b (cf. also Job 10:9; 34:15; Sir 40:11a; Ps 104:29), although they disagree as to whether these parallels signal literary dependence. Charles C. Forman ("Koheleth's Use of Genesis," *JSS* 5 [1960]: 256-63; "The Pessimism of Ecclesiastes," *JSS* 3 [1958]: 336-43) has argued on the basis of the verbal similarities between Eccl 3:20 and Gen 3:19 and a number of thematic parallels dispersed throughout Ecclesiastes (including the centrality of the term "vanity, void"—*hbl* הבל = Abel) that the wisdom book may represent an extended midrash on Gen 3–11. Tremper Longman III (*The Book of Ecclesiastes* [NICOT; Grand Rapids: Eerdmans, 1997], 91, 119, 177, 268) has called attention to affinities between Eccl 1:5 and Gen 1:11, 29; 2:9; Eccl 3:11 and Gen 1; the "naming" common to Eccl 7:1 and Gen 1–2; and the notion that light may exist independently of a light source (Eccl 12:2 and Gen 1).

The argument from thematic parallels cannot, however, sustain the thesis of a literary relationship between Ecclesiastes and Genesis. Furthermore, a comparison of biblical texts that allude to the creation of humanity from the dust of the earth demonstrates that they reflect a common tradition without evidencing literary interdependence. (Cf. Gen 2:7; 3:19; Eccl 3:19-20; 12:7; Ps 104:29; Job 10:9; 34:15).

On the one hand, all these texts agree that human beings return (שוב, *shub*) to the dust (עָפָר, *'afar*). On the other, however, the more extensive texts disagree in language regarding the animating force (Gen 3—נְשָׁמָה, *nishmah*; Eccl 3:19; 12:7; Ps 104:29—רוּחַ, *ruach*), describing the use of dust as the material (Gen 3:19—לקח, *lqh*; Eccl 3:20; 12:7—היה, *hyh*), and denoting the earth as the source of the dust (Gen 2:7; 3:19—אֲדָמָה, *'adamah*; Eccl 12:7—אֶרֶץ, *'erets*). Clearly, the Teacher had in mind the tradition recorded in Gen 2–3, but he did not have before him the text.

25. M. Fox, *Qoheleth and His Contradictions*, 194. He does not suggest the same emendation in v. 14, however.

26. *Untersuchungen zur Eigenart des Buches Qohelet* (BZAW 183; New York: de Gruyter, 1989), 64. Similarly, Dominic Rudman (*Determinism in the Book of Ecclesiastes* [JSOTSup 316; Sheffield, England: Sheffield Academic Press, 2001], 91) comments, ". . . [*'lm*] is the whole of which each individual [*'t*] ('time') is a part," although he understands the issue in terms of divine determinism. The issue for the Teacher does not concern the ability of human beings to act freely, but is an epistemological problem. Even with the capacity to conceive of *'lm*, they cannot *know* the work of God in its duration (v. 11). Therefore, human beings should concentrate on conducting their own lives satisfactorily.

27. T. Longman, *The Book of Ecclesiastes*, 80.

28. Ibid., 130.

29. "Überwindung des Todesgeschicks in der alttestamentlichen Frömmigkeit vor und neben dem Auferstehenungsglauben," *ZThK* 73 (1976): 259-82. Compare also Bernd Willmes, *Menschliches Schicksal und ironische Weisheitskritik im Kohelethbuch: Koheleths Ironie und die Grenzen der Exegese* (Biblisch-Theologische Studien 39; Neukirchen: Neukirchener, 2000), 132.

30. Ecclesiastes 12:7 notwithstanding. As M. Fox comments, ". . . Qoheleth assumes that the spirit returns to God but takes this event to mean death and nothing more, and this assumption does not prevent a *hebel*-judgment in the next verse" (*Contradictions*, 309).

31. So also D. Michel, *Untersuchungen zur Eigenart*, 118.

32. Noting the doubled *yodh* in the verb describing God's creation of Adam, *Genesis Rabbah* XIV:III posits two acts of creation: the first bestowed upon humankind the traits of the upper world (humans stand like the ministering angels, they speak, have understanding, see) and the second the traits of the lower world (like the beasts, humans eat, drink, have sex, defecate, and die)

33. Morna D. Hooker ("Adam in Romans 1," *NTS* 6 [1959-1960]: 297-306), for example, catalogued a number of verbal and thematic parallels beginning with the typically rabbinic redundancy "in the likeness of the image" in Rom 1:23. Here Paul cites Ps 106:20 (LXX 105:20), expanding it with the addition of εἰκών, *eikōn*, "image," an obvious allusion to "in our likeness and in our image," Gen 1:26. Elsewhere, Paul typically uses the added term to denote either the *imago dei* or the *imago Christi* (Rom 8:29; 1 Cor 11:7; 15:49; 2 Cor 3:18; 4:4; Col 1:15; 3:10). First Corinthians 11:7 establishes the correlation in Paul's usage between "image" and "glory" as synonyms for the divine image imprinted on humankind at creation. Furthermore, Paul utilizes key terms (τὰ πετεινὰ, *ta peteina*, "birds"; τὰ τετράποδα, *ta tetrapoda*, "four footed animals"; and τὰ ἑρπετά, *ta herpeta*, "reptiles") from the Greek version of the account of God's creative activity (Gen 1:20-25). Romans 1:24 probably alludes to the first pair's sense of shame at the nakedness of their bodies. Paul's exposition of the three results of human sin replicates the sequence of events that unfold in Gen 3: idolatry, sexual complications, and all other sins. Genesis 1:2 and Rom 1:20 both describe the original state of creation as "invisible" (ἀόρτά, *aorta*). Humanity's false claim to wisdom only masks a return to the darkness (ἐσκοτίσθη, *eskotisthē*, Rom 1:22; cf. Gen 1:2) that characterizes the chaos before cosmos. In addition to Gen 1–3, Rom 1 also evidences Paul's familiarity with the Wisdom of Jesus Ben Sirach, an apocryphal wisdom text that stands in Ecclesiastes' tradition of interpreting the accounts of the creation and "fall" (see especially Sir 13 and compare Rom 1:20 with Sir 2:23 and 7:26).

34. See above, p. 1.

35. J. Connor, "Original Sin," 222, citing E. Gutwenger, "Die Erbsünde," 437-38, notes that the "powers of sin and death" to which Paul refers are extra-personal in the text, not hereditary characteristics *of* persons, and that these powers, in Paul's view, are universally effective because all actually sin.

36. The logic here is perplexing and seems to contradict Paul's statements in 1:18-32 and, especially, 2:12-16. Romans 5:13 seems to suggest that the heathen of 1:18-32 are free from guilt, although

Notes

Paul surely knew the story of the flood. Timo Laato (*Paul and Judaism: An Anthropological Approach* [South Florida Studies in the History of Judaism 115; Atlanta: Scholars, 1995], 134) concludes that it must refer to God's decision not to log these sins in the "book of life" to be opened at the last day. Charles H. Dodd (*The Epistle of Paul to the Romans* [MNTC; New York: R. Long & R.R. Smith, 1932], 82) relates "sin" here to his understanding of 3:23, which describes a state of "being short of God's glory." This sin "does not carry guilt, where there is no intention to act contrary to what is known to be right." Douglas J. Moo (*The Epistle to the Romans* [NICOT; Grand Rapids: Eerdmans, 1996], 332) argues that v. 14 "expresses Paul's view that sin can be charged explicitly and in detail to each person's account only when that person has consciously and knowingly disobeyed a direct command that prohibits that sin." Death, on the other hand, reigns supreme from Adam to Moses (v. 14; cf. 3:25). The key moment, then, comes in v. 20—the advent of the law. Paul seems to mean the Mosaic law here, since the law available to all human beings in the form of what might now be termed the conscience (see Rom 1:19) is not linked to a single historical moment. He has argued, however, that this more universal law implies an awareness of sin very similar to that produced by acquaintance with the Mosaic Torah. Similarly perplexing is the reference to "those who did not sin in the same way that Adam . . . transgressed." For now, it is essential to focus attention on what can be clearly garnered from Paul's discussion. These obscurities, now noted, must be resolved elsewhere.

37. E. Gutwenger (*loc. cit.*) argues, indeed, that for Paul the universality of sin follows from the universality of redemption.

38. "Some Observations on the Origin of Sin in Judaism and St Paul," *CBQ* 31 (1969): 28-29.

39. Cf. Gal 3:27, which employs the image of "putting on clothing": "For those who were baptized *into* Christ have *put on* Christ."

40. See, for example, Rom 16:7, "who was *in* Christ before me," and Eph 4:15, "to grow *into* Christ."

41. Cf. 2 Cor 5:17: "Anyone who is *in* Christ is a new creation...."

42. Indeed, Paul may have in mind a "corporate" understanding of the term "adam," which, in Hebrew, normally refers to "humankind" instead of to an individual human being. Only the "Adam" of Gen 3 may be in reference to an individual, although many interpreters argue, in keeping with the mythic character of the text, that even Gen 3 refers to the race instead of the individual. See J. Connor, "Original Sin," 222, citing E. Gutwenger, "Erbsünde," 437-38.

Analyzing the two schools of interpretation regarding Rom 5:12-21 (i.e., all Adam's descendants inherit his sin and guilt automatically vis-à-vis Adam's descendants replicate Adam's sin), H. Blocher offers a similar solution, observing that

> Both kinds of interpretations . . . appear to share a disjunctive presupposition: *either* we are condemned for our own sins (and Adam's role is reduced to that of a remote fountainhead, losing much of its significance) *or* we are condemned for his sin (and the equity of that transfer is hard to see). Now, what if this "either/or" were misleading? What if there were a third possibility?

Indeed, Blocher's modified "federal" view holds that, since sin cannot be imputed before it has been defined, "the role of Adam and of his sin in Romans 5 is *to make possible the imputation, the judicial treatment, of human sins.*" That is, "before the Law of Moses was promulgated, sin was imputed and therefore death reigned owing to the relationship of all humans to Adam, the natural and legal head or mediator." H. Blocher, *Original Sin*, 77.

43. Marriage provides another analogy of the "shift of realms" (7:1-6).

44. The Greek term, like its Hebrew counterpart, covers a rather wide semantic field, ranging from "principle," "instruction," and "criterion" to the more specific "covenantal law." Paul uses it in the sense of "criterion" in Rom 3:27 and in the rather surprising expression "the law of the spirit of life in Christ Jesus" in Rom 8:2. Given the fact that the reference to the hostility toward "God's law" on the part of unregenerate individuals in Rom 8:7 appears toward the culmination of Paul's exposition

of the universal need of sinful humanity for faith in Christ, it is unclear whether he means the Torah in the strict sense, or, as seems more likely, the common core of God's will revealed either in the covenant or in the principle of wisdom.

45. Although he may have understood the Torah concept in a somewhat idiosyncratic fashion. As traditionally understood, Paul rejected Jewish reliance on the salvific role of the Mosaic law, arguing that Jewish efforts to attain salvation through obedience to the law fails without exception, that the law can only bring condemnation, and so forth. Scholars increasingly recognize that this summary of Paul's doctrine conflicts with several fundamental truths. First, nowhere does the Old Testament ascribe a saving role to the Torah. Second, mainstream Judaism holds and has long held a view of the Torah that is by and large consistent with the Old Testament's understanding of the Torah as the expression of God's will for God's people, not as the *means to become* God's people. Third, as a trained rabbi, Paul would have been familiar with both the Bible and mainstream Jewish thought. Consequently, either Paul argued against a straw opponent or Paul rejected only some peculiar *interpretation/conceptualization* of Torah.

For a recent, insightful analysis of the problem see Stephan Davis (*The Antithesis of the Ages: Paul's Reconfiguration of Torah* [CBQMS 33; Washington: Catholic Biblical Association, 2002]), who argues that "when Paul wrote negatively about Torah he was not addressing Torah *per se*, but rather a particular mode of envisioning Torah" (p. 3). Davis terms this early Jewish concept of Torah the "eternal," "cosmic," or "ontological" Torah, "Torah as God's cosmic force, an entity that acts as an intermediary between God and humanity . . . the Word or Wisdom by which God created the world and the instrument of final judgment" (p. 4).

46. Although the theological basis for the prophets' oracles against the nations is nowhere made explicit, it is noteworthy that all the major prophets, along with the minor prophet Amos, addressed the sins and shortcomings of Israel's Gentile neighbors. Amos 1–2 offers an instructive case study. To what criterion of righteousness does Amos hold Israel's neighbors accountable? Since they are not parties to the Mosaic covenant, they cannot be charged with willful rebellion against God's revealed will. Instead, Amos charges them with violations of what might be termed "standards of common decency." Every human being of good conscience, Amos seems to assume, will recognize the moral repugnance of terrorizing civilian populations by "slashing open the bellies of pregnant women in Gilead" in a campaign of "ethnic cleansing." The underlying principle, then, is that even Assyria (or Ashdod; the text is uncertain) and Egypt know what is "right" (3:9-10). For Amos and the major prophets, this understanding of "right" is the common heritage of humankind. See further John Barton, *Amos' Oracles against the Nations* (Cambridge: Cambridge University Press, 1980); idem, "Natural Law and Poetic Justice in the Old Testament," *JTS* 30 (1979): 1-14.

47. Cf., for example, Paul's statement that the Gentiles sometimes behave in such a way as to constitute "a law unto themselves" with Aristotle's statements in *Nicomachean Ethics* 1128^{a}31 and *Politics* 1284^{a}14, and see the discussion in J. Barr, *Biblical Faith and Natural Theology*, 15, 19, 51-53, 75-76.

48. Paul does not explicitly specify whether this knowledge is innate, as suggested by the expression "written on their hearts," or acquired through experience, as indicated by the discussion of the revelation of God in the created order found in Rom 1 and by the Rom 7 discussion of the movement from innocence to accountability. It may well be that Paul did not consider the distinction.

49. Several preliminary issues are at stake here: Does Paul describe the Christian or the non-Christian? Is this section autobiographical or speculative? The larger passage divides into two subsections. Verses 7-13 deal with the notion that sin apart from the law is not sin (see above). Paul obviously has in mind Gen 3 here. The exegesis is intriguing. Does v. 9 refer to a specific moment? James addresses a similar issue with respect to the manner in which desire gives rise to sin. In a discussion of the source of temptation, which may have been intended to counter a misunderstanding of part of the Lord's Prayer (see James B. Adamson, *The Epistle of James* [NICNT; Grand Rapids: Eerdmans, 1976], 69; it has long been recognized that James functions as something of a commentary on the Sermon on the Mount with close affinities also to the *Didache*), James rejects the notion that God can be such a source. Significantly, neither does he appeal to Satan or the "evil inclination"

often cited in the Jewish texts of the day, "but to a psychological analysis" (James H. Ropes, *A Critical and Exegetical Commentary on the Epistle of St. James* [ICC 40; Edinburgh: T. &. T. Clark, 1948], 155-56) that clearly has in view Gen 3 and resonates with overtones of Jesus' discussion of obedience to the law found in the so-called "antitheses" in the Sermon on the Mount and with Rom 7. At issue is the moment when "desire," itself morally neutral, becomes "sin," i.e., when it seeks "to convert its relativity into an absolute and its finitude into infinity" (John Baillie, cited in Adamson, 70).

50. Paul's statement in Rom 1:18-32 seems on its face to be unambiguous, but exegetes uncomfortable with any hint of natural theology in Paul often deny that Paul could possibly have held such a position, or they argue that it is not central to his argument, or that Paul borrows language here from another source but does not endorse it (for a discussion of the various scholarly approaches, see J. Barr, *Biblical Faith and Natural Theology*, 40-57).

51. For such a study, see the very refreshing analysis offered recently by J. Barr (*Biblical Faith and Natural Theology*).

52. Consequently, as Barr comments, "the traditional boundaries between revealed and natural theology cannot be sustained or must be reconsidered . . . " (*Biblical Faith and Natural Theology*, 42).

53. J. Barr, *Biblical Faith and Natural Theology*, 54-55.

54. W. Lowe, *Evil and the Unconscious*, xiii.

3. Sin: Failure to Embrace Authentic Freedom

1. H. Cox, *On Not Leaving It to the Snake* (New York: Macmillan, 1964), ix.

2. L. Mercadante, *Victims and Sinners: Spiritual Roots of Addiction and Recovery* (Louisville: Westminster John Knox, 1996), 37-39. Feminism's understanding of sloth must be distinguished from the traditional concept of sloth as indolence, the sin of omission. In the traditional understanding, sloth can still be an expression of pride: one can be so egocentric and self-satisfied as to be unwilling to relate to others, including God. See A. McFadyen, *Bound to Sin: Abuse, Holocaust and the Christian Doctrine of Sin* (Cambridge: Cambridge University Press, 2000), 139.

3. S. Dunfee, "The Sin of Hiding: A Feminist Critique of Reinhold Niebuhr's Account of the Sin of Pride," *Soundings* 65 (1982): 317.

4. In S. Ray's view, Niebuhr fails to sustain the paradoxical relationship between the competing logics of human freedom and finitude in his descriptions of some dimensions of society: "Niebuhr's discursive logic of social sin puts members of the *Negro community* in the odd position of being inherently sinners through their cultural location, yet unable to sin because the freedom necessary to offer the opportunity to be irresponsible is unavailable to them by virtue of their cultural location." Ray concludes that Niebuhr's discourse equates victim and sinner, implying "absolute environmental determinism." Victims' failures to overcome the strictures of the flawed environment tragically doom them to sin. They can do no other. (S. Ray, Jr., *Do No Harm: Social Sin and Christian Responsibility* [Minneapolis: Fortress, 2003], 69, 72).

5. R. Niebuhr, *Nature and Destiny of Man: A Christian Interpretation, Vol. I: Human Nature* (New York: C. Scribner's Sons, 1941), 179.

6. Dunfee, "The Sin of Hiding," 319.

7. A. McFadyen, *Bound to Sin*, 137-38.

8. S. Dunfee, "The Sin of Hiding," 320.

9. A. McFadyen, *Bound to Sin*, 137-38; cf. S. Dunfee, "The Sin of Hiding," 322-27. For more on the feminist critique of traditional, pride-oriented definitions of sin, see J. O'Connor, "Sin and Salvation from a Feminist Perspective," in *Problems in the Philosophy of Religion: Critical Studies in the Work of John Hick* (ed. Harold Hewitt, Jr.; New York: St. Martin's Press, 1991), 72-81 and John Hick's "Reply," *op. cit.*, 82-85.

10. Mitchell Dahood (*Psalms I: 1-50* [AB 16; Garden City: Doubleday, 1966], 239) translates "your servants are beaten and your people stumble."

Notes

11. The text is difficult. Many commentators hypothesize different vowels for the consonants משברים (mshbrym) to render "waves of the sea" instead of MT's "breaches, crashing." Of greater moment is the significance of the hithpael form of חטא. Robert Gordis (*The Book of Job: Commentary, New Translation and Special Studies* [New York: Jewish Theological Seminary of America, 1978], 487-88) lists four commonly proposed translations and three rabbinic uses of the verb in this form: (1) to miss, lose the way; (2) to fall into confusion; (3) to be beside oneself; (4) to withdraw, flee; (5) to importune; (6) to behave affectionately toward someone; and (7) to appease, placate. He accepts the repointing of the noun and translates, following rabbinic usage, "the waves importune Him." Edouard Dhorme (*A Commentary on the Book of Job* [trans. H. Knight; London: Nelson, 1967], 639) translates "the waves of the sea draw back." At any rate, the verb describes some reaction to the awesome character of Leviathan.

12. J. González has offered an insightful reading of Gen 2–3 from this perspective: "The usual interpretation of the passage in Genesis 3 regarding the temptation is that the serpent tempted the human creatures by declaring that they would be 'like God.' Seen in this light, the primal sin is pride. But as the story now stands, after the two creation narratives of Genesis 1 and 2, it would seem that the serpent was not promising them anything new. They were already 'like God' (Gen. 1:26-27). Perhaps then we ought not to interpret this passage as pointing to inordinate pride . . . but rather to inordinate humility based in a lack of trust. They were already like God. They were to have dominion over all the beasts, and therefore presumably also over the serpent. And yet they refused to stand up as 'others' before the tempter. In listening to the serpent and refusing to claim their godlikeness, they denied their for-otherness. . . . The result is not only their undoing but also that of the serpent and of all creation over against which they had denied their for-otherness" (*Mañana: Christian Theology from a Hispanic Perspective* [Nashville: Abingdon, 1990], 137-38).

13. Eleven of seventeen occurrences of the qal active participle appear in Proverbs and Ecclesiastes.

14. So Roland Murphy, *Ecclesiastes* (WBC 23A; Dallas: Word, 1992), 26-27; see also 100 ("bungler"). Given the etymology of the root, however, the expression "emptied" incorrectly implies that morality is inherent to *ht'*.

15. So Choon-Leong Seow, *Ecclesiastes: A New Translation with Introduction and Commentary* (AB 18C; Garden City: Doubleday, 1997), 157, 311. See also Tremper Longman III, *The Book of Ecclesiastes* (NICOT; Grand Rapids: Eerdmans, 1998), 110, 237; M. Fox, *A Time to Tear Down and a Time to Build Up: A Rereading of Ecclesiastes* (Grand Rapids: Eerdmans, 1999), 189-91, 300; and idem, *Qoheleth and his Contradictions* (JSOTSup 71; Sheffield, England: Almond, 1989), 188-90. Fox often translates "offender."

16. The Teacher of Ecclesiastes argues that incompetence is simply inefficient. It only makes for more work ("to the bumbler [*ht'*] he gives the task of gathering and heaping," Eccl 2:26). In the Teacher's reckoning, the common lot of humanity is labor or toil. The question is whether one can, by working wisely and well, find value intrinsic in one's labor. The unwise can only toil. As one might expect, Israelite Wisdom literature views ignorance and incompetence not in psychological or analytical terms, but primarily in terms of their real, negative consequences.

17. See the previous chapter, pp. 31-33.

18. Michael Fox, *Proverbs 1-9: A New Translation with Introduction and Commentary* (AB 18A; New York: Doubleday, 2000), 29, 33.

19. See M. Fox, *Proverbs 1-9*, 133.

20. Cf. Seow, *Ecclesiastes*, 311 calls attention to the "ruler among fools" mentioned in Eccl 9:17 as the context for the wisdom comparison in v. 18.

21. M. Fox (*A Time to Tear Down*, 300) observes: "Incompetence or obtuseness . . . undoes the efficacy of wisdom. . . . " Cf. T. Longman, *Ecclesiastes*, 231 and R. Murphy, *Ecclesiastes*, 100.

22. M. Fox (*Proverbs 1-9*, 38-43) helpfully surveys words employed in Proverbs for varieties of "fools" and "folly," the opposite of wisdom. Given the significance of wisdom in Proverbs as the key to living life as God intends, one should understand these terms as synonyms for "sin." They describe

a range of conditions from simple ignorance and immaturity, which in the view of Proverbs can be corrected—indeed, the purpose of the book is to provide corrective instruction for such individuals—to callous obstinacy, which may be beyond remedy. (1) At one extreme, the naïve *peti* (פֶּתִי) simply has not yet learned wisdom. Immature, inexperienced, and gullible, such persons may be taught (Prov 8:5; 9:4; 19:25; 21:11). In fact, Proverbs is addressed primarily to them (1:4). They must choose to learn (1:22), however, in order to avoid the danger that, untutored in wisdom and righteousness, their simplicity may evolve into truly perverse folly of the morally blind (14:18). (2) One can be *ba'ar* (בַּעַר), possessed of "animal-like brutishness" (Prov 30:2; 12:1; cf. Pss 73:22; 92:6; Jer 10:14, 21). Such ignorance is not itself morally culpable, but it renders one vulnerable to error and moral corruption. The antidote is the pursuit of wisdom. (3) One can be "empty-headed" (*hasar leb*, חֲסַר לֵב), ill-equipped, unable, or unwilling to make prudent decisions (Prov 6:32; 12:11; 17:18; 24:30; cf. Jer 5:21; Hos 7:11; Eccl 10:3). (4) The "oaf" (*kesil*, כְּסִיל) acts out of a stupidity (*kesilut*, כְּסִילוּת) that results from an active unwillingness to learn or from complacency (Prov 1:32; 3:26; 12:23; 14:8, 16; 15:2, 14; 17:12; 18:7; 19:10; 21:20; 26:6, 7, 9, 11; 28:26; 29:11; cf. Pss 49:11; 78:7; 85:9; 92:7; 94:8; Job 4:6; 8:14; 31:24; Eccl 2:14; 4:5, 13; 5:2; 7:4, 5, 6, 9; 10:2, 12, 15). Because the oaf does not understand right living, and does not care to take the effort to come to understand, the oaf is prone to pragmatic and moral blunders. Such stupidity can "twist [the oaf's] values so that he [*sic*] easily slides into wickedness and stays there ([Prov] 10:23; 13:19)." (5) The arrogance and insolence characteristic of the "mocker" לֵץ, *lets* (Prov 1:4; 3:34; 9:7-8; 13:1; 14:6; 15:12; 19:25, 29; 21:11, 24; cf. Isa 28:14-15; 29:19-21; Ps 119:51; Sir 3:28; 15:8; 38:18) prevents the mocker from attaining wisdom because the mocker cannot and will not submit to instruction. (6) True "fools" (*'ewilim*, אֱוִילִים) intentionally refuse to make moral choices. They are not necessarily unintelligent in pragmatic matters, but they are stupidly and willfully blind regarding God's plan (cf. Isa 19:12-15) for creation.

23. See Hubert Frankemölle, *1. Petrusbrief, 2. Petrusbrief, Judasbrief* (Neue Echter Bibel; Wurzburg: Echter, 1987), 105.

24. Clearly, 2 Pet 2 and Jude stand in some relationship to one another. Not only do the two passages treat substantially the same topic (false teachers), utilizing the same or similar argumentation (comparisons to the fallen angels, Sodom and Gomorrah, Balaam, the thematic of inappropriate desire, ἐπιθυμία, *epithumia*), but a number of verbal parallels confirms some direct relationship ("gloom"—Jude 6; 2 Pet 2:4; walking "after the flesh"—7; 2:10; authority—8; 2:10; "blaspheming glorious ones"—8; 2:10; daring/to dare—9; 2:10; "blasphemous/reviling judgment"—9; 2:12; "blaspheming what they do not know/in ignorance"—10; 2:12; "by nature"—10; 2:12; "irrational animals"—10; 2:12; "[Balaam's] wages"—11; 2:15; "stains"—12; 2:13; "dining together"—12; 2:13; "dry clouds/wells—12; 2:17).

Several factors suggest Peter's dependency on Jude. First, all of Jude appears in some form in 2 Peter. It is much more likely that the Petrine author would have utilized and adapted Jude as a source than that the author of Jude would have excerpted only this portion of 2 Peter (see, for example, John N. D. Kelly, *A Commentary on the Epistles of Peter and of Jude* [Harper's New Testament Commentaries; New York: Harper & Row, 1969], 226). Second, all of the differences between the two passages can be explained as Petrine "improvements" of Jude's style (Jude's "dry clouds," a nonsensical statement, for example, becomes "dry fountains") or as evidence of Peter's later date. Although some manuscripts of 2 Pet 2:13 agree with Jude 12 in reading "agape [feasts]," ἀγάπαις *agapais*, instead of the graphically similar ἀπάταις (*apatais*) reflected in the translation and interpretation favored here, it is more likely that scribes would have harmonized a divergent 2 Pet 2:13 to the Jude text than that they would have introduced a variant into the tradition. Thus, the Petrine text must be considered a conscious alteration by the author, perhaps because circumstances had changed since the writing of Jude. H. Frankemölle (*1. Petrusbrief*, 105) suggests that, by the date of the later writing, the rift between the heretical teachers and the orthodox community had grown to the point that they no longer participated in the *agape*. Similarly, 2 Peter ameliorates Jude's reliance on literature ultimately classified as non-canonical (*Enoch, Assumption of Moses*), omitting entirely Jude's direct reference to *Enoch* and abbreviating the accounts of the angel's sin and Michael's struggle for the body of Moses. This attitude (of embarrassment?) may indicate that 2 Peter was composed at a time when or in a place where the subsequent predominant evaluation of these works as extra-canonical was already emerging.

25. The discussion above assumes that the "false teachers" held some form of gnostic doctrine. Alternatively, Richard Bauckham (*Jude, 2 Peter* [Word Biblical Commentary 50; Waco: Word, 1983], 11-13), noting the absence of any strain of cosmological dualism in the opponents' apparent position, argues that they can best be described as "charismatic antinomians."

26. Both lists are abbreviated forms of a standard list employed in Jewish paraenesis to warn against repeating these behaviors (Sir 16:7-10; CD 2:17–3:12; 3 Macc 2:4-7; *T. Napht.* 3:4-5; *m. Sanh.* 10:3). See R. Bauckham, *Jude, 2 Peter,* 46.

27. See James C. VanderKam, *Textual and Historical Studies in the Book of Jubilees* (HSM 14; Missoula, Mont.: Scholars Press, 1977); idem, *Enoch and the Growth of the Apocalyptic Tradition* (CBQMS 16; Washington: Catholic Biblical Association, 1984).

28. The literature differs as to the name for these angels as a group: *2 Enoch* calls them the "Grigori" whereas the other literature agrees that they are the "Watchers." Lists of individual members of the group vary widely, especially with respect to the name of its leader (even *1 En.* 6–11 preserves variant traditions concerning Shemihazah and Asael).

29. See also CD 2:17-19; 1QapGen 2:1; *Tg. Ps.-J.* Gen 6:1-4; *2 Apoc. Bar.* 56:10-14; and cf. 1 Pet 3:19-20; 1 Cor 11:10.

30. Robert Henry Charles, *The Apocrypha and Pseudepigrapha of the Old Testament in English, Vol II: Pseudepigrapha* (Oxford: Clarendon, 1963 = 1913), 191-92.

31. R. Bauckham, *Jude, 2 Peter,* 79.

32. The Bible (Deut 34) reports only that when Moses died, God concealed his burial place. No account of a dispute between the archangel Michael and the devil over Moses' body appears in Scripture, or in *extant* extra-biblical materials either. Based on patristic references to such an account in the so-called *Assumption of Moses,* which has survived only in fragments, scholars often assume that Jude 9 must be based on the now lost ending to this work. For a very thorough discussion of the problems associated with reconstructing the ending of the *Assumption of Moses* as the source for Jude 9, see R. Bauckham, *Jude, 2 Peter,* 67-76.

33. Jude 8; 2 Pet 2:10. Scholars debate the precise references of the key terms κυριότης, *kuriotēs,* "authority, dominion," and δόξα, *doxa,* "glory." Outside Jude and 2 Peter, *kuriotēs* appears only in the parallel passages Eph 1:21 and Col 1:16, in which its plural form seems to refer to a class of angels. Jude and 2 Peter employ the singular form, however. In *Hermas, Sim.* v.6.1, and other post-biblical texts, it refers to the lordship of God. The cases cited in both Jude and 2 Peter, however, do not deal with God's authority in a direct sense, but with the principle of order built into creation. In this sense, then, Jude and 2 Peter charge the false teachers with disdain for the very moral fabric of God's good creation, in J. N. D. Kelly's words, "a blasphemous rebellion against the divinely established order of existence" (*Peter and Jude,* 338).

Relatedly, scholars have suggested that the *doxas* (plural) of Jude 8 and 2 Peter 2:10b refers to angels (so J. N. D. Kelly, *Peter and Jude,* 337 and others; cf. *2 En.* 22:7, 10; *Asc. Isa.* 9:32; *Allogenes* 50:19; 52:14; 55:17-18, 34; 57:25; cf. also 1QH 10:8; 11QPs^aZion 22:13), church dignitaries (so Charles Bigg, *A Critical and Exegetical Commentary on the Epistles of St. Peter and St. Jude* [ICC 46; Edinburgh: T. & T. Clark, 1975], 279 and others), or even the powers of state (so Bo Reicke, *The Epistles of James, Peter and Jude* [AB 37; Garden City, New York: Doubleday, 1964], 167).

34. R. Bauckham, *Jude, 2 Peter,* 58.

35. *Bib. Ant.* 18:13; cf. *Tg. Ps.-J.* Num 24:14, 25; 31:8; Philo, *Mos.* 1 295-300; Josephus, *Ant.* 4.126-130; *y. Sanh.* 10:28d; and cf. Rev 2:14. See R. Bauckham, *Jude, 2 Peter,* 81.

36. J. Segundo, et al. (*Evolution and Guilt* [trans. J. Drury; A Theology for Artisans of a New Humanity 5; Maryknoll, N.Y.: Orbis, 1974], 72), see the story of the Gerasene maniac (Mark 5:1-20; Luke 8:26-39) as illustrative of the notion that Jesus saves from this captivity to one's animal nature, the condition of being not-yet-human:

Notes

Here we see what liberation from diabolic possession means. If we compare the "before" and "after," we find the following features. *Before* the man moves around purposelessly, has no human domicile, makes inarticulate cries, suffers to no good purpose, and has brutal strength but does no positive work. *After* he displays common sense, is capable of speech and dialogue and tranquility, and can look for a proper social function.

In other words the demonic in the gospel is not the temptation that follows man's full development; it is the prehuman, presocial stage from which Christ and his followers are commissioned to free man. Man is in bondage to a power . . .

37. So Ernst Käsemann, *Commentary on Romans* (trans. G. Bromiley; Grand Rapids: Eerdmans, 1980), 94.

38. Scholars have suggested a number of solutions. Leon Morris (*The Epistle to the Romans* [Pillar New Testament Commentary; Grand Rapids: Eerdmans, 1988]) catalogues six possibilities suggested in the literature: (1) the apocalyptic radiance awaiting the justified; (2) "the divine standard for human life"; (3) God's image; (4) God's approval (as in John 12:43); (5) God's presence and communion; and (6) "sanctifying grace."

39. Charles Kingsley Barrett, *A Commentary on the Epistle to the Romans* (HNTC; New York: Harper, 1958), 103.

40. Cf. Moyer Hubbard, *New Creation in Paul's Letters and Thought* (SNTSMS 119; Cambridge: Cambridge University Press, 2002), 157-60.

41. J. Murphy-O'Connor, *Becoming Human Together: The Pastoral Anthropology of St. Paul* (Good News Studies 2; Collegeville, Minn.: Liturgical Press, 1982), 33-45; citation 44.

42. *Op. cit.*, 76.

43. Compare C. Gestrich, *The Return of Splendor in the World: The Christian Doctrine of Sin and Forgiveness* (trans. D. Bloesch; Grand Rapids: Eerdmans, 1997), 55: "Man is a flawed being. However, what he lacks through no fault of his own (constitutionally) is not a sure instinct, physical strength, and skill or the ability to adapt. *Rather, he lacks sufficient strength to be human in freedom, love, and dignity.* Put differently, he lacks the strength to maintain a reliable, constant humanity. To echo Kierkegaard, he lacks the strength to become a self on his own."

44. "The Person as Resonating Existential," *American Catholic Philosophical Quarterly* 66 (1992): 47 [39-56]. Others also stress the idea that one must grow into full and true personhood. P. Kerans, for example, comments that "one becomes a person by freely accepting responsibility for an emerging pattern of meaning in one's life. A person is one who stands by his story, who has attained the integrity (i.e. wholeness) whereby his actions and words reflect who he is and what his life stands for" (*Sinful Social Structures* [New York: Paulist, 1974], 45).

45. L. Mercadante, *Victims and Sinners*, 44-45.

46. Cf. H. Doweiko, "Substance Use Disorders as a Symptom of a Spiritual Disease," in *Addiction and Spirituality: A Multidisciplinary Approach* (eds. Oliver Morgan and Merle Jordan; St. Louis, Mo.: Chalice Press, 1999), 33-53. Sartre (*Being and Nothingness*, 625ff; cited in W. Lowe, *Evil and the Unconscious* [AAR Studies in Religion 30; Chico, Calif.: Scholars Press, 1983], 51) maintains that the common human response to the anxiety of existence is to accept some inauthentic, predefined, and predetermined modality. Bernard Lonergan terms this acceptance of the lie a *bias*, " . . . the choice, because of what we perceive to be a potential threat to our well-being, to eliminate from consideration data upon which we base our understanding, judgment, and decision. The result is a deliberate or semi-deliberate refusal to engage in the process of self-transcendence" (cited in Nancy Ring, "Sin and Transformation From a Systematic Perspective," *Chicago Studies* 23 [1984]: 308). Lonergan identifies four of these "biases": (1) the dramatic bias: the denial of affect (failure to acknowledge the real affective layer of our lives; lobotomized); (2) the individual bias: the denial of intersubjectivity; (3) the group bias: the inflation of intersubjectivity; and (4) general bias of common sense: the refusal to see future implications of immediate decisions (Ring, "Sin and Transformation," 308-12).

Notes

47. Howard Clinebell (*Understanding and Counseling Persons with Alcohol, Drug, and Behavioral Addictions: Counseling for Recovery and Prevention Using Psychology and Religion* [rev. ed.; Nashville: Abingdon, 1998], 51-52) suggests that dependency develops when two or more of five types of causative factors converge in the life of a particular individual. In addition to psychological wounds, these causative factors include: (1) biochemical properties of the substance make it inherently addictive; (2) physiological factors making some people more susceptible (there seems to be a genetic component to this susceptibility); (3) sociological and cultural factors that condition individuals to behave in certain ways (i.e., low rates of alcoholism in some cultures, high in others); (4) religious, existential, or philosophical dynamics—"Some belief and value systems, by which individuals and groups attempt to create meaning and purpose in their lives, are pathogenic or sickness causing."

48. L. Jampolsky, "Healing the Addictive Mind," in *Addiction and Spirituality: A Multidisciplinary Approach* (eds. Oliver Morgan and Merle Jordan; St. Louis, Mo.: Chalice Press, 1999), 66.

49. *Understanding and Counseling*, 51.

50. A. McFadyen, *Bound to Sin*, 114-15.

51. "In closed congregational systems where there is 'original shame,' one will find a legalism that requires perfection, an assault on the worth of people who do not (and by definition, cannot) maintain the rules. Therefore one may identify a theological anxiety that relationship to and with God is always in jeopardy. This anxiety usually leads to more shame and despair, increasing rigidity, alienation and distance, and the development of an 'acceptable appearance' requiring increasing control to maintain" (Laurel A. Burton, "Original Sin or Original Shame," *Quarterly Review* 8 [1988]: 38).

52. H. Clinebell, *Understanding and Counseling*, 60.

53. McFadyen, *Bound to Sin*, 123.

54. One can observe this process of co-opting the victim's will and thought to create a false framework of reality in many forms of indoctrination. George Orwell's fictional account of O'Brien's indoctrination of Wilson (*1984* [New York: The New American Library, 1961], 204-8) chillingly resembles first-person accounts of Latin American victims, such as those recorded by Lois A. Lorentzen in "Writing for Liberation: Prison Testimonials from El Salvador" (in *Liberation Theologies, Postmodernity, and the Americas*, D. Batstone, et al., eds. [New York: Routledge, 1997], 128-47).

55. McFadyen, *Bound to Sin*, 124.

56. A. McFadyen, *Bound to Sin*, 123-24.

57. *Op. cit.*, 147.

58. The Bible offers an interesting example of this dynamic with respect to the role of women. After Adam and Eve's adventure with the tree of knowledge, God describes the resulting situation of disorder in the relationship between the sexes. This disorder is the consequence of their actions; it is not God's purpose and plan. Instead of seeking the kingdom of God in harmony and balance, defenders of patriarchy often argue that the distortion (the way things are) is God's intention (the way things should be).

59. Compare C. Gestrich's observations (*The Return of Splendor*, 259) concerning the contemporary church's apparent reaction to the realization of the role of systemic sin, a reaction that threatens to shift the church's focus entirely away from the complicit role, however slight, of "victims" in their own oppression. The church must call victims, addicts, and the oppressed to the fullness of their humanity; the church must give them the courage and the tools to assert their Christlike nobility.

A. McFadyen (*Bound to Sin*, 118) observes that the complicity of the German populace in the holocaust exemplified the maintenance of a false reality through quiet assent to its basic premises. "This prevented them also from experiencing their participation in genocide as related to a mode of active willing which would render them *personally* accountable and responsible for their actions. For willing appears here more like a passive acceptance of reality, the order of which is constituted outside of the self, than a decision which rests ultimately on the internally generated freedom of the self in its willing."

60. A. McFadyen (*Bound to Sin*, 117) demonstrates that this mechanism of more or less passive cooperation with a false portrayal of reality was instrumental in the Nazis' success in executing the

Notes

holocaust. Even Germans who might have found Auschwitz repugnant were seduced into passive complicity.

61. Maria M. Fortune, "The Transformation of Suffering: A Biblical and Theological Perspective," in *Violence Against Women and Children: A Christian Theological Sourcebook* (eds. Carol J. Adams and Maria M. Fortune; New York: Continuum, 1998), 89.

62. *Bound to Sin*, 141-42. McFadyen identifies the feminist scholars who prefer each of these terms.

63. L. Mercadante, *Victims and Sinners*, 150 and especially citations in nn. 17-18.

64. A. McFadyen, *Bound to Sin*, 144.

65. W. Lowe (*Evil and the Unconscious*, 83) notes that tragedy expresses this paradox in terms of the "givenness" of the situation confronting the protagonist, its "facticity," and the protagonist's responsibility, "complicity," nonetheless.

66. But not, of course, exclusively there. It is evident in most situations of "loss of self." Even the will of the victims of the holocaust was co-opted, for example. Individual Jews confronted the choice between their own deaths and cooperation with the exterminators: "In the extermination camps . . . willing one's own survival meant an at least passive willing of others' destruction" (A. McFadyen, *Bound to Sin*, 126).

67. *Op. cit.*, 124-25.

68. A. McFadyen, *Bound to Sin*, 121: "...the fact that childhood sexual abuse tends to effect a distortion in survivors' basic patterns and structures of intentionality (including willing) constitutive of identity strongly suggests that the distortion of willing might be traceable back into the situation of abuse itself."

69. Cf. *op. cit.*, 114: "The presence of a history of abuse in the background of a significant proportion of abusers strongly suggests that their own disposition to abuse is not an artefact of their pure internality, having no explanation other than their free and arbitrary decision."

70. "Healing the Addictive Mind," 59-60.

71. "The Spirituality of Recovery: Recovery Is Learning to Love," in *Addiction and Spirituality: A Multidisciplinary Approach* (eds. O. Morgan and M. Jordan; St. Louis, Mo.: Chalice Press, 1999), 162-64.

72. *Op. cit.*, J. W. Ciarrocchi, "Spirituality for High and Low Rollers," 181.

73. H. Clinebell, *Understanding and Counseling*, 113-14.

74. N. Ring, "Sin and Transformation," 307-8.

75. H. Cox, *On Not Leaving*, x.

76. With reference to victims of child sexual abuse, McFadyen (*Bound to Sin*, 121) rightly insists that since "abuse [is] coincident with age-related disparities in power, status and knowledge . . . the child's willing cannot be operative as a cause of abuse. It also means, incidentally, that she is unable effectively to resist the abuse. For her will simply does not have the required potency, given her lack of power, status and knowledge relative to those significantly older than she is, either to initiate or to resist. Since it is impossible for the child to free herself from these disparities, there is no possibility here of genuine consent—of her freely willing to permit the abuse."

77. L. Jampolsky, "Healing the Addictive Mind," 66. Cf. L. Brakeman's reading of the story of the Gerasene demoniac as a counterpart to the slavery of addiction, "By Love Possessed," in *Addiction and Spirituality: A Multidisciplinary Approach* (eds. O. Morgan and M. Jordan; St. Louis, Mo.: Chalice Press, 1999), 195-213; and L. Mercadante, *Victims and Sinners*, 13.

78. *Understanding and Counseling*, 181.

79. L. Mercadante, *Victims and Sinners*, 23.

80. L. Jampolsky, "Healing the Addictive Mind," 57-58.

81. *Childhood and Society* (2nd ed.; New York: W. W. Norton, 1963), 262-63.

82. "Substance Use Disorders as a Symptom of a Spiritual Disease," in *Addiction and Spirituality: A Multidisciplinary Approach* (eds. O. J. Morgan and M. R. Jordan; St. Louis, Mo.: Chalice Press, 1999), 49.

83. "The religious sense of the absolute qualifies the will-to-live and the will-to-power by bringing them under subjection to an absolute will, and by imparting transcendent value to other human

Notes

beings, whose life and needs thus achieve a higher claim upon the self." Reinhold Niebuhr, *Moral Man and Immoral Society: A Study in Ethics and Politics* (Louisville: Westminster John Knox, 2001), 63.

84. S. Ray, *Do No Harm*, 49-50; cf. J. O'Connor's observation that human beings experience the pull between other-centeredness and self-centeredness as a "balancing-act" ("Sin and Salvation," 72-81).

85. E. Larsen, "The Spirituality of Recovery," 162-64.

4. Sin as Basic Mistrust

1. Ralph Waldo Emerson, "Immortality," http://www.rwe.org/comm/index.php?option=com_content&task=view&id=52&Itemid=229.

2. See above, pp. 31-33.

3. See, for example, Adam S. van der Woude, "אמן *'mn* firm, secure," *Theological Lexicon of the Old Testament* I (eds. Ernst Jenni and Claus Westermann; trans. M. Biddle; Peabody, Mass.: Hendrickson, 1997), 134-57; Erhard Gerstenberger, "בטח *bṭḥ* to trust," *TLOT* I, 226-30; Rudolf Bultmann, "πιστεύω, κτλ," *Theological Dictionary of the New Testament* 4 (ed. Gerhard Friedrich; trans. G. Bromiley; Grand Rapids: Eerdmans, 1968), 174-228.

4. Cf. the delightful reading of this passage by Hermann Gunkel (*Genesis* [trans. M. Biddle; MLBS 1; Macon: Mercer, 1997], 15-18, 28-31), still quite insightful despite the passage of time.

5. The tradition seems to have undergone a rather complex history of growth, which need not concern us here. The definitive study of the history of the tradition continues to be George W. Coats, *Rebellion in the Wilderness: The Murmuring Motif in the Wilderness Traditions of the Old Testament* (Nashville: Abingdon, 1968). See also Terry L. Burden, *The Kerygma of the Wilderness Traditions in the Hebrew Bible* (American University Studies, Series VII, Vol. 163; New York: Peter Lang, 1994).

6. In many respects, Ezek 20 represents a special case. It departs from the other "murmuring" texts in that it focuses not on Israel's lack of confidence in God's provision but on outright rebellion in the sense of disobedience of God's statutes and ordinances.

7. See G. W. Coats, *Rebellion in the Wilderness*, 29-43.

8. Apparently, the people's mistrust was a contagion affecting even Moses and Aaron: "Because you did not trust ['mn] in me, to show my holiness before the eyes of the Israelites, therefore you shall not bring this assembly into the land that I have given them" (Num 20:12).

9. See Walter Grundmann, "ἁμαρτάνω," *TDNT* 1 (ed. Gerhard Kittel; trans. G. Bromiley; Grand Rapids: Eerdmans, 1967), 302-3 and Karl H. Rengstorff, "ἁμαρτωλός," *op. cit.*, 329.

10. *Mark 8:27–16:20* (WBC 34B; Nashville: Thomas Nelson, 2001), 103.

11. *The Gospel According to St. Mark: The Greek Text with Introduction, Notes and Indexes* (London: Macmillan, 1952), 242. See also *ExT* 68 (1957): 240-44.

12. Rainer Metzner (*Das Verständnis der Sünde im Johannesevangelium* [WUNT 122; Tübingen: Mohr Siebeck, 2000]) classifies texts dealing with sin in John's Gospel in three thematic groupings: (a) in the miracle stories the sin concept occurs "in the context of the Pharisaic Torah question"; (b) in settings dealing with the fact that Jesus, the Revealer, announces the sin of the world (8:21, 24, 34, 46; 9:39-41; 15:22-24; 16:8ff.; 19:11); and (c) 1:29 (cf. 6:51; 10:11-18; 11:49-52; 15:13; 17:19; 18:14; 1 John 1:7; 2:2; 3:5, 16; 4:10) and 20:23 (cf. Matt 16:19; 18:18) deal with the removal/forgiveness of sin.

The miracle stories play out against the backdrop of the Pharisees' conviction, shared by Jesus' disciples (9:2), that illness is the consequence of sin (5:14; 9:34) and their claim that Jesus is a sinner (9:24, 25) because he violated the Sabbath (5:10, 16; 9:14, 16). In effect, the Pharisees' concept of sin is oriented entirely toward the fixed will of God as stated in the Torah (9:31). See R. Metzner, *Verständnis*, 24-25.

13. Incidentally, many scholars consider the reference to excommunication in vv. 22-23 a reflection of the situation faced by the early church; see also v. 34.

14. Rudolph Schnackenburg, *The Gospel According to St. John*, II (New York: Seabury Press, 1980), 256.

15. R. Metzner, *Verständnis*, 77-78.

16. S. Kierkegaard devoted an entire work (*The Concept of Anxiety*) to an analysis of anxiety. In *The Sickness Unto Death: A Christian Psychological Exposition for Upbuilding and Awakening* (eds. H. Hong and E. Hong; Princeton: Princeton, 1980), he defines sin in relation to the sense of despair that can arise from anxiety over the tension between human freedom and human limits. "Sin is: *before God, or with the concept of God, in despair not to will to be oneself, or in despair to will to be oneself*" (77). Cf. Stephen J. Duffy, "Our Hearts of Darkness: Original Sin Revisited," *Theological Studies* 49 (1988): 597-622, and J. D. Korsmeyer, *Evolution and Eden: Balancing Original Sin and Contemporary Science* (New York: Paulist, 1998), 66-67. Ted Peters (*Sin: Radical Evil in Soul and Society* [Grand Rapids: Eerdmans, 1994], 11-17) follows in the Kierkegaardian tradition to outline "seven steps down the path to radical evil": (1) anxiety, (2) unfaith (untrust), (3) pride, (4) concupiscence, (5) self-justification, (6) cruelty, and (7) blasphemy.

17. *Evil and the Unconscious* (AAR Studies in Religion 30; Chico, Calif.: Scholars Press, 1983), 79. Lowe summarizes the analysis offered by Norman O. Brown in *Life Against Death: The Psychoanalytical Meaning of History* (New York: Random House, 1959), 113.

18. See, especially, *Childhood and Society* (2nd ed.; New York: Norton, 1963), 247-51.

19. See, especially, *Stages of Faith: The Psychology of Human Development and the Quest for Meaning* (San Francisco: Harper and Row, 1981), 120.

20. *The Nature and Destiny of Man: A Christian Interpretation* I (Library of Theological Ethics; Louisville: Westminster John Knox, 1996), 252.

21. R. Niebuhr, *Nature and Destiny of Man* I, 179. S. Dunfee ("The Sin of Hiding: A Feminist Critique of Reinhold Niebuhr's Account of the Sin of Pride," *Soundings* 65 (1982): 319) argues that, in fact, the situation is even more complex than Niebuhr recognized. The two primary forms of sin may overlap. In the effort to overcome finitude, one chooses idolatry—hiding in the finite; in the attempt to escape freedom, one seeks to control the chaos in one's life—the sin of pride.

22. *Victims and Sinners: Spiritual Roots of Addiction and Recovery* (Louisville: Westminster John Knox, 1996), 20.

23. Gestrich's translator has "fundamental confidence"; he apparently did not know Erickson.

24. C. Gestrich, *The Return of Splendor in the World: The Christian Doctrine of Sin and Forgiveness* (trans. D. Bloesch; Grand Rapids: Eerdmans, 1997), 60-62.

25. *Childhood and Society*, 248.

26. L. Mercadante, *Victims and Sinners*, 31.

5. The Objective Nature of Sin: Intention Is (Relatively) Insignificant

1. Miguel de Unamuno, *The Tragic Sense of Life* (trans. J. Crawford Flitch; New York: Dover, 1954), 17.

2. J. Harold Ellens, "Sin or Sickness: The Problem of Human Dysfunction," in *Seeking Understanding: The Stob Lectures, 1986-1998* (Grand Rapids: Eerdmans, 2001), 454.

3. This problem has given rise to the dispute among Protestant theologians concerning whether justification by faith should be regarded in *forensic* or in *ethical* terms. That is, while there is no dispute regarding the fundamental assertion that God justifies the sinner as an expression of God's faithfulness in response to the sinner's faith, theologians debate whether God justifies by merely *declaring* the guilty party to be innocent or whether God alters the character of the guilty party, making the sinner just by sanctifying and transforming. In the Lutheran tradition, Dietrich Bonhoeffer expressed awareness of the hollow character of the conventional view of sin and salvation in the phrase "cheap grace" (see *The Cost of Discipleship* [trans. R. H. Fuller and I. Booth; London: SCM, 1959]).

Notes

4. *Sin Reconsidered* (New York: Paulist Press, 1984), 5.

5. Libertinism is the notion that, since God's grace through faith in Jesus Christ frees believers from condemnation under the law, believers are entirely free of the law's ethical demands.

6. "The Bible and Han," in *The Other Side of Sin: Woundedness from the Perspective of the Sinned-Against* (eds. A. S. Park and S. L. Nelson; Albany: State University of New York Press, 2001), 51. See also idem, *The Wounded Heart of God* (Nashville: Abingdon, 1993) and L. Mercadante, *Victims and Sinners: Spiritual Roots of Addiction and Recovery* (Louisville: Westminster John Knox, 1996), 150, especially citations in nn. 17-18. In a similar vein, Susan L. Nelson, who examines the phenomenon of untrust discussed in the previous chapter of this study under the rubric of "refusal [of grace]," observes that

> . . . while persons whose postures of refusal are born of a broken heart may actually participate as perpetrators in ongoing situations of refusal (e.g. battered children becoming batterers; those wounded by trusted others refuse to risk the vulnerability of their basic relationality) and thus can be said to be guilty of sin, their 'salvation' or 'reconciliation' entails not only repentance and the receiving of forgiveness (where appropriate), but *more basically* a process of healing that includes remembering their experience of being refused, grieving their loss, accepting their vulnerability, forgiving themselves for being so vulnerable, seeking restitution (where possible), and learning to reconnect and trust again. Where theologies have focused on sin as the problem of human alienation, they have failed to address these situations of brokenheartedness and to offer healing and hope to the brokenhearted. They have also, perhaps inadvertently, compounded the confusion and brokenheartedness of those who have been refused by reinforcing their sometimes inappropriate construal of themselves as wretched sinners.

See "For Shame, for Shame, the Shame of It All: Postures of Refusal and the Broken Heart," in *The Other Side of Sin: Woundedness from the Perspective of the Sinned-Against* (eds. A. S. Park and S. L. Nelson; Albany: State University of New York Press, 2001), 74-75.

In the same vein, J. H. Ellens ("Sin or Sickness: The Problem of Human Dysfunction," in *Seeking Understanding: The Stob Lectures, 1986-1998* [Grand Rapids: Eerdmans, 2001], 460, 489) suggests that the church should abandon the "blame-justification equation," that is, (anxiety/shame/guilt/blame) + (justice/penalty/punishment/expiation) = (justification/forgiveness/restoration/equilibrium), and employ the "grace-wholeness equation," that is, (pain/shame/guilt/anxiety) + (passion/compassion/mercy/grace) = (forgiveness [and other therapies]/affirmation/healing/actualization).

7. Somewhat surprisingly, given the centrality of intention to the dominant Western view of sin, the first Christian thinker to advocate intention as a defining characteristic of sin was Abelard (1079–1142); that is, not until the eleventh century did a Christian thinker propose that, in order to be classified as sin, an act must both produce an evil outcome *and* have been intended to do so. See John Marenbon, *The Philosophy of Peter Abelard* (Cambridge: Cambridge University Press, 1997), 251-64.

8. A. McFadyen, *Bound to Sin: Abuse, Holocaust and the Christian Doctrine of Sin* (Cambridge: Cambridge University Press, 2000), 27.

9. P. Ricoeur, "From Existentialism to the Philosophy of Language," *Philosophy Today* 17 (1973): 89. Theologians in the Augustinian tradition face the same dilemma. Augustine's notion that evil is an absence, a privation, rather than an essence runs the risk of identifying finitude itself with sin and guilt. For him, God is not responsible for evil since God did not create it. Rather, God created a finite world. The limitations of creatureliness result inevitably in error/wrong/injury. (Cf. W. Lowe, *Evil and the Unconscious* [AAR Studies in Religion 30; Chico, Calif.: Scholars Press, 1983], 102.)

10. P. Tillich describes a situation in which humans are "forced to choose between a vacuous innocence and a guilty autonomy" (W. Lowe, *Evil and the Unconscious*, 111). Thus, on the one hand, finitude, which is given, issues in error/sin, and on the other, freedom, which must be exercised, issues in alienating autonomy.

Notes

11. W. Lowe, *Evil and the Unconscious*, 114.

12. L. Mercadante, *Victims and Sinners*, 30. Pelagius was Augustine's theological opponent on the question of the role of free will in human behavior. He held that human beings are truly and entirely free, that is, that a given human being could, at least theoretically, choose not to sin. Augustine's view of original sin disallowed even the theoretical possibility of human sinlessness. Manicheans, on the other hand, were dualists who argued that purity belongs only to the spiritual realm. As physical creatures, human beings are inherently evil. Augustine argued, rather, that physical human beings were created good, but by an act of will, fell into sinfulness. That is, human sin is not an essential characteristic of being human (ontology), but is a secondary, historical characteristic of human behavior; sin is inevitable because of inheritance from Adam, not because of design by God.

13. As J. H. Ellens ("Sin or Sickness," 453) observes: "Our information is inadequate, our experience too limited, our vision too blurred, our inherent qualities insufficient, our maturity incomplete. We are cast out of the womb of Eden without a vote. We cannot catch hold of our Father's hand unless he reaches out and clasps ours in his. We long mystically and confusingly for home. Meanwhile, we stumble often, ever struggle, and blindly stagger, looking for the light." Furthermore, "if we are to take the biblical terminology seriously . . . we are forced to the conclusion that the Bible is saying more about our pathology than our moral perfidy, more about our lostness than our chosen lousiness."

14. See Mark E. Biddle, "The 'Endangered Ancestress' and Blessing for the Nations," *JBL* 109 (1990): 599-611.

15. Compare R. Knierim, *Hauptbegriffe für Sünde*, 68: "Neither the motive nor the attitude of the actor is qualified, but his act."

16. The noun הַטָּאת usually connotes the remediation of the effects of wrong done, in which case it is sometimes translated "sin offering," although this translation overlooks the fact that the הַטָּאת remediates wrongs committed against both human and divine parties, both intentionally and unintentionally. In fact, it also remediates wrongful circumstances or conditions involving inanimate objects (Exod 30:10; Lev 8:15; 14:49, 52; Ezek 43:20, 22, 23; 45:18) and for which no actor is discernible, that is, in which "guilt" cannot pertain (Lev 12:6, 8; 14:13, 19, 22, 31; 15:15, 30; Num 8:7, 8, 12; 19:9, 17). Since the priestly literature, the most common context for the term, focuses on the ritual aspect of such remediation, not on assessing responsibility for the wrong committed, and since the same term describes the remediation of intentional and unintentional wrongs alike, the context often leaves unclear the degree of volition involved in the commission of the act.

17. See Mark E. Biddle, "Murder," in *The Mercer Dictionary of the Bible* (ed. Watson E. Mills; Macon: Mercer University Press, 1990), 588-90.

18. The root is common Semitic with cognates in Akkadian ("to miss, sin"), Ugaritic ("to sin"), Aramaic ("to sin"), Arabic ("to commit an error"), and Ethiopic ("to not find"). The verb occurs in the Bible 237 times and the various nouns 358 times (including 2x in Aramaic). Its usage is highly concentrated in the priestly traditions. In biblical Hebrew, the verb has the following meanings: "to miss, err" (qal), "to recognize that one has erred" or "to remediate an error" (piel), "to cause to do wrong" or "to let oneself slip into error" (hiphil), and "to remove one's wrong" (hithpael). Related nouns denote: (1) the act of wrongdoing, the wrong done (חֵטְא *het'*, חֲטָאָה *het'ah*, חַטָּאָה *hatta'ah*, חֲטָאָה *hata'ah*, and חַטָּאת *hatta't*); (2) the actor, the offender (חַטָּא *hatta'*); (3) the state of the actor following the wrong, "guilt" (חֵטְא *het'*, חֲטָאָה *hata'ah*); and (4) the means for remediating the act, the "sin offering" (חַטָּאת *hatta't*).

The most common uses of the root (including the qal of the verb and the various nouns) in the Hebrew Bible apply to actions in the context of relationship either with another human being, in which case translators often render it as "to wrong" or "to offend," or with God, when the term takes on connotations of the English "sin." In keeping with the inherent focus on the nature of the act and not the character of the actor's intention, however, in both of these realms of relationship the term may describe either *unintentional* wrongs or *intentional* offenses. Since the term itself implies nothing of the actor's attitude, context determines the degree of intentionality involved in a given case. Not surprisingly, in a number of instances, the context supplies no clues. Texts that clearly belong to one of four categories defined by the identity of the offended party and the intention of the offender include the following: (1) *intentional wrongs committed against a person*—Judg 11:27; 1 Sam 24:12 [11 Eng.]; 2 Sam 19:20; 1 Kgs 8:31; 2 Kgs 18:14; Prov 14:21; (2) *unintentional wrongs committed against a person*—Gen 31:26; 40:1; 41:9; 1 Sam 20:1; 26:21; 1 Kgs 1:21; 18:9; Jer 37:18; (3) *intentional wrongs against God*—Gen 4:7; 13:13; 18:20; 39:9, passim; Exod 9:27, passim; Lev 26:18, 21, 24, 28; Num 5:6, 7; 14:40; 16:22, 26; 21:7, passim; Deut 1:41; 9:16, 21, 27, passim; Josh 7:11, 20; 24:19; Judg 10:10, 15; 1 Sam 2:17; 7:6; 12:10, 19, 23, passim; 2 Sam 12:13; 24:17; 1 Kgs 8:33, 34, 35, 36 (and parallels), passim; 2 Kgs 3:3; 10:29, 31, passim; Isa 1:4; 3:9; 6:7 passim; Jer 2:35; 3:25, passim; Ezek 3:20, 21; 14:13, passim; Hos 4:7, 8; 8:11, 13, passim; Amos 5:12; 9:8, 10; Mic 1:5, 13; 3:8; 6:7, 13; 7:9; Zeph 1:17; Pss 4:4; 25:7, 18, passim, Job 1:5, 22; 2:10, passim; Prov 5:22; 10:16; 13:6, passim; Eccl 8:12; Lam 1:8; 4:6, 13, 22; 5:7, 16, passim; Dan 4:27; 9:5, 8, 11, 15, 16, 20, 24; Neh 1:6; 6:13, passim; 2 Chr 7:14; 25:4; 28:13; 33:19; (4) *unintentional wrongs against God*—Gen 20:6; Lev 4:1–5:26 [6:7 Eng.]; Num 15:27-28; 22:34; Ezek 45:20.

19. Hebrew מעל, *m'l*, "to trespass" (5:20 [6:1 Eng.]), in the sense of the "misappropriation or misuse of sancta" (so Jacob Milgrom, *Leviticus 1-16: A New Translation with Introduction and Commentary* [AB 3; New York: Doubleday, 1991], 320).

20. So Nobuyoshi Kiuchi, *The Purification Offering in the Priestly Literature* (JSOTSup 56; Sheffield: Sheffield, 1987), 31-34.

21. So J. Milgrom, *Leviticus 1-16*, 338 and frequently elsewhere.

22. *Loc. cit.*

23. *Leviticus* (BKAT 3/3; Neukirchen: Neukirchener, 1992), 189.

24. Daniel Friedman (*To Kill and Take Possession: Law, Morality, and Society in Biblical Stories* [Peabody, Mass.: Hendrickson, 2002], 136) observes that post-biblical Jewish tradition regards Jephthah's actions as illegal (Josephus, *Ant. Jud.* 5:7:10) and describes Jephthah as an ignoramus (see *Midr. Tanh. Behuqqotay* 5).

25. Alternatively, fear at what he had inadvertently done, by reflex. The question of whether the primary force of the ancient Israelite taboo *actually* resided in the ancient Israelite belief in the inherent danger of the sacred or was a *real* force misses the point for the purposes of this discussion.

26. For a discussion of Deuteronomy's principles of interpretation regarding the commandment against killing and Jesus' endorsement and extension of these principles, see M. Biddle, *Deuteronomy* (Smyth & Helwys Bible Commentary 4; Macon, Ga.: Smyth & Helwys, 2003), 311.

27. See J. Adamson, *The Epistle of James* (NICNT; Grand Rapids: Eerdmans, 1976), 69 on James as a commentary on the Sermon on the Mount with close affinities also to the *Didache*.

28. J. H. Ropes, *Epistle of St. James*, 155-56.

29. John Baillie, *Invitation to Pilgrimage* (New York: Scribner, 1942), 56; cited in J. Adamson, *Epistle of James*, 70.

30. Cf. Mark E. Biddle, *Polyphony and Symphony in Prophetic Literature: Rereading Jeremiah 7-20* (SOTI 2, Macon: Mercer, 1996), 103-11.

31. The Greek term τέλειος has connotations of being suited to the objective and can be translated "complete, perfect, whole, mature," etc. The traditional translation of Matt 5:48, "Be perfect as your heavenly Father is perfect," suggests a standard beyond attainment. In the context of the Sermon on the Mount, with its call for purity of will, singleness of vision, and commitment to one master and its warnings against hypocrisy (two-facedness), anxiety (two-mindedness), and inconsistency of being and behavior, Jesus seems to be calling for "wholeness" in the sense of integrity, consistency of being and doing, of identity and action. Hence the translation offered above.

32. Since the human will is so complex, according to Matthew's Jesus, it is not always possible to conclude from the evidence of good fruit that the tree is good. Wolves wear sheep's clothing. For an insightful discussion of this complexity in Matthew's record of Jesus' teaching, see Dan O. Via, Jr., *Self-Deception and Wholeness in Paul and Matthew* (Minneapolis: Fortress, 1990), 77-132, esp. 96-97.

Notes

33. Ironically, the healing stories in the Gospels play out against the backdrop of the Pharisees' conviction, shared no doubt by the populace and certainly by Jesus' disciples (John 9:2), that illness is the consequence of sin (John 5:14; 9:2ff., 34). The Pharisees further claim that Jesus is a sinner (John 9:24, 25) because he violated the Sabbath (John 5:10, 16; 9:14, 16) by healing. In effect, the Pharisees' concept of sin is oriented entirely toward the fixed will of God as stated in the Torah (John 9:31; see R. Metzner, *Das Verständnis der Sünde*, 24-25).

34. Compare Louis Ruprecht, Jr., *Tragic Posture and Tragic Vision: Against the Modern Failure of Nerve* (New York: Continuum, 1994), 90.

35. "Usually" because, on the example of hurricanes, in certain instances, victims unwisely and arrogantly refuse the advice of authorities to evacuate danger zones, or to build further inland in the first place, or to employ certain technologies in construction. In such cases, "victims" are complicit in their suffering.

36. See the discussion of the complicity of certain victims in their victimization above, pp. 67-70.

37. Northrop Frye, *Anatomy of Criticism* (New York: Atheneum, 1966), 162; cf. George Steiner, *The Death of Tragedy* (Oxford: Oxford University Press, 1961), 9, 128, 222.

38. John Morreall, *Comedy, Tragedy, and Religion* (Albany: SUNY Press, 1999), 86.

39. John F. Haught, "Evolution, Tragedy, and Hope," in *Science and Theology: The New Consonance* (ed. T. Peters; Boulder, Colo.: Westview Press, 1998), 236.

40. See the discussion in John McDowell, *Hope in Barth's Eschatology: Interrogations and Transformations Beyond Tragedy* (Ashgate New Critical Thinking in Theology & Biblical Studies; Burlington, Vt.: Ashgate, 2000), 20-21.

41. Interestingly, Laius incurred the curse by abducting Chryssipus, son of King Pelos, who had given Lauis sanctuary. Before that, there had been generation after generation of deception and evil in Laius' family, culminating in Oedipus' fate. He is doomed even though he perpetrates no willful wrong. The system of sin, unaddressed and unrighted, creates such disharmony in the universe that even "good" acts (trying to avoid patricide) become tainted.

42. Sophocles, "Oedipus Rex," in *Ten Greek Plays in Contemporary Translations* (ed. L. R. Lind, ed.; trans. A. Cook; Boston: Houghton Mifflin, 1957), 134. The translation "sin" should not mislead. The Greek text of the last clause reads οὐδ᾽ ὁρᾶν ἵν εἰ κακοῦ *oud' oran in ei kakou* ("ΟΙΔΙΠΟΥΣ ΤΨΡΑΝΝΟΣ," in *Sophocles: With an English Translation* [vol. 2; trans. F. Storr; The Loeb Classical Library; New York: G. P. Putnam's Sons, 1939], 36). *Kakou/kakos* refers, quite generically, to anything "bad" or "wrong." Thus, Teiresias does not explicitly charge Oedipus with *hubris*, or even with *hamartia*.

43. J. Morreall offers a "Tragic Profile" involving five viewpoints characteristic of tragedy. Tragedy regards at least some suffering to be: (1) inexplicable, (2) unavoidable, (3) pointless, (4) unredeemable, and (5) worthy of resistance (*Comedy, Tragedy, and Religion*, 44).

44. L. Ruprecht, Jr. (*Tragic Posture and Tragic Vision* [1994], 72) attributes this fundamental insight to Hegel.

45. *Comedy, Tragedy, and Religion*, 76-77.

46. Alasdair MacIntyre, *After Virtue* (2nd ed.; South Bend, Ind.: University of Notre Dame Press, 1984), 179, 243; cited in L. Ruprecht, Jr., *Tragic Posture and Tragic Vision*, 143.

47. *Christianity, Tragedy, and Holocaust Literature* (Contributions to the Study of Religion 41; Westport, Conn.: Greenwood Press, 1995), 150-51.

48. J. McDowell, *Hope in Barth's Eschatology*, 55. No less than K. Barth can, for example, contend that, in the coming of Christ, "the tragedy of human existence is dissolved" (*The Doctrine of God* [vol. 2, pt. 1 of *Church Dogmatics*; trans. T. Parker; Edinburgh: T. & T. Clark, 1957], 374).

49. L. Ruprecht, Jr., *Tragic Posture and Tragic Vision*, 16-17.

50. L. Ruprecht, Jr. (*Tragic Posture and Tragic Vision*, 72; cf. 213), following Hegel, takes the plight of the heroine of Sophocles' *Antigone* as the paradigm for this root of tragedy. She faced the dilemma of a legal right and a moral right in competition. To choose either would result in tragedy.

51. L. Ruprecht, Jr., *Tragic Posture and Tragic Vision*, 126.

52. Cf. L. Ruprecht, Jr., *Tragic Posture and Tragic Vision*, 182.

Notes

53. Cf. L. Ruprecht, Jr., *Tragic Posture and Tragic Vision*, 128.

54. Nicholas Lash, *The Beginning and End of Religion* (Cambridge: Cambridge University Press, 1996), 207: "There are scars, it seems, in heaven." Cf. Donald MacKinnon, *Explorations in Theology 5* (London: SCM Press, 1979), 192.

55. Donald MacKinnon, *Borderlands of Theology and Other Essays* (London: Lutterworth Press, 1968), 92ff.

56. M. Steele, *Christianity, Tragedy, and Holocaust Literature*, 155, citing Lawrence Langer.

57. L. Ruprecht, Jr., *Tragic Posture and Tragic Vision*, 229.

6. *Guilt as a Condition and a Consequence: Sin and Systems*

1. T. S. Eliot, "Choruses from 'The Rock,'" no. II, *The Complete Poems and Plays: 1909-1950* (New York: Harcourt Brace, 1980), 101.

2. In what may be a hopeful sign that the system may be coming to some awareness that the black-and-white approach to all crimes lacks the nuance sufficient to describe reality, the Supreme Court ruled six to three on *Atkins v. Virginia* (01-8452) in June of 2002 that the execution of the moderately retarded (IQ of 70 or less) violates the "cruel and unusual punishment" clause of the Eighth Amendment to the Constitution. The ruling applies only to capital punishment, however, and does not address the problem of defining justice for the mentally and emotionally ill or disadvantaged.

3. Every state in the Union allows for the transferal of juveniles to the jurisdiction of adult courts, usually as a result of a decision from the bench. Fourteen states even mandate treatment of juveniles as adults under certain conditions. Fifteen assign the decision to the prosecuting attorney. The United States is one of only six countries in the world to execute persons who were under the age of eighteen when the crime was committed (Iran, Nigeria, Pakistan, Saudi Arabia, and Yemen are the others). With nine executions of minor criminals in the last decade, the United States leads the world in this category. Fortunately, perhaps, at the time of this writing (Fall 2004), the Supreme Court has under review *Roper v. Simmons* (03-0633), a case dealing with the propriety of the death penalty for juveniles sixteen to seventeen years of age that has the potential to reverse a Supreme Court ruling issued in 1989 in *Stanford v. Kentucky* (492-361), which upheld the constitutionality of the death penalty for juveniles over fifteen years of age.

4. On 10 December 2003, Florida's Fourth District Court of Appeals overturned the conviction of Lionel Tate, who was twelve at the time of the incident, in the first-degree murder of his neighbor Tiffany Eunick (six years old). The court found that Tate was too young to materially participate in his own defense—that is, he was too young to understand the court proceedings and their implications.

5. Marc Ambinder, "'You Helped This Happen': Falwell's Controversial Comments Draw Fire," n.p. [cited 6 May 2004]. Online: http://abcnews.go.com/sections/politics/DailyNews/WTC_Falwell010914.html. To be entirely fair, under pressure Falwell issued an apology only a few days later (Sept. 18, 2001; Jerry Falwell, "Jerry Falwell Apologizes," n.p. Cited 6 May 2004. Online: http://www.nljonline.com/state.htm):

> Last Thursday during an appearance on the 700 Club, in the midst of the shock and mourning of a dark week for America, I made a statement that I should not have made and which I sincerely regret. I apologize that, during a week when everyone appropriately dropped all labels and no one was seen as liberal or conservative, Democrat or Republican, religious or secular, I singled out for blame certain groups of Americans.
>
> This was insensitive, uncalled for at the time, and unnecessary as part of the commentary on this destruction. The only label any of us needs in such a terrible time of crisis is that of "American."

Notes

I obviously did not state my theological convictions very well and I stated them at a bad time. During the difficult weeks ahead there will be much discussion about the judgment of God. It is a worthy discussion for all of us at a time when we are reminded of the fleeting nature of life itself, but it is a complicated discussion.

I do not know if the horrific events of September 11 are the judgment of God, but if they are, that judgment is on all of America—including me and all fellow sinners—and not on any particular group.

My statements were understandably called divisive by some, including those whom I mentioned by name in the interview. This grieves me, as I had no intention of being divisive.

In conclusion, I blame no one but the hijackers and terrorists for the barbaric happenings of September 11.

6. The noun and its Aramaic cognate, derived from the verbal root עוה ('wh), occur only in the Bible and in dependent middle Hebrew and Jewish Aramaic literature. The verbal root is related to Arabic 'awa, "to bend," or ġawa, "to diverge from the way." Hebrew also attests the nominal derivatives עוים ('iwim), "reeling" (Isa 19:14), עַוָּה ('awwah, Ezek 21:32), עִי ('iy, Jer 26:18; Mic 1:6; 3:12; Ps 79:1; Job 30:24; cf. place-name "Ai"), and מְעִי (me'iy, Isa 17:1 txt?), all with the meaning "ruin."

7. Unlike ht', חטא, 'awon does not also function as a term for the remediation or removal of guilt. That is, there is no 'awon sacrifice. A number of instances of עָוֹן in the Masoretic text seem to reflect confusion with עֳנִי, "affliction." See 2 Sam 16:12 and Ps 31:11 [10]. Following Carl Heinrich Cornill, many scholars and the NRSV, JB, and REB translations emend "their guilt" in Ezek 32:27, which yields no sense, to read "their shields," an emendation based on the assumption of scribal confusion regarding the first letter of the word between צ and ע. Although this emendation has no textual support, it is based on a common confusion and it produces a sensible text.

8. R. Knierim, *Hauptbegriffe*, 239-43; idem, "עָוֹן 'awon perversity," *TLOT* 2 (Peabody, Mass.: Hendrickson, 1997), 864.

9. Notably, instances of the term as a designation of the act of wrongdoing itself comprise the clear minority of usages. See Exod 34:9; 1 Sam 3:13; Isa 43:24; 50:1; 57:17; 59:2; Jer 5:25; 11:10; 16:18; Ezek 7:19; 14:3, 4, 7; 16:49; 18:30; 28:18; 29:16; 36:3; 43:10; 44:12; Mal 2:6; Pss 38:18; 49:5; 130:3; Job 13:23; 22:5; 31:11, 28; Dan 9:13; Ezra 9:13; cf. also a series of uses in which the term seems to encompass the transition from act to the resultant state of guilt (Lev 16:21; Num 5:15; 2 Sam 22:24 [= Ps 18:24 (23)]; 1 Kgs 17:18; Isa 53:5; Jer 13:22; 16:17; 18:23; 36:3; 50:20; Hos 4:8; 12:9 [8 Eng.]; Pss 36:3; 51:9; 59:5 [3]; 78:38; 85:2; 89:32; 130:3; Lam 2:14; Dan 9:16).

10. Although, in a few texts, elements of legal culpability can be heard (2 Kgs 7:9; Isa 22:14; Job 11:6; Ps 32:2).

11. In biblical Hebrew, the verbal root appears in the basic meaning "to bend/twist/contort" (piel, Isa 24:1—YHWH "twists" the face of the earth; Lam 3:9—YHWH "bends" the path of the sufferer by blocking it off) and "to be bent/twisted/contorted" (niphal, Isa 21:3—being "bent over" in childbirth; Ps 38:7 [6]—being "bowed down" in suffering; Prov 12:8—a "twisted" mind contrasted with having good sense). In certain contexts, especially those with a political component, it connotes deceit, treachery, or disloyalty (qal, Esth 1:16—Vashti's disobedience; Dan 9:5, paralleled with מרד, mrd, "to rebel"; niphal, 1 Sam 20:30, again paralleled with מרד, mrd; hiphil, 2 Sam 19:20—Shimei's act of disloyalty; Jer 9:4 [5]—paralleled with דבר שקר, dbr shqr, "speaking lies"). With certain direct objects (hiphil, Jer 3:21—"perverting their way" parallel to "forgetting YHWH"; Job 33:27—"perverting the right") and, finally, on its own, in deuteronomistic diction, reflecting the common usage of the noun (hiphil, 2 Sam 7:14; 24:17; 1 Kgs 8:47 || 2 Chr 6:37), the verb denotes wrongdoing in a religious sense.

12. Other prophets compare the effects of 'awon to the degeneration of vines of purest stock into a wild state (Jer 2:20-22) or to a cause for stumbling (Hos 5:5; 14:2-3 [1-2 Eng.]. For the idea that 'awon encompasses the act and the resultant twisted condition see also, for example, Gen 4:13; Num 5:31; 14:34; 15:31; 1 Sam 25:24; Isa 64:5-8 [6-9]; Jer 3:13; Ezek 24:23; Ps 69:28; Prov 5:22.

Notes

13. See also Jer 25:12.
14. See also, for example, Isa 64:5-8 [6-9 Eng.]: "Our *'awonot*, like the wind, take us away."
15. For the idea of solidarity with ancestors in perpetuating ancestral sin, see also Jer 14:20; Ezra 9:6-7; Neh 9:2.
16. Cf. Lev 26:39; Isa 14:21. See M. Biddle, *A Redaction History of Jeremiah 2:1-4:2* (AThANT 77; Zurich: TVZ, 1990), 138-45 (esp. 143-44 n. 23), for a discussion of scholarship on the question of the supposed evolution of Israelite thought from collectivism to individualism.
17. It is important to remember with regard to time references that, from the standpoint of the Gospel writers, the predicted persecution of the "prophets and apostles" (Luke 11:49), to include "crucifixions and scourgings in the synagogue" (Matt 23:34), is taking place or has taken place.
18. Matthew and Luke share the following wording. Where they employ synonyms or variant forms of a common term, the translation appears in italics: "Woe to you . . . because you build the *memorials* of the prophets . . . *You witness against yourselves*. . . . Because of this . . . I *send you* prophets. Some of them you will kill and *persecute in various ways*. . . . *So that you may be held accountable* for the blood spilt . . . from the blood of Abel . . . to the blood of Zechariah . . . *who was killed* between the *sanctuary and the altar*. Truly, I say to you, *it shall come upon* this generation."
19. Most notably, Matthew's references to crucifixion, the synagogue, and persecutions "from town to town" seem to reflect his concern with Christianity's increasingly troubled relationship with the synagogue. In turn, this provides a setting for his theology of history, stamped with a deuteronomistic imprint. The Pharisees bring the cumulative guilt of the generations for rejecting God's messengers to its full measure (v. 32) by rejecting Jesus and, subsequently, his apostles. In Matthew's view, the Jewish Wars with Rome were the consequence. See, Odil Hannes Steck, *Israel und das gewaltsame Geshick der Propheten: Untersuchungen zur Überlieferung des deuteronomistischen Geschichtsbildes im Alten Testament, Spätjudentum und Urchristentum* (WMANT 23; Neukirchen: Neukirchener Verlag, 1967), 289-316.
20. Not in historical order (cf. the prophet Uriah, who died by order of King Jehoiakim, who ruled 608–597, during Jeremiah's lifetime; see Jer 26:20-23). Second Chronicles 24:20-22 records Zechariah's death at the hands of the people on the command of King Joash (i.e., in the late ninth/early eighth cent. BCE, over two centuries *before* Uriah's death). The Hebrew canon ends with the books of Chronicles.
21. See also Gen 19:15; Ps 107:17.
22. In several instances, in fact, the Old Testament uses the phrase in tandem with the expression פקד חטא (*pqd ht'*, "to visit sin"; Jer 14:10; Hos 8:13; 9:9), on which see immediately below.
23. Cf. Hos 7:1 (Hebrew גלה, *glh*, "to uncover, reveal"); Ps 90:8; Job 10:6 בקש, *bqsh*, "to seek out"); 20:27 (גלה, *glh*).
24. See also Gen 44:16; 1 Sam 3:10-14; Isa 27.9, Lam 4:2.
25. Karl Rahner argues that sin is its own result/punishment. An imposed punishment is extrinsic to the act and, necessarily then, somewhat artificial. "The punishments of sin are the persistent objectifications of the bad moral decisions, being themselves contrary to the true nature of the free subject. . . . [Punishment] can and must be the connatural intrinsic consequence of sin." See Ron Highfield, *Barth and Rahner in Dialogue: Toward an Ecumenical Understanding of Sin and Evil* (American University Studies VII/62; New York: Peter Lang, 1989), 161-62, who cites Rahner's "Sin II: The Punishment of Sin," *Encyclopedia of Theology: The Concise Sacramentum Mundi* (ed. K. Rahner; New York: Crossroad, 1975), 1587.
26. *Prolegomena Eines Alttestamentlers zur Erbsündenlehre* (Quaestiones Disputatae 37; Freiburg/Basel/Wien: Herder, 1968), 78-93; see below, pp. 132-34.
27. Cf. above, pp. 41-44.
28. E. Käsemann, *Commentary on Romans* (trans. G. Bromiley; Grand Rapids: Eerdmans, 1980), 44.
29. See above, pp. 98-100.

Notes

30. The Hebrew term סלח, *slh*, "to forgive," appears only forty-seven times in the Hebrew Bible. Of these, eight occur with *'awon* as object. Thirteen appear in priestly materials following the verb כפר, *kpr*, "to cover, atone," to describe the result of the sacrifice for sin (Lev 4:20, 26, 31, 35; 5:10, 13, 16, 18, 26 [6:7 Eng.]; 19:22; Num 15:25-26, 28). Three instances refer not to forgiveness of sin but to pardoning the obligation of a woman's vow if her father or husband chooses not to ratify it (Num 30:6, 9, 13 [5, 8, 12 Eng.]). Only the remaining twenty-three instances (sixteen if one reduces the number to account for the parallels between 1 Kgs 8 and 2 Chr 6, Solomon's prayer dedicating the temple) employ the verb in the absolute sense, that is, without object, to refer to the forgiveness of sin. These usages fall generally into three categories: (1) prayers for forgiveness (1 Kgs 8:30, 34, 36, 39, 50 ‖ 2 Chr 6:21, 25, 27, 30, 39; 2 Kgs 5:18 [2x]; Amos 7:2; Dan 9:19); (2) assurances of forgiveness (Isa 55:7; Jer 50:20; 2 Chr 7:14); and (3) refusals to forgive (Deut 29:19 [20 Eng.]; 2 Kgs 24:4; Jer 5:1, 7 [2x]; Lam 3:42). Cf. the discussion in J. J. Stamm, "סלח *slh* to forgive," *TLOT* 2 (eds. E. Jenni and C. Westermann; trans. M. Biddle; Peabody, Mass.: Hendrickson, 1997), 797-803.

31. Interestingly, the concentration in Jeremiah is in a layer of materials dealing with the fears of the exilic community that Judah's disregard for the covenant may have effectively ended the covenant relationship.

32. Surprisingly, given the concentration of prayers for forgiveness and deliverance there, the verb "to forgive" occurs only twice in the Psalter, both with *'awon* as the object. This distribution supports the observation that the Bible prefers language describing the deactivation of sin's afterlife. Mere disregard for sin does nothing to disrupt the continuation of sin's effects.

33. See Johann Jakob Stamm, *Erlösen und Vergeben im AT: Eine Begriffsgeschichtliche Untersuchung* (Berlin: Francke, 1940), 57.

34. *Hauptbegriffe*, 220-21.

35. The similar expression with object nouns from the root חטא, *ht'*, "sin/error/wrong," is virtually synonymous (Lev 18:22, 32; 19:17; 22:9; 24:15).

36. Again, the similar expressions with object nouns from the roots חטא, *ht'* and פשע, *psh'*, "rebellion, transgression," are virtually synonymous (Gen 50:17; Exod 23:21; Josh 24:19; 1 Sam 25:28; Job 7:21; Ps 32:1).

37. Priestly ritual associates washing one's garments with purification from sin. The idea seems to be that it is necessary to cleanse away all residual guilt/consequences. See Exod 19:10, 14; Lev 6:20; 11:25, 28, 40; 13:6, 34, 54, 55, 56, 58, etc; Num 8:7, 21, etc.

38. The verb נקה (*nqh*) without the prepositional phrase appears prominently in the credo concerning the heritage of *'awon* passed from generation to generation (Exod 20:7 ‖ Deut 5:11; Exod 34:7; Num 14:18) discussed above (see p. 121 and n. 15).

39. As is evident in the papyri materials from the western Mediterranean in reference to release from a legal obligation such as a contract or a debt. See R. Bultmann, "ἀφίημι, ἄφεσις, παρίημι, κτλ," *TDNT* 1 (ed. G. Kittel; trans. G. Bromiley; Grand Rapids: Eerdmans, 1967), 509-14.

40. James and 1 Peter have the same phrase, which seems to be based on Prov 10:12, perhaps under the influence also of Ezek 28:18, almost verbatim—although it is unclear whether one borrowed from the other. Its recurrence in *1 Clem.* 49:5; *2 Clem.* 16:4; and *Didasc.* 2:5, where it is attributed to Jesus, suggests that it circulated widely, i.e., proverbially, in the early church. Cf. also Sir 5:6; *Pss. Sol.* 84:2 and see the discussion in Albrecht Oepke, "καλύπτω, κάλυμμα, κτλ," in *TDNT* 3 (ed. G. Kittel, ed.; trans. G. Bromiley; Grand Rapids: Eerdmans, 1967), 558.

41. Cf. Otto Procksch, "λύω, αναλύω, κτλ," *TDNT* 4 (ed. G. Kittel, ed.; trans. G. Bromiley; Grand Rapids: Eerdmans, 1967), 329.

42. See A. Oepke, "λούω, ἀπολούω, λουτρόν," *TDNT* 4 (ed. G. Kittel, ed.; trans. G. Bromiley; Grand Rapids: Eerdmans, 1967), 295-307.

43. James Moffatt, *A Critical and Exegetical Commentary on the Epistle to the Hebrews* (ICC; New York: Charles Scribner's Sons, 1924), 212.

44. Frederick Fyvie Bruce, *The Book of Hebrews* (NICNT; rev. ed.; Grand Rapids: Eerdmans, 1990), 351.

Notes

45. A. McFadyen, *Bound to Sin: Abuse, Holocaust and the Christian Doctrine of Sin* (Cambridge: Cambridge University Press, 2000), 32, 34.

46. Paul's notion of universal bondage to sin by virtue of descent from Adam is also in tension with Judaism and, as some understand it, the Old Testament. "At this point Paul differs from Judaism. For Paul sin does not consist only in the individual act. Sin is for him a state which embraces all humanity. The individual is always in this all-embracing state of sin, and thus he does not have the Jewish freedom of choice which constitutes the Jewish conception of sin. . . . " W. Grundmann, "ἁμαρτάνω F. Sin in the New Testament," *TDNT* 1 (ed. G. Kittel; trans. G. Bromiley; Grand Rapids: Eerdmans, 1967), 309-10.

47. Cf. R. Highfield's discussion of Karl Rahner's position on this question in *Barth and Rahner in Dialogue: Toward an Ecumenical Understanding of Sin and Evil* (American University Studies VII/62; New York: Peter Lang, 1989), 94.

48. Steven Kepnes, "'Turn Us to You and We Shall Return': Original Sin, Atonement, and Redemption in Jewish Terms," in *Christianity in Jewish Terms* (eds. T. Frymer-Kensky, et al.; Boulder, Colo.: Westview Press, 2000), 295, 296.

49. M. Volf, "The Lamb of God," 314-15 (in *Christianity in Jewish Terms*).

50. W. Grundmann, "ἁμαρτάνω F. Sin in the New Testament," 313.

51. The Gospel of John addresses the same state of affairs as Paul's notion of sin as a power that binds, although with even greater economy of language: Jesus came to "take away [αἴρειν, *airein*] the sin of the world" (John 1:29; cf. 1 John 3:5).

52. D. Friedman, operating within the framework of modern legal theory, disagrees with the interpretation offered here: "Years after the event, the house of David was beset by tragedies, including rape, murder, and rebellion. But the attempt to relate these disasters to crimes committed many years before is unconvincing. It becomes an effort to seek justice where there is none, to see our world in an unrealistically positive light. These catastrophes could be attributed to other acts of David; for example, Absalom's revolt could be viewed as retribution for David's seizure of Saul's throne" (*To Kill and Take Possession: Law, Morality, and Society in Biblical Stories* [Peabody, Mass.: Hendrickson, 2002], 85). The problem with this, of course, is that, in the words of Nathan, the editor/redactor of the Succession Narrative connects David's sin with Bathsheba and against Uriah with the actions of David's son.

53. It is difficult to determine from the text how Nathan viewed the nature of the relationship between David's sin and the death of Bathsheba's son. As narrated ("YHWH struck the child," 2 Sam 12:15b), God's role in the child's death seems somewhat arbitrary, retributive, and unfair, certainly so from the child's perspective. While it is tempting to speculate that the child's death resulted as a "natural" consequence of the conditions of his birth, especially the stress Bathsheba must have experienced (cf. 2 Sam 11:27; 12:24), exegetical honesty requires one to note that, in this instance, as the text relates it, God acted to take from David and Bathsheba the gain of their sin. From a redactional perspective, it should also be noted that the death of Bathsheba's first son paves the way for the birth and rise of her second, Solomon. Some have even suggested that the account of the death of the first may be a fictive defense of Solomon's legitimacy.

54. Whether God absolutely cannot reverse the course of events set into motion by David's choices or cannot do so and remain true to God's character—that is, that God chooses self-restriction in these matters in order to protect human free agency—is a distinction without a difference when seen from the human perspective. In either case, whether as an inherent characteristic or a freely chosen limitation, God does not relate to human beings from a stance of omnipotence. God cannot or does not override the course of human history; God redeems it.

55. See 2 Sam 14:8-11, 28-33 where the concern for the "guilt" loose in the world because of the manslaughter of one of the widow's sons at the hands of the other, now sole surviving, son functions as an analogy to Absalom's status because of his revenge on Amnon.

56. See Mark E. Biddle, "Contingency, God, and the Babylonians: Jeremiah on the Complexity of Repentance," *RevExp* 101 (2004): 247-65.

Notes

57. See M. Biddle, "Contingency," 255-58.

58. Significantly, several passages in Jeremiah, especially the so-called "Prose Sermons" (Jer 7, 11, for example) and "symbolic acts" (Jer 13), record God's words to Jeremiah but do not indicate that Jeremiah ever delivered them publicly. See M. Biddle, *Polyphony and Symphony in Prophetic Literature: Rereading Jeremiah 7-20* (SOTI 2; Macon: Mercer, 1996), 64-86; cf. notes to Oxford Annotated.

59. Although Jeremiah is remarkably silent on the matter, 2 Kings observes that not even the reforms (2 Kgs 23) of Manasseh's son, Josiah, celebrated as one who "did right in the sight of YHWH, and walked in all the way of his father David . . . turning aside neither to the right or to the left" (2 Kgs 22:2), could rob the unfolding consequences of Judah's history of sin of its momentum.

60. See M. Biddle, "Contingency," 258-62.

61. *The Return of Splendor in the World: The Christian Doctrine of Sin and Forgiveness* (trans. D. Bloesch; Grand Rapids: Eerdmans, 1997), 259.

62. See above, pp. ix-xi.

Subject Index

Aaron, 124, 157
Abel, 29
Abelard, viii, 97, 105, 159
Abimelech, 98
Absalom, 131
Abraham, 29, 120
abuse/abuser, 67-70, 71, 72, 156
Adamson, James B., 158, 161
Adapa, 144
addict/addiction, 50, 67-68, 71, 72
Adonijah, 132
Ahaz, 83
Alienation, 19
Ambinder, Marc, 163
Amnon, 131, 168
angst/anxiety, 85-87, 90, 154-55, 158
Anselm, viii
anthropology, xi, 3, 8
Antichrist, 26, 27
Antigone, 110
apostasy, 21, 29-30
Aristotle, 109, 149
Atkins v. Virginia, 163
Augustine/Augustinian(ism), viii, xvi, 1-3, 5, 36, 66, 143, 160

Baillie, John, 150, 161
Balaam, 62, 152
Balak, 62
baptism, 38
Barr, James, xix, xx, 41-43, 140, 149-50
Barrett, Charles Kingsley, 154
Barth, Karl, 41, 43, 163
Barton, John, 149
Baruch, 133

basic trust v. basic mistrust, 18, 90-93, 138, 151, 159
Bathsheba, 130-31, 167
Bauckham, Richard, 153
Baumann, Urs, 143
Biddle, Mark E., 145, 160-61, 165, 168
Bigg, Charles, 153
Birch, Charles L., 142
Blake, William, 97
blasphemy, 87-89, 146
Blocher, Henri, 141-43, 148
Bonhoeffer, Dietrich, 159
Brakeman, L., 156
Brown, Norman O., 158
Bruce, Frederick Fyvie, 167
Buddhism, vii
Bultmann, Rudolf, 157, 166
Burden, Terry L., 157
Burton, Laurel A., 155

Calvinism, 110
Carthage, Council of, 2
Chardin, Teilhard de, 6, 142
Charles, Robert Henry, 153
Christlikeness, 5-7, 63, 65, 73
Ciarrocchi, Joseph W., 141, 156
Clendenin, Daniel, 140
Clifford, Richard J., 145
Clinebell, Howard, 67-68, 72, 155-56
Coats, George W., 157
Cobb, John B., 142
comedy, 110-12
complicity, 52, 67-70, 139, 155-56, 162
Connor, James, 3, 142, 147-48
Connor, Robert, 66
Cornill, Carl Heinrich, 164

Subject Index

corporate existence, xiv, xvi, xvii
Cox, Harvey, 50, 140, 144, 150, 156

Dahood, Mitchell, 150
Davis, Stephan, 149
despair, 70-71, 76, 158
Dhorme, Edouard, 151
Dodd, Charles H., 148
Doweiko, Harold, 73, 141, 154
Duffy, Stephen J., 158
Dunfee, Susan, 50, 140, 144, 150, 158

Eastern Orthodox theology, xvi, 5, 7, 8, 140, 142
economics, xi
Edwards, Jonathan, 116
egoism, 17, 18
Ellens, J. Harold, 158-60
Ellingsworth, Paul, 146
Elliot, T. S., 163
Emerson, Ralph Waldo, 157
Enoch, 29
Erikson, Eric, 18, 71, 72, 91, 92, 94, 144
Esau, 127-28
Evans, Craig A., 86
evolution, 6
existentialism/ist, xii, xvii, 7-9, 19, 143

fall, the/fallen/fallenness, 2-5, 7, 8, 143
fallen angels, 58-60
falling short, 51-57, 64
false teachers, 58-62
Falwell, Jerry 116, 163
feminism/ist, xvi, xviii, 12, 50, 69, 77, 144, 150
finitude/freedom polarity, 11, 32-33, 44, 47, 66, 90, 97, 105, 111, 114, 150, 158, 160
folly, 32, 151-52
Forman, Charles C., 146
Fortune, Maria M., 156
Fowler, James, 18, 91, 92, 144
Fox, Michael, 146, 147, 151
Frankemölle, Hubert, 152
Freud, Sigmund, 90
Freudianism, vii, 7
Friedman, Daniel, 161, 167

Frye, Northrop, 162

Gaffney, James, 9, 96, 142
Gerstenberger, Erhard, 157
Gestrich, Christof, 92, 136, 140, 143, 154-55, 158
Gnosticism, docetic, 27, 58, 146; libertine, 58, 96, 159; neo-, 47, 74, 117
González, Justo, 11-12, 140, 142, 151
Gordis, Robert, 143-44, 151
Gregory, St., the Theologian, 5
Grundmann, Walter, 157, 167
Gunkel, Hermann, 157
Gutwenger, Eric, 141-42, 147-48

han, 96-97
Hauck, Frederick, 145
Haught, John F., 162
Hegel, 112
Heise, Jürgen, 145
Hertzberg, Hans Wilhelm, 145
Hick, John, 150
Highfield, Ron, 166-67
Holocaust, xvii, 3, 111, 122, 156
Hooker, Morna D., 147
Hubbard, Moyer, 154
hubris/pride/arrogance, xvi, xviii, 1, 12, 18, 19, 21, 50-51, 67, 75, 109-10, 144, 150-51, 158
Hulsbosch, Ansfried, 6, 142

imago dei, xii, xiii, 3-12, 31 44, 47-48, 77, 89, 95, 96, 139, 147, 151
incarnation, 27, 28, 31, 47, 63, 88
individualism, (hyper-), xvi, xviii, 19, 114-15, 117, 120, 128, 140
integrity, 106
intergenerational responsibility, 120-22, 140
Irenaeus, xvi, 5, 6
Isaac, 128

Jacob, 127-28
Jampolsky, Lee, 67, 70, 141, 155, 156
Jephthah, 102-3, 110, 112, 161
juridical/legal model, viii, ix, xii, xiv, xvi, 1, 3, 13, 17, 19, 67, 95-96, 115, 117, 119

Subject Index

Käsemann, Ernst, 154, 166
Kellermann, Ulrich, 33
Kelly, John N. D., 152, 153
Kepnes, Steven, 129, 167
Kerans, Patrick, 144, 154
Kierkegaard, Søren, 7, 90, 141, 158
Kiuchi, Nobuyoshi, 161
Knierim, Rolf, 118, 125, 145, 160, 164
Kohlberg, Lawrence, 144
Köhler, Ludwig, 145
Korah, 62
Korsmeyer, Jerry D., 141-43, 158

Laato, Timo, 148
Langer, Lawrence, 163
Larsen, Earnie, 70, 157
Lash, Nocholas, 163
Lee, Dorothy, 145
liberation theology, xvi, xviii, 12, 77
Lonergan, Bernard, 154
Longman, Tremper, 33, 146, 147, 151
Lorentzen, Lois A., 155
Lowe, Walter, 90-91, 144, 150, 154, 160

MacIntyre, Alasdair, 110, 162
MacKinnon, Donald, 163
Malina, Bruce J., 37
Manasseh, 132-33, 168
Manicheanism, 97, 160
Marenbon, John, 159
Marx/Marxism, vii
McCormick, Patrick, 140, 141
McDermott, Brian, 141, 142
McDowell, John, 162, 163
McFadyen, Alistair, 68, 69, 128, 141, 150, 155, 156, 159, 167
Mercadante, Linda, 50, 91, 97, 142, 143, 150, 154, 156, 158-60
Metzner, Rainer, 157, 158, 162
Michael (archangel), 61, 153
Michel, Diethelm, 32, 147
Milgrom, Jacob, 102, 161
Miller-McLemore, Bonnie J., 143
Moffatt, James, 167
Moo, Douglas J., 148
Morreall, John, 110, 162
Morris, Leon, 154

Moses, 29, 61, 103, 153, 157
Murphy, Roland, 151
Murphy-O'Connor, Jerome, 65-66, 141, 154

Nathan, 130
natural theology, xv, 35, 41-43, 150
Nellas, Panayiotis, 5, 142
Nelson, Susan L., 159
Nephilim/Watchers/Grigori, 60-61, 153
Niebuhr, Reinhold, 17-18, 50, 73, 74, 91, 141, 144, 150, 157, 158

O'Connor, June, 140, 150, 157
O'Shea, Kevin, 140
Oedipus, 109-10, 162
Oepke, Albrecht, 167
omega point, 142
original sin, 1-9, 16, 34, 35, 37, 96, 129, 142, 143
Orwell, George, 155

Park, Andrew Sung, 96-97
Parousia, 26
Pascal, Blaise, 144
Pelagius/Pelagian(ism), 2, 97, 143, 160
perfectionism, 23-28, 30, 45, 46, 107, 155
personagenesis, 66, 71, 154
personality development, 17-19, 75, 90, 94, 144
perversion, 119, 128-30, 134-38, 164-65
Peters, Ted, 158
Piaget, Jean, 144
Plein, Ina, 145
polygenism, 3
polyphyletism, 3
Porter, Stanley E., 142
practical atheism/ist, 93
process theology, 109
Procksch, Otto, 167
psychiatry/psychoanalysis, xvii, 14, 90
psychology, xi, xii, xvii, xviii, 72

Rahner, Karl, 144, 165-67
Ray, Stephen G., Jr., 141, 144, 150, 157
rebellion, 21, 33, 46, 48, 91, 139, 141, 145, 149, 157

Subject Index

Reformation, 2
Reicke, Bo, 153
Rendtorff, Rolf, 102
Rengstorff, Karl, 157
restitution/restoration, 103-4, 116, 124-27, 139
Ricoeur, Paul, 97, 159
Ring, Nancy, 154-56
Robertson, Pat, 116
Rondet, Henri, 141, 142
Roper v. Simmons, 163
Ropes, James H., 150, 161
Rosscup, James, 145
Rudman, Dominic, 147
Ruprecht, Louis, 111, 112, 113, 162, 163

Sarah, 29
Sartre, Jean-Paul, 141, 154
Saul, 102-3
Scharbert, Josef, 124
Schmitz-Moormann, Karl, 141, 142
Schnackenburg, Rudolph, 158
Schoonenberg, Piet, 141, 143
Segundo, Juan Luis, 140, 153
Seow, Choon-Leong, 151
sloth/sensuality, 50, 75, 91, 139, 144, 150
Smalley, Stephen, 24
sociology, xi, xii
sola scriptura, xv
Sophocles, 110, 162, 163
soteriology, xviii, 113
Stamm, Joahnn Jakob, 166
Stanford v. Kentucky, 163
Steck, Odil Hannes, 165
Steele, Michael, 111, 163
Steiner, George, 162
Stoic/Stoicism, 26, 39
Strecker, Georg, 25-26

Suchocki, Marjori Hewitt, 141-42

Tamar, 131
Taylor, Vincent, 88
Tertullian, viii
theodicy, 111-12
theosis/deification/Christification, 140, 142
Tillich, Paul, 7, 19, 143, 160
Torah/law, 22, 35, 38-41, 63, 148, 149, 157
tragedy/tragic, 108-14, 138, 162, 163
Trent, Council of, 143
Troy, Crawford Howell, 145
Tsirpanlis, Constantine, 142

Unamuno, Miguel de, 158
undifferentiated faith, 91
universalism, 37
unpardonable/unforgivable sin, 28, 85, 89, 105, 107
Uzzah, 103

Van der Woude, Adam S., 157
VanderKam, James C., 153
Vanneste, Alfred, 141, 142, 143
Via, Dan O., 162
victim/victimization, 50, 69, 72, 139, 150, 156, 162
Volf, Miroslav, 129, 141

Weger, Karl-Heinz, 143
Westcott, Brooke Foss, 145
Whybray, R. Norman, 33
Wiley, Tatha, 141, 142, 143
Willmes, Bernd, 147
wisdom/wisdom, 31, 32, 39, 54-55, 63

Zechariah, 122, 165

Scripture Index

HEBREW BIBLE

Genesis
- 1–2 ....146, 151
- 1–3 ....10, 34, 43
- 1 ....10, 146
- 1:2 ....12, 147
- 1:11 146
- 1:20-25 147
- 1:26-27 ....12, 65, 151
- 1:26 147
- 1:27 33
- 1:29 146
- 2–3 ....32, 147, 151
- 2 ....10, 11, 33
- 2:7 ....33, 146, 147
- 2:9 146
- 2:15 83
- 3–11 146
- 3 ....xvii, xviii, 1, 2, 4, 5, 14, 32, 34, 35, 44, 146-51
- 3:1b-5 12
- 3:6 52
- 3:19 ....15, 146, 147
- 3:22 4
- 4:7 ....xiv, 129, 161
- 4:8 62
- 4:13 ....118, 125, 165
- 5:3 4
- 6:1-4 ....59, 153
- 8:21 129
- 10:14 146
- 11:4 46
- 12:17-20 98
- 13:13 161
- 15:16 ....118, 120
- 18:17-33 133
- 18:20 161
- 19:15 ....118, 165
- 20:1-18 98
- 20:6 161
- 22:14 94
- 27:30 146
- 31:26 ....145, 161
- 39:9 161
- 40:1 161
- 41:9 161
- 44:4 146
- 44:16 165
- 44:28 146
- 50:17 ....145, 166

Exodus
- 3:5 103
- 4:10 52
- 5:16 51
- 5:20 146
- 9:27 161
- 13:17 78
- 14:10 78
- 14:11-12 ....78, 79
- 14:15 78
- 14:31 80
- 15:22-27 81
- 15:24 ....77, 78
- 16:2 77
- 16:3 78
- 16:6-7 81
- 16:7-10 77
- 16:8 80
- 16:12 81
- 17:1-7 ....29, 81

Scripture Index

17:2	78, 80, 81	5:6	126
17:3	77, 78	5:10	126, 166
17:4	78	5:13	126, 166
17:7	80, 81	5:14-19	101, 103
19:10	166	5:15	25, 98
20:3	21	5:16	126, 166
20:4-6	21	5:17-18	25
20:5	121, 124	5:17	98, 125
20:7	166	5:18	98, 166
20:9	83	6:1-7	101, 102
20:16	102	6:1	101, 161
22:8	145	6:3	101
23:1-2	102	6:4	101
23:21	145, 166	6:7	166
28:3	55	6:20	166
28:38	124, 125	7:11	125
28:43	125	8:15	160
30:10	160	10:15	125
31:6	55	11:8	102
32:30	126	11:25	166
34:7	121, 124, 125, 166	11:26	102
34:9	125, 164	11:27	102
		11:28	166
Leviticus		11:40	166
4:1–6:7	98, 161	12:6	160
4–5	101, 107	12:8	160
4	102	13:6	166
4:2	25, 98, 100, 102	13:34	166
4:3-21	101	13:54-56	166
4:13	25, 98, 100, 101, 102	13:58	166
4:20	166	14:1-32	98
4:22-26	101	14:13	160
4:22	25, 98, 100, 101, 102	14:19	160
4:26	126, 127	14:22	160
4:27-35	101	14:31	160
4:27	25, 98, 100, 101, 102	14:33-53	98
4:31	166	14:49	160
4:35	126, 166	14:52	160
5:1–6:7	101	15:15	160
5:1-13	101	15:30	160
5:1-6	102	16:16	126, 144
5:1	101, 102, 105, 125	16:21	124, 144, 164
5:2-4	98	16:22	125
5:2-3	101	16:30	126
5:4	101, 102	16:34	126
5:5-6	102	17:16	125
5:5	101	18:22	166

Scripture Index

18:25	124
18:32	166
19:8	124
19:17	166
19:22	126, 166
20:17	125
20:19	125
22:9	166
22:16	118, 125
24:15	166
26:18	161
26:21	161
26:24	161
26:28	161
26:39	165

Numbers

5	123
5:6-7	161
5:15	123, 164
5:31	123, 164
8:7	126, 166
8:8	161
8:12	161
8:21	166
11:1	78
11:4-5	78
11:4-6	53, 79
11:10	78
11:13	78
11:18	78, 79
11:20	79
11:23	80, 81
14:1	78
14:2-3	78, 79
14:2-4	53
14:2	77
14:11	80
14:18	121, 124, 125, 144, 166
14:19-20	125
14:22-23	80, 81
14:27	77
14:28	81
14:34	125, 165
14:35	78
14:36	77
14:40	161

15:25-26	166
15:27-28	98, 161
15:27-31	25
15:28	166
15:30-31	27
15:31	165
16:3	78
16:11	77, 80
16:13-14	80
16:22	161
16:26	161
16:41	77, 78
17:10	77
18:1	118, 125
18:23	118, 125
19:9	161
19:17	161
20:1-13	29
20:3-5	78-79
20:3	78
20:5	78
20:12	157
20:13	78
21:5	78, 79
21:7	78, 161
22:34	98, 161
24:14	153
27:14	29
30:5	166
30:8	166
30:12	166
31:8	153
35:9-34	98
35:11	99, 104
35:15	99
35:16-18	99
35:20-21	98, 99, 104
35:22-23	104
35:25-28	99
35:30-34	99

Deuteronomy

1:26	78
1:27-28	78, 79
1:27	78
1:30-32	80
1:41	161

Scripture Index

1:43 78
5:7 21
5:9-10 121
5:9 124
5:11 166
5:13 84
5:20 102
7:7 83
9:7 78
9:15 118
9:16 161
9:21 161
9:23-24 78
9:23 . . . . .78, 83
9:27 161
17:12 25
17:16 83
19 . . . . .104, 105
19:1-13 98
19:4 . . . . .99, 104
19:11-13 99
19:11 . . . . .98-99, 104
19:15 118
19:16-18 102
21 110
21:1-9 . . . . .98, 124
21:6-9 99
21:22-23 105
22:8 100
28:52 83
29:20 166
30:1-20 22
30:6 22
30:11 22
30:14 22
34 153

Joshua
6:1-21 84
7:11 161
7:20 161
20:1-6 98
20:3 104
20:5 . . . . .99, 104
20:6 99
22:17 119
22:20 119

24:19-20 21
24:19 . . . . .144, 161, 166

Judges
6:15 52
7:16-22 84
10:10 161
10:15 161
11:27 161
11:29-40 102
20:16 51

1 Samuel
2:17 161
3:10-14 165
3:13 164
3:14 125
5–6 103
7:6 161
8 83
10 83
12:10 161
12:19 161
12:23 161
14:24-46 161
14:41 118
20:1 . . . . .118, 161
24:10-14 145
24:11 . . . . .144, 161
25:24 165
25:28 . . . . .144, 166
26:21 161

2 Samuel
3:8 124
6:1-7 103
7:14 165
11 viii
11:14-15 130
11:26-27 130
11:27 167
12:7-15 130
12:7 ix
12:9-10 131
12:10-14 ix
12:11 131

Scripture Index

12:13 . . . . .ix, 126, 161
12:14 131
12:15 167
12:24 167
13:1-19 131
13:3 55
14:8-11 168
14:28-33 168
14:32 118
15:3-6 131
16:12 164
19:19 123
19:20 . . . . .161, 165
22:24 164
24:10 126
24:17 . . . . .161, 165

1 Kings
1:21 161
2:9 55
8 166
8:30 166
8:31 161
8:33 161
8:34 .161, 166
8:35 161
8:36 .161, 166
8:39 166
8:47 165
8:50 .144, 166
12:19 144
17:18 . . . . .118, 123, 164
18:9 161

2 Kings
1:1 144
3:3 161
3:5 144
3:7 144
5:18 166
7:9 . . . . .118, 164
8:20 .144, 145
8:22 .144, 145
10:29 161
10:31 161
18:14 161
21:1-18 133

22:2 168
23 168
24:2-4 133
24:4 166

1 Chronicles
21:8 126
22:15 55

2 Chronicles
2:7 55
6 166
6:21 166
6:25 166
6:27 166
6:30 166
6:37 165
6:39 166
7:14 .161, 166
10:19 144
21:8 144
21:10 144
24:20-22 165
25:4 161
28:13 161
29:24 126
33:19 161

Ezra
7:14 63
7:26-27 63
9:6-7 .120, 165
9:13 164

Nehemiah
1:6 161
4:5 126
6:13 161
9:2 . . . . .120, 165
9:17 . . . . .79, 80

Esther
1:16 164

Job
1:5 161
1:22 161

2:10	161	38:4	120
4:6	152	38:6	164
5:24	51	38:18	164
7:20	57	40:12	120
7:21	125, 126, 144, 166	44:6	84
8:4	144	49:5	164
8:14	152	49:6	84
10:6	165	49:11	152
10:9	146	51:2	126
10:14	126	51:5	144
11:6	164	51:7	126
13:23	144, 164	51:9	164
14:17	125, 144	52:7	84
20:27	165	59:3	144, 164
22:5	164	65:3	144
30:24	164	69:28	165
31:11	144, 164	73:22	152
31:24	84, 152	78:7	152
31:28	164	78:17	78
31:33	144	78:18-20	78
33:9	144	78:18	81
33:27	165	78:19-20	79
34:15	146	78:19	78
35:6	144	78:22	80
41:25	51	78:32	80
		78:38	125, 164

Psalms

4:4	161	78:40	78
4:5	84	78:41	81
5:10	145	78:56	78, 81
9:10	84	79:1	164
13:5	84	79:8	123
18:23	164	79:9	126
19:1-4	42	81:7	29
19:12	126	82:6-8	143
19:13	25	85:2	125, 164
21:7	84	85:9	152
22:4-5	84	89:32	124, 144, 164
25:7	144, 161	90:8	165
25:11	118, 125	92:6	152
25:18	161	92:7	152
31:10	164	94:8	152
31:11	118	95:7-8	29
32:1	126, 144, 166	103:3	118, 125
32:2	164	103:12	144
32:5	119, 125, 131, 144	104:1-4	42
36:3	164	104:29	146
		106:7-12	80

Scripture Index

106:7	78	8:17	56
106:14	81	8:20	55
106:20	147	8:22-31	55, 63
106:24	80	9:4-6	56
106:25	78	9:4	152
106:32	29	9:7-8	152
107:17	144, 165	10:12	166
109:14	123	10:16	161
119:51	152	10:23	152
119:89-90	42	11:28	84
130:3	164	12:1	152
145:3	84	12:8	164
		12:11	152
Proverbs		12:23	152
1:1	152	13:1	152
1:7	56	13:6	161
1:20-23	56	13:19	152
1:22	152	14:6	152
1:24-25	57	14:8	152
1:29-33	57	14:16	152
1:32	152	14:18	152
2:1-22	56	14:21	161
2:1-8	56	14:26	84
2:1-4	57	15:2	152
2:5	57	15:12	152
2:6	57	15:14	152
2:9-16	55	16:6	125
2:9	55, 56	16:20	84
2:20-22	55	16:22	56
3:5-10	84	17:12	152
3:5	84	17:18	152
3:6	56	18:4	56
3:19-20	55	18:7	152
3:19	63	19:2	57
3:21-24	56	19:8	56
3:26	152	19:10	152
3:34	152	19:25	152
4:4-9	56	19:29	152
5:22	161, 165	20:2	57
6:32	152	20:9	126
7:1-4	63	21:11	152
8	39, 42, 54, 65	21:16	57
8:1-5	56	21:20	152
8:5	152	21:24	152
8:6-9	55	22:19	84
8:9	55	24:9	57
8:10-11	56	24:13-14	56

Scripture Index

24:30	152
26:6	152
26:7	152
26:9	152
26:11	152
27:12	57
28:2	145
28:24	145
28:25	84
28:26	152
29:7	55
29:11	152
29:25	84
30:2	49, 62, 152

Ecclesiastes

1:5	146
1:16	31
1:32	152
2:13	31
2:14	152
2:15	31
2:21	31
2:26	151
3	32, 44
3:1-8	32
3:9	32
3:11	32, 146, 147
3:14	32
3:15	32
3:18	33
3:19-20	32, 146
3:19	146
3:20	33, 146
3:26	152
4:5	152
4:13	152
5:2	152
5:13-17	94
6:32	152
7:1	146
7:4	152
7:5	152
7:6	152
7:9	152
7:11-2	31
7:16-18	32
7:19	31
7:23	31
7:26	57
8:1	31
8:7	31
8:12	161
8:16-17	32
9:16	31
9:18	31, 57
10:2	31, 152
10:3	152
10:10	31
10:12	31, 152
10:14	32
10:15	152
11:5	32
12:2	146
12:7	146, 147

Isaiah

1:2-3	22
1:4	119, 161
1:28	21
3:3	55
3:9	161
5:18-23	119
5:18	118
6:7	118, 161
7:4	83
7:9	83
13:11	124
14:21	165
17:1	164
19:12-15	152
19:14	164
21:3	164
22:14	27, 125, 164
24:1	164
26:21	124
27:9	125, 165
28:14-15	152
29:19-21	152
31:1	83
33:24	125
40–55	82
40:6-7	88
40:15	82

Scripture Index

40:17	.82
40:20	.55
43:24	.164
43:25	.144
43:27	.144
44:22	.144
48:8	.21, 145
50:1	.144, 164
53:5	.144, 164
53:12	.144
55:7	.166
57:4	.21, 145
57:17	.164
58:1	.144
59	.119
59:2	.119, 164
59:8	.119
59:10	.119
59:12	.144
59:13-15	.119
59:13	.21
64:6-9	.165
64:9	.123
65:6-7	.121, 123
65:20	.51

Jeremiah

1:6	.52
2:5	.81
2:6	.81
2:8	.21, 81
2:11-13	.81
2:11	.41, 81
2:12-13	.22
2:20-22	.165
2:22	.126
2:26-37	.83
2:29	.21, 81
2:35	.161
2:36-37	.81
3:6-10	.21
3:13	.21, 165
3:21	.165
3:22-25	.133
3:25	.161
4:1-2	.132
4:4	.22
4:14	.126
5:1	.166
5:6	.21, 144
5:7	.166
5:17	.83
5:21	.152
5:25	.164
7	.168
7:1-15	.132
7:16–8:3	.132
7:16-20	.133
7:26	.121
7:27	.133
9:5	.165
9:13	.121
9:17	.55
10:14	.152
10:21	.152
11	.168
11:1-13	.132
11:10	.121, 164
11:14-17	.132, 133
11:18-20	.133
12:1-6	.133
13	.168
13:22	.164
13:25	.83
14:1-9	.133
14:10	.123, 165
14:11-12	.133
14:19-22	.133
14:20	.165
15:1-4	.133
16:1-9	.132
16:1-4	.133
16:11-12	.121
16:17	.164
16:18	.164
17:1	.22
17:2	.121
17:5-8	.84
17:9	.106
18:1-11	.132
18:23	.125, 164
19:1-15	.132-33
19:4	.121
23:7	.121

Scripture Index

25:9	133
25:12	124, 165
26:1-6	132
26:18	164
26:20-23	165
31	121
31:29-30	121
31:31-34	22, 120
31:34	125
32:18	121
33:8	125, 131
34:13-18	121
36:3	124, 125, 164
36:31	121
37:18	161
44:9-10	121
44:21-23	121
45	133
46:25	83
48:7	83
50:20	164, 166

Lamentations

1:2-13	123
1:8	161
2:14	123, 164
3:9	164
3:42	145, 166
4:2	165
4:6	161
4:13	161
4:22	124, 161
5:7	121, 161
5:16	161

Ezekiel

2:3	145
3:20	161
3:21	161
4:4	125
4:5	125
4:6	125
7:19	164
14:3	164
14:4	164
14:7	164
14:10	125
14:11	21
14:13	161
16	21
16:15	83
16:49	164
18	121
18:19	125
18:20	125
18:30	164
20	157
20:13	78
20:21	78
20:38	145
21:23	123
21:24	123
21:29	144
21:32	164
23	21
24:23	165
28:12-14	143
28:18	164, 166
29:16	83, 123, 164
32:27	164
33:8	126
36:3	164
36:26	22
36:33	126
37:23	21, 144
39:24	144
43:10	164
43:20	98
43:22	98
43:23	98
44:10	125
44:12	125, 164
45:18	98
45:20	98, 161

Daniel

4:27	161
9:5	161, 165
9:8	161
9:11	161
9:13	164
9:15	161

Scripture Index

9:16 . . . . .161, 164
9:19 166
9:20 161
9:24 . . . . .125, 161

Hosea
1–3 21
2:5 82
2:8 82
4:7 161
4:8 . . . . .161, 164
5:5 165
7:1 165
7:11 152
7:13 . . . . .21, 145
8:1 21
8:11 161
8:13 . . . . .123, 161, 165
9:7 123
9:9 . . . . .123, 165
10:13 83
11:1-2 22
12:8 164
13:12 119
14:1-2 165
14:2 125

Amos
1–2 145
1 145
1:3 123
1:6 123
1:9 123
1:11 123
1:13 123
2 145
2:1 123
2:4 123
2:6 123
3:2 . . . . .118, 124
3:9-10 149
4:4 21
5:12 161
7:2 166
9:8 161
9:10 161

Micah
1:5 .21, 144, 161
1:6 164
1:13 . . . . .144, 161
3:8 . . . . .145, 161
3:12 164
6:7 . . . . .144, 161
6:13 161
7:9 161
7:18-19 125
7:18 144

Zephaniah
1:17 161

Zechariah
3:4 126
3:9 126
4:6 84
12:3 30
12:10 30

Malachi
2:6 164

NEW TESTAMENT

Matthew
5:8 106
5:17-48 104
5:22 . . . . .104, 105
5:23-24 105
5:25-26 105
5:45-46 106
5:48 . . . . .1-6, 161
6:1-4 106
6:5 106
6:12 85
6:14-15 85
6:16-18 106
6:22-23 106
6:24 106
6:25 87
6:26 86
6:27 87
6:30 87

Scripture Index

6:31 87
6:32 86
6:33 106
6:34 87
7:7-11 87
7:20 106
7:21-23 106
12:31-32 . . . . .87-88, 146
13:41 85
16:19 157
18:1-6 85
18:2 85
18:5-6 85
18:7 85
18:15 . . . . .51, 85
18:18 157
18:21 . . . . .51, 85
19:13-15 85
19:20 . . . . .64, 86
19:21 64
19:22 86
23:29-36 121
23:30 122
23:31-32 122
23:34 .122, 165
23:35 122
23:36 122
26:28 . . . . .85, 126
26:52 124
27:4 51

Mark
1:4 126
2:5 85
2:9-10 85
2:17 85
2:27 14
3:28-30 . . . . .87-88, 146
5:1-20 153
8:38 85
9:24 . . . . .75, 87
9:42 85
9:43-48 85
10:13-16 86
10:14 85
10:15 85
10:20 86

10:24 86
10:51 54
11:25 85

Luke
6:32-34 85
7:47-48 85
8:26-39 153
11:4 85
11:47-51 121
11:47 122
11:48 122
11:49 165
11:50 122
11:51 122
12:8-10 87-88
12:10 146
12:22 87
12:24 86
12:25 87
12:26 87
12:28 87
12:29 87
12:30 86
13:2 85
15:7 85
15:10 85
15:14 64
15:18 51
15:21 51
17:2 85
17:3-4 85
17:3 51
17:4 51
18:1-6 85
18:16 85
18:17 85
18:18 86
18:21 86
19:13-15 85
22:35 64
24:7 85
24:47 . . . . .85, 126

John
1:1-18 65

Scripture Index

1:3	.6
1:29	157, 167
1:38-39	.25
2:3	.64
3	.35
4:40	.25
5:2-9	.53
5:6	.53
5:10	.158
5:14	51, 85, 157, 162
5:16	158, 162
6:27	.25
6:48-58	.27
6:51	.157
6:56	.25
8:7	.85
8:11	51, 85
8:21	.157
8:24	88, 157
8:31	.25
8:34	.157
8:35	.25
8:46	.157
8:52	.89
9	89, 107
9:1	.89
9:2-3	51, 162
9:2-4	.158
9:2-5	.89
9:2	xi, 107, 157, 162
9:3	85, 106, 107
9:13-17	.89
9:14	158, 162
9:16	158, 162
9:18-23	.89
9:24-34	.89
9:24	158, 162
9:25	158, 162
9:31	.158
9:34	157, 158, 162
9:35-41	.89
9:39-41	.157
9:41	.24
10:11-18	.157
11:4	.65
11:40	.65
11:49-52	.157

12:43	65, 154
13:34	.24
14:10	.25
14:17	.25
15:1-11	.25
15:4-7	.25
15:9-10	.25
15:13	.157
15:22-24	.157
15:22	.24
15:24	.24
16:8-11	.157
17:19	.157
17:22	.63
18:14	.157
19:11	24, 85, 157
20:23	85, 157

Acts

2:38	.126
5:31	.126
7:55	.65
15:9	.127
22:16	.127
25:8	.51

Romans

1–7	34, 35, 44
1	34, 35, 149
1:18-32	41, 124, 147, 150
1:19	43, 148
1:20	43, 147
1:21-22	.43
1:21	.43
1:22	.147
1:23	42, 63, 65, 147
1:24	124, 147
1:26	.124
1:28	.124
2–3	.39
2:12-16	.147
2:12	.40
2:13	.39
2:14-16	.39
2:15	.40
2:17-25	.39

185

2:18	.39
2:20	.39
2:26-27	.40
2:27	.39
3:9	.40
3:14	.148
3:19	.40
3:20	.148
3:21-22	.90
3:21-26	.63
3:23	.64, 65, 148
3:25	.40, 64, 148
3:27	.148
3:28	.39
3:31	.39
4:7	.126, 127
4:13-16	.39
4:15	.40
5–7	.143
5	.148
5:2	.65
5:12-21	.35, 129, 148
5:12-14	.36
5:12	.36
5:13-14	.36
5:13	.40, 147
5:14	.40
5:18-19	.36
5:20	.40
5:21	.2, 4
6:3-11	.37-38
6:12	.130
6:20-23	.129
7	.40, 41, 149, 150
7:1-6	.148
7:1-25	.39
7:1	.39
7:5	.39, 40
7:6	.39
7:7–8:4	.65
7:7-13	.149
7:7-11	.39
7:7	.40
7:8-11	.40
7:9	.149
7:13	.39, 40
7:15-25	.39

7:15	.130
8:2	.148
8:7	.149
8:9	.26
8:19-23	.130
8:29-30	.65
8:29	.65, 147
15:7	.65
16:7	.148

1 Corinthians

1:7	.64
5:7	.127
6:11	.127
6:18	.51
7:28	.51
7:36	.51
8:8	.64
8:12	.51
10:31	.65
11:7	.65, 147
11:10	.153
12:24	.64
15:21-22	.38
15:34	.51
15:43	.65
15:49	.65, 147

2 Corinthians

3:18	.65, 66, 147
4:4-6	.65
4:4	.65, 147
4:6	.65
4:7	.xi
4:15	.65
5:4	.36
5:17	.148
11:5	.64
11:9	.64

Galatians

1:6-9	.xvi
3:27	.148
4:8	.62
5:1	.62
6:7	.124

Scripture Index

Ephesians
1:7 126
1:21 153
4:13 66
4:15 .66, 148
4:23 66
4:26 51
5:26 127

Philippians
1:11 65
2:5 74
2:11 65
3:12 36
3:19 62
3:21 65
4:10 36
4:12 64

Colossians
1:14 126
1:15-16 65
1:15-20 65-66
1:15 . . . . .63, 65, 147
1:16 153
1:28 . . . . .65, 66
3:10 . . . . .65, 66, 147

2 Thessalonians
2:1 26
2:3-12 26
2:4 26
2:9 26

1 Timothy
5:20 51

Titus
2:13 65
2:14 127
3:5 127
3:11 51

Hebrews
1:1 94
1:3 127
2:1-3 28
2:9-10 28
2:18 . . . . .29, 30
3:12-19 . . . . .29, 107
3:14 28
3:17 51
4:1 64
4:14-15 29
4:15 30
5:1-2 .vii, 113
5:1-4 107
5:2 30
6:4-6 .29, 146
9:14 127
9:22 .126, 127
9:23 127
10:23 28
10:26-31 . . . . .30, 146
10:26 51
10:29 30
10:32-34 28
10:39 28
11 29
11:1 94
11:33-38 29
11:37 64
12:12-17 127-28
12:15 64
12:16-18 .146
13:3 28

James
2:9 105
2:19 76
4:17 105
5:20 127

1 Peter
2:20 51
3:19-20 153
4:8 127

2 Peter
1:3-15 58
1:3 58
1:4 59
1:5-7 . . . . .59, 61

1:8	59
1:9	59, 127
2	58
2:1	58
2:2	58
2:4-22	58
2:4-10a	59
2:4	152
2:5	58
2:6	58
2:7	58
2:10	60, 61, 152, 153
2:10b-16	59
2:12	62, 152
2:13	152
2:15	152
2:17-22	59
2:17	152
2:18-19	62
2:18	58
2:19-22	62

1 John

1:7	23, 127, 157
1:8-10	23, 24, 25, 27
1:8	25
1:9	126, 127
2:1	24
2:2	157
2:5	24
2:6	25
2:9	24
2:10	25
2:12	126
2:14	25
2:17	25
2:18-29	26
2:18-24	27
2:18	26
2:19	25
2:22-23	26
2:24	25, 26
2:27-28	25
2:27	26
2:28	26
2:29	26
3	26

3:2	28
3:5	157
3:4-10	23, 24, 26, 27
3:4	25, 26, 27
3:5	25, 167
3:6	24, 25, 26, 27
3:7	26
3:8	25, 26
3:9	24, 25, 26, 27
3:10	26
3:11-24	26
3:15	25
3:16	157
3:17	25
3:24	25
4:1-21	26
4:1-3	27
4:2-3	27
4:2	26
4:3	26
4:7-12	28
4:10	157
4:12	25
4:14-15	26
4:15-16	25
5:1-12	27
5:1	27
5:5-12	27
5:6	27
5:16-18	23, 27

2 John

1:2	25
1:9	25

Jude

4	58
5-16	58
5-8	59
6	60, 152
7-8	60
7	152
8	152, 153
9-13	59
9	152
10	62, 152

Scripture Index

11 152
12 152
14-18 59
18 58

Revelation
2:14 153
15:8 65
21:11 65
21:23 65

APOCRYPHA

3 Maccabees
2:4-7 153

Sirach
2:23 147
5:6 167
7:26 147
16:7-10 153
40:11 . . . . 14, 33

OLD TESTAMENT PSEUDEPIGRAPHA

2 Apocalypse of Baruch
56:10-14 153

Ascension of Isaiah
9:32 153

1 Enoch
6-11 59
7:1-6 59
7:1 60
9:9 60
10:4-7 60
10:11-15 60
12:4 59
15:3-4 59
15:6-7 60
64:1–69:1 60
64:1-2 59
69:4-6 59

106:12-16 59

2 Enoch
18 59
22:7 153
22:10 153

Jubilees
4:21-24 59
5:1-7 59
5:2 60
5:6-7 60
7:21-25 59
7:21 60
8:3-4 59
10:5 59
21:22 27
26:34 27

Psalms of Solomon
84:2 167

Testament of Gad
6:3-7 27

Testament of Issachar
7:1 27

Testament of Naphtali
3 59
3:4-5 153
3:5 60

Testament of Reuben
5:6 59

Testament of Zebulun
1:5 146

QUMRAN

1QapGen
2:1 153

1QH
10:8 153

Scripture Index

1QPs^aZion
22:13 153

1QS
5:11-12 25
8:17 27
8:21–9:2 .25, 27

CD
2:17–3:12 153
2:17-19 153
3:14-15 25

NEW TESTAMENT PSEUDEPIGRAPHA

1 Clement
49:5 166

2 Clement
16:4 166

Didache
2:5 166
11:7 146

Hermas, *Similitudes*
v.6.1 153

"CLASSICAL" SOURCES

Allogenes
50:19 153
52:14 153
55:17-18 153

55:34 153
57:25 153

Josephus, *Antiquities of the Jews*
4:126-130 .153
5:7:10 161

Josephus, *Biblical Antiquities*
18:13 153

Philo, *Moses*
1:295-300 .153

RABBINIC SOURCES

Aboth
v.26 30

Midr. Tanh. Behuqqotay
5 161

m. Sanhedrin
10:3 153

y. Sanhedrin
10:28d 153

Sanhedrin
107b 30

Targum Pseudo-Jonathan
Gen 6:1-4 .153
Num 24:14 153
24:15 153
31:8 153